Guard *Your* Heart

Don't Give It Away

TEWANNAH AMAN

Book cover design and interior formatting by Nelly Murariu at PixBeeDesign.com

I dedicate this book to my Lord and Savior, Jesus Christ.
He has rescued me and set me free! I owe Him everything.
I want to thank Him for my husband, John, who's been one of
the greatest blessings in my life. I want to thank Him for the
calling that He has placed on my life. He has led me to where
I am today. I am humbled to be used as an instrument
to lead others to freedom in Christ.

He is my one true love!!!

Introduction

*A*re you tired of being in relationships that take you down a dead-end street? Are you ready to experience healing from the hurts and pains of your past? Then this book is for you! This material will help you draw closer to the Savior. You will find out how you can break free of sinful behavioral patterns and live a life fully devoted to Him. As you embrace His deep and abiding love, you can discover true freedom in Christ.

Walk with me as I share the incredible adventure on which the Lord has taken me. As you do, you will discover that your identity need not be wrapped up in the things you have done or the people who have influenced you.

I always longed for someone to love me unconditionally and accept me for who I am. But no matter how hard I tried, I never felt like I was good enough, so I struggled with a deep sense of insecurity. As I drew closer to Jesus, He began to reveal Himself in ways that showed His amazing love for me. I have finally found that sense of acceptance and wholeness through my relationship with Christ. No one knows the depths of my heart like He does, and no one can satisfy the longings of my soul like He has. I pray that you will embrace these truths and come to understand the person that you truly are in Christ.

I know that God has guided and directed my steps to lead me to where I am today. I have gone through many twists and turns in my life. I have learned a lot in the years since I accepted Jesus into my heart. I have shed many a tear and been forced to come face-to-face with my sinful nature. But I also have experienced a oneness with the Savior that I never thought possible. I want you to experience that, too. He is no respecter of persons. He desires a close, intimate relationship with you.

If you have accepted Christ as your Savior, you are a daughter of the King. You have been adopted into His royal family. You are on a quest of discovery. And what you will find is an amazing Father who desires to give an abundance of blessings and good things to His children.

It is like being on a treasure hunt. Only to discover that Christ is the treasure. And walking with Him produces riches that money can't buy. He wants to take a life that is ordinary and make it extraordinary. He has a miraculous plan for you, and it will unfold as you embark on this incredible journey!

I wish I'd known sooner the relationship that I could have with my Savior. I didn't understand how to make Him the priority of my life. The ungodly thinking and behavioral patterns that were established while growing up led me to make some very foolish decisions that brought a lot of turmoil in my life.

I believed that people could make me happy. I allowed relationships with men to interfere in my walk with Christ. I spent several years filling my heart with the things of this world, only to experience brokenness, pain and regret. I now understand why my life was a vicious cycle. I didn't have godly wisdom and understanding to walk away from the hurtful situations that were consuming my life.

But my past does not define who I am today. As I began to live for Him, the cycle of broken relationships–some might call "romantic roulette"— began to break. God brought me numerous counselors and teachers who directed me to the cross and helped guide me in the healing process. I praise Him for sending individuals that helped me make decisions to live for Him, instead of continuing down my own foolish road. They encouraged me to trust Him at His Word! Their wise and godly counsel spoke into my life, and I'm praying that God will use this book, if you'll let Him, to speak into yours.

I've taught and counseled thousands of women in the years that I've been in ministry. The things I've gone through are parallel to what many of you have experienced. I've had so many ladies tell me that my story sounds just like theirs. It's almost as if we've walked the same road.

Well, we actually have. Like you, I've experienced similar feelings of rejection, insecurity, fear, and bondage in relationships. And for so many, it was hard to break free. You held on until there was nothing left to hold onto.

You no longer want to stay in a relationship that is like a heavy weight to your heart. There must be a better way! Ladies, there is. Hang onto hope! It doesn't disappoint (Romans 5:5). You can have healthy relationships. That should bring a smile to your face and a spring to your step!

God guided and helped me understand what I needed to do to overcome the pain and heartache that plagued me for years. As you read these pages, the Holy Spirit will minister to your heart.

As He brings up those things that have caused pain, let His Word be a soothing balm to your soul. Meditate on His truths. The Word has the power to heal your heart. His Holy Spirit will comfort and strengthen you and give you joy for the journey.

It is not a coincidence that you are reading *Guard Your Heart* right now. He is moving in your life, just as He moved in mine. I listened when someone encouraged me to take His Hand and follow Him in the way of righteousness. I pray that you will do the same.

I am excited to be on this adventure with you. I am humbled that He would redeem what I've gone through so others can experience freedom in Him. Rejoice! You are a new creation in Christ.

"Old things have passed away; behold, all things
have become new" (II Corinthians 5:17).

My Prince Has Come

Haven't we all felt like Cinderella, hoping that one day our Prince would come? Didn't you believe that you'd met that special someone? How did the relationship end up making you feel? Haven't you wondered if there really is a prince charming out there for you?

Well, Cinderella had almost given up hope when, suddenly, a knock comes at the door. There is a beautiful carriage with white stallions awaiting her. "This must be a dream," she thinks. "How could this be happening to me? I feel so unworthy."

The coachman takes her hand and leads her to a beautiful white gown and places a diamond tiara on her head. It's the most beautiful dress she has ever seen. He whispers to her, "You have a special invitation to the ball. The Prince is waiting for you! Hurry, we mustn't be late!" Tears begin to well up in her eyes.

She arrives at the ball and feels like she doesn't belong there. The Prince glances across the room and their eyes meet! He makes His way toward her. She can't believe He is coming for her. She feels so undeserving of His attention. She can't even stand in His presence. She stumbles to the ground and bows before Him, tears streaming down her face. He kneels down and gently lifts her head, brushing the tears away. He looks into her eyes and says, "I've chosen you. You are the one. I love you. I will never leave you. You are my princess." He places the glass slipper on her foot, and it fits!! It is just the right size. Her heart is overflowing with love and gratitude.

He smiles and whisks her off to the dance floor! She is in the arms of her beloved. She feels loved and accepted. She feels a sense of peace that she's never known before. All the suitors that came before weren't the one. They were all counterfeits! Jesus—He is her Prince. He is her Knight in shining armor! He rescued her and set her free. You can see the joy on her face. The pain is gone. This story does have a happy ending.

This is a metaphor for the relationship that we can have with God through Jesus Christ. The light of God surrounds me, the love of God enfolds me, the power of God protects me, and the presence of God watches over me. Wherever I am, He is there! Walk with me as we discover that, "As the bridegroom rejoices over the bride, so shall your God rejoice over you" (Isaiah 62:5).

Remember how Cinderella felt before the fairy godmother came to visit her? She felt so alone....so rejected. Sound familiar? And, in the twinkling of an eye, she became a princess. That's what God does when we accept Him. We become a daughter of the King. A precious child of God. And He washes away our sin! He is a real-life miracle worker. He wants you to feel a true sense of belonging. He wants you to know just how much you are loved.

You are His Cinderella, and He adores you. As you draw close to Him, it will feel like you are the only one on the dance floor. He only has eyes for you. The Prince wishes to dance with you. Will you take His hand? He wants to lead you to the Promised Land.

Contents

Chapter 1   Daughter of the King   1

Chapter 2   First Things First   19

Chapter 3   The Armor Of God   41

Chapter 4   Renewal Begins   71

Chapter 5   Friends First   93

Chapter 6   There Is A Love Worth Waiting For   129

Chapter 7   Boy Meets Girl   161

Chapter 8   Freedom In Christ   195

Chapter 9   Encouragement For The Journey   227

Chapter 10   Salvation is the Key   245

About the Author   250

CHAPTER 1
Daughter of the King

Once upon a time there was a little girl named Ashley. She had long dark hair and big brown eyes. Her heart overflowed with anticipation, as she dreamed about all the things she'd do when she grew up. She loved watching the sunrise from her bedroom window. Ashley's future looked so bright.

Cinderella was her favorite fairy tale. The most exciting part was when the prince slipped the shoe on Cinderella and it fit. She fantasized about the day she'd meet her prince. She believed it was possible to live happily ever after! She was convinced that dreams do come true.

For Ashley, life was simple. She loved playing with friends. They'd ride bikes to the park and play on the swings. Hide-n-seek was a favorite pastime for the neighborhood kids. How she loved watching the ducks paddle in the pond. She knew every one of them by name. Everyday she'd visit with the squirrel who lived in the backyard tree. His name was Sammy! Her life was filled with adventure.

Ashley was growing up so fast. Before you knew it, she was a teenager. She had never felt attracted to anyone. But then came the first crush. Puberty was setting in! And then there was the guy who gave Ashley his charm bracelet, which made her feel so special. And, she'll never forget the guy who took her Ken Rosewall sneakers and wrote his name on them—

with indelible ink, no less! The boy had left his mark! Ashley was not happy!

But then it happened! There he was! The one she believed would make her dreams come true. There, standing before her, was her prince! Just like in the fairy tale. She had never felt like this before. Ashley was in love! She imagined the pumpkin turning into a glistening carriage, as visions of Cinderella slippers danced in her head.

The young man told her she was beautiful, and that she was the only one. He said their love would last forever and he'd never leave her side. He promised her the world. All the attention made her feel like a princess. She had never experienced such happiness.

She finally felt accepted and loved. All she ever wanted was for someone to understand her. It wasn't long before she gave him her heart. It felt so good to have someone there who acted like he really cared.

Everything was perfect for the first few months. It seemed like they were made for each other. All they wanted to do was be together. Was this going to be Ashley's happy ending? Sadly, it's the beginning of a very sad love story. The boyfriend became controlling and jealous. She didn't know why things were changing. She felt so unsettled by all his demands. "Don't all relationships have some form of jealousy and control?" she thought.

And then he started to drift away. Out of desperation, she begged him to stay. But nothing she said mattered anymore. And then, just like that, he was gone. It was over. Why did he leave? She could feel her heart breaking! There was such a deep sense of loss. She was trying to make sense of what happened.

Ashley wasn't going to give up. She was sure he'd return. Why would she wait for someone who didn't want to be with her anymore? She was afraid to let go of her dream. She was trying to put the pieces of her broken heart back together again. She finally decided that she wasn't getting involved in another unhealthy relationship. She was wiser now, or so she thought.

The Cycle Continues

And then another guy came along. She was so excited about the potential for this new relationship. "Maybe now," she thought, "This would be the happily ever after I've longed for." Everything seemed so perfect. Everything she liked to do, he wanted to do too. They had so much in common. Ladies, haven't we experienced that before? You were convinced that he was the man of your dreams. And then things began to fall apart. Things weren't perfect anymore. Their fear of abandonment caused them to be very possessive. Their jealousy created many an argument. Another word for their relationship could be combustible. They didn't know how to work things out. Conflict resolution was not in their vocabulary.

They refused to give each other the freedom to grow so they could become what God intended them to be. They fell into very destructive behavioral patterns, but no matter how abusive it got, they continued to hold on to the relationship, while it hung by a thread. You would think that one of them would realize it wasn't meant to be. But not Ashley! She dug her heels in, determined to never give up. She was in it for the long haul.

She decided that she'd rather be with him than be alone. The thought of not having someone in her life prompted fear and anxiety to set in! Her belief was that it's better to have someone than no one at all. She found herself paralyzed and unable to move forward. And, if she did break up with him, there was no guarantee that the next relationship would be any better.

She had so many fears circling in her mind. How do you start over? How do you leave a relationship you've spent so much time trying to build? Would anyone ever really love her unconditionally? And if there was someone out there, where was he? Why was he so hard to find?

One day she looked in the mirror and tried to make sense of the years gone by. What had she become? She spent so much time trying to make someone else happy that she got lost in the process. She had poured so much into the relationships, trying to make them work. But instead of them making her feel better about herself, they only made her doubt her value and self-worth. The rejection had made her feel so insecure. She realized that she had clung to men in a desperate attempt to gain acceptance. The result was the exact opposite. She was confused and didn't know what to do.

Transformation Begins

Prior to falling into a pattern of unhealthy relationships, she was invited to a Bible study where she heard the *Good News* that Jesus died for her. That is where she received Christ as her Savior. Something happened to Ashley's heart that day! She knew that God was real. She knew that Jesus was alive! She believed!! She was excited about living a life for the King. She was going to church on Sundays and Bible studies every week.

But ungodly relationships got in the way and interfered in her walk with the Lord. And for several years, she went astray. Instead of seeking after God for acceptance and love, she tried to find that in relationships with the opposite sex. It never worked. All it caused was a greater sense of insecurity and inadequacy. But God always had His hand on her, and He would work mightily to draw her back to Himself.

The Holy Spirit was moving in her heart. She began to desire a close relationship with the Lord. She started reading the Bible and going back to church. Her hard heart was softening to the things of God. She started seeking His Word for direction in her life.

Rays of spiritual light were breaking through the emotional prison she had created for herself. God was at work. The door of the prison cell was opening. All the lies she had believed from the past were being exposed to the light of His Word. She discovered that she has amazing value and worth. God was going to use her mightily for His purposes. She understood that she wasn't a failure, and things weren't hopeless. He was going to redeem all the sinful things that had happened in her life. It wasn't too late. The sun was rising, and a new day was dawning.

God's Word was beginning to take root in her heart and mind, and she began seeing herself through His eyes. Her confidence began to grow as she put her trust in Him. He was doing a new thing! God began to infuse her with His power and strength, and she began to move in His direction. Her eyes began to open to His amazing love.

My Rock And My Fortress

"For You are my rock and my fortress; Therefore, for Your name's sake, lead me and guide me. Pull me out of the net which they have secretly laid for me, For You are my strength. Into Your hand I commit my spirit; You have redeemed me, O Lord, God of truth" (Psalm 31:3-5).

God put her on a path of healing and restoration. She realized that she had been in bondage to sin and unhealthy relationships for far too long. She finally walked away from the relationship that had been an idol in her life! Sadly, she didn't even realize it was an idol.

She wanted to live a life of righteousness and purity. She was experiencing meaning and purpose like she never had before. God began using all the painful experiences she'd gone through to help direct others to the cross. He healed her wounds from the past, and she now had a deep desire to help other's experience that same restoration and healing.

Ashley is me and this, in brief, is my story. There were so many times that I got lost, and I didn't know which way to go. I'd find myself at a crossroad and I'd take another wrong turn. You might feel that way right now.

His sovereign hand of love and protection led me through the valley! He will lead and guide you, too. He never left my side! He is with you. There is so much to live for. The Prince is riding in on His white stallion to rescue you! And this time, He's not just a prince, He's the King of Kings!! Follow Him and bask in the warmth of His embrace. May the love of Jesus flow through every compartment of your heart.

"A man's heart plans his way, but the Lord directs his steps" (Proverbs 16:9).

I pray that you will take the message in this book to heart and that you will let Him be the Lord of your life–your one and only! I pray that you will discover that nothing else compares to a relationship with the Savior. He is in love with you.

I hope you will embrace the truth of these wonderful words:

"Oh, taste and see that the Lord is good; blessed is the man who trusts in Him! Oh, fear the Lord, you His saints! There is no want to those who fear Him.

The young lions lack and suffer hunger; but those who seek the Lord shall not lack any good thing" (Psalm 34:8-10).

Created In His Image

As we seek Him, our eyes will open to who we truly are in Christ. And that is the key to overcoming our feelings of insecurities from the past. We were created in His image and likeness (Genesis 1:26). We were wired for greatness. We were wired to shine. He wants us to represent Him in all that we do. And that His glory would radiate through and through.

When you look in the mirror, don't you tend to see your flaws and imperfections? If I asked you to name something that you don't like about yourself, what would your answer be? Some would want a total makeover. But God doesn't want us feeling insecure about our appearance. He doesn't want us obsessing about the way we look.

I was concerned about that for years. When I was younger, I had numerous people tell me that I needed to change certain things about the way I looked. I was only a young girl. It left me broken and confused. It is so hard to be content with yourself, as it is. When people say negative things about you, it makes you feel even more inferior. I thought that if I made those changes, then I'd be accepted. All I wanted was for people to like me. That was such an unhealthy, destructive way to think.

It's a challenge to accept our imperfections, isn't it? The enemy wants to point out all the negatives. That's his goal. He doesn't want us to feel like we're good enough. He doesn't want you to know just how amazing you are and how much God wants to use you.

And then the secular world around us reinforces those feelings of insecurity. The images plastered all over magazine covers are of women who are shapely and beautiful. It's as if you'll experience happiness if you achieve a certain look. But that's not true.

There are so many women that have spent thousands of dollars and done everything in the book to be beautiful. But no matter what they did, it was never enough. We will never experience perfection, no matter how hard we try. I remember when I had thoughts like, "Maybe if I were funnier? Prettier? Smarter?" If we feel inadequate, then we will feel insecure. And we'll always be unhappy with ourselves and want change.

We don't have to believe the lies that we need to fit a certain stereotype to feel worthy and deserving of love. God will enable us to accept ourselves for who He created us to be. And even though you don't like everything about yourself, He molded you a certain way for a divine purpose. And all that He created is good! You weren't an accident or a mistake.

God wants you to understand that He wove you together in your mother's womb. When He stitched you together, He was purposeful in His design.

"You formed my inward parts; You covered me in my mother's womb. I will praise You, for I am fearfully and wonderfully made; Marvelous are your works, and that my soul knows very well" (Psalm 139:13–14).

He is in the business of transforming us from the inside out. He can take our inadequacies and imperfections and use them for His glory. Don't allow your flaws to interfere with the work God is calling you to do. Don't let the fear of rejection stymie the movement of the Holy Spirit in your life. Let Him take you to new spiritual heights as you step out in faith. Allow Him to create beauty from the brokenness.

You Are Beautiful

"So, the King will greatly desire your beauty; because He is your Lord, worship Him" (Psalm 45:11).

When I came upon this Scripture, I was taken aback. I couldn't comprehend that He is captivated by my beauty. I know that I'm not to be full of pride and arrogance, but He does want me to realize how beautiful and special I am to Him. He wants me to understand the deep, abiding love He has for me. Even though I felt so inadequate deep down inside, His Words were bringing such assurance and confidence into my life. I began letting His truths resonate within my heart, and they literally transformed the way I felt about myself and others.

Haven't we always dreamed of finding someone that believed we are truly beautiful? We do have someone, and it is Jesus. God is so amazingly beautiful and, as you seek His face, you will radiate loveliness, just as our Savior does. He wants your life to sparkle for the Son.

"He has no stately form or majesty that we should look upon Him, nor appearance that we should be attracted to Him" (Isaiah 53:2 NASB).

That's Jesus. I believe that if He'd been "Mr. GQ," people would have been drawn to His looks. The emphasis needed to focus on what's inside the heart. As we draw close to Him, we will reflect His awesome love and power. God wants people to be in awe of Him! He wants to pour out His heart of compassion into the lives of those around you in need of His grace. His love will be a light that shines through the darkness to lead others to the Savior.

Let God reveal Himself through you. Ask the Lord to help you share His amazing grace. May you seek to know Him and make Him known to others. You will have countless testimonies of His mighty and strong arm moving in your life. Have your way, Lord Jesus, have your way!

Shine On Me

Have the negative circumstances in your life caused you to feel like a wilted flower? Have you found it hard to lift your head? Has the sun beaten down on you to where you feel drained and lifeless?

Just like the rain perks up a thirsty flower, the Word of God will bring nourishment and refreshment to your soul. Just as a plant tilts toward the sun to absorb light, we need to set our sights on Jesus, so His presence will be made manifest through us. He can help you to bloom again

My favorite flower is the rose. I love to look at the petals and examine its unique beauty. When I think of how many different rose blossoms there are, I stand in wonder! And that's just one of the many flowers that blanket His creation. And just think, you are more beautiful than all the flowers put together.

When He made you, He really did break the mold. You have a fingerprint that is unlike any other. There is no one else with your DNA. No one has your unique gifts and talents. No matter how many billions of people have come before you, and no matter how many will come after, there is only one you. You are precious! You are valuable! In Him, you are worthy!

He wants you to grasp how He can achieve His will in and through you—and make your life one of individual beauty. It's encouraging to know that no matter what you've gone through, He can bring good out of your thorny past.

It's comforting to know that He will create a beautiful fragrance from the hurts you've experienced. What type of aromatic scent will come from the Son shining down on you? What types of beautiful flowers will grow as a result of the work He will do in your life? Will your life radiate His brilliance?

A Warm Blanket

How many like to curl up under a warm blanket when it gets cold outside. I live in South Florida, so there aren't many chances to do that during the year. But I do love when the temperature drops below 70.

God's love is like that blanket we cuddle up with. It wraps around to keep us safe and warm. It is a shield of protection that surrounds us. For many of us, it's hard to comprehend that kind of love because of the experiences that have occurred in our life.

We've been so rejected by people, that it's hard to believe unconditional love really does exist. But it does and it is exhibited in His nail-scarred hands! We need to understand the magnitude of our sin, and the sacrifice that God made so that we can experience a close, intimate relationship with Him. He suffered a painful, cruel and agonizing death for our sake!

He paid the ultimate price for you and for me. There is no one that will ever express a greater love for you than what was shown on the cross. I pray that you will desire, above all else, a deep oneness with Him. Let Him be the Lord of your life. I pray that your heart will overflow with a passion for the Savior. He wants to redeem your life for His glory.

"For He made Him who knew no sin to be sin for us, that we might become the righteousness of God in Him" (II Corinthians 5:21).

His acceptance of us isn't based on performance. If it was, we'd never be good enough. How many of you have fallen into performance and acceptance traps? I used to think that I had to perform a certain way and do everything right. Perfection was the key. It was an awful way to live. I remember being so overwhelmed when I'd fail. I felt so stupid.

The thoughts were, "Didn't I know better? What was I thinking? What was wrong with me?" That type of thinking plagued me, and sometimes to the point of paralysis. We have been so discouraged because we didn't match up to other people's standards.

There have been individuals in our lives who made us feel like we had to jump through hoops of acceptance to win their love. We'd try so hard to gain their approval, but nothing we did was ever good enough. That was one of the main reasons I'd feel like such a failure. Then I'd obsess over things said and done, out of concern that I might have disappointed or offended someone. I was consumed by what others thought of me and that thinking kept me in bondage for years.

Thank God, I've learned that my goal in life is to please my Savior. If I'm constantly worried about what others think of me, I won't be focused on living for Him. I did that for too many years. It was so emotionally draining. At times it really did take everything out of me! I'm so thankful that He freed me from that thought process, as I began to make Him the priority of my life. His love has engulfed my soul, renewed my heart and enabled me to live freely for Him.

A Testimony Of His Grace

I always longed to feel special in a relationship. I always wanted to be someone's number one. I yearned for someone to accept me for who I am and love me unconditionally. I cried out for that when I was young. There were so many hurtful things that happened to me while growing up that left me a very wounded vessel. My heart ached to hear words of validation from others. I longed to be affirmed and understood. But, no matter how hard I tried, I was never able to experience the acceptance I longed for.

I found myself seeking approval from people who only left me feeling more rejected and alone. I had to have my heart broken many times before I realized that no one could meet all my needs. There wasn't going to be anyone able to heal the hurts from my past or minister to those deep cuts to my heart. No one, except Jesus! As I cried out to Him, He restored my heart. He washed away so many of the hurts and pains from my past. I am in awe of how He's worked in my life to bring me to where I am today. I've found someone who truly does love me, in spite of myself. With Jesus as my Savior, I've experienced a completeness that I wasn't able to receive from any human being.

He wants to heal your broken heart. He knows the deep pain you've been through, and He wants to help you rise above all the challenges and difficulties that you've faced. He will work all things together for your good. He wants to redeem all the things that have happened to you. Trust Him to do that! In fact, He is the only One who can.

God's Divine Timing

God wants to be your great encourager, counselor and comforter. He is your champion. He is on the sidelines rooting for you. He is the captain of your ship, the quarterback of your team, the pilot of your plane, the composer of your orchestra, the writer of your music. He is your all in all!

He wants me to be an instrument that He can use to accomplish great and mighty things for the Kingdom of God. He longs to give me the desires of my heart as I delight myself in Him. I have a oneness that enables me to experience an intimacy that brings amazing joy, peace and harmony into my life. I see Him intervening in so many ways throughout my day. As I continue to make Him the priority, I see His hand guiding me along. There are constant revelations of His movement in my life. He's always there to lift me up and encourage me.

How precious is Your love for me, O God!! That is His love for you, too!! He wants to experience that closeness with you. He wants to be the answer to your prayers. He wants to be the One that comforts and strengthens you. He wants to be the One who brings you peace and contentment. He wants to receive all the glory for working things out in your life. I've learned that He is the only one able to minister to the depths of my heart.

I remember being depressed about a few things going on in my life. I felt burdened by the struggles I was facing. While on my way to Walmart, I prayed for the Lord to bring me someone to talk to. I got into the pet food aisle and ran into a friend I hadn't seen in months. She asked how I was, and I said that everything was alright. She kept prodding me, because she was convinced something was wrong.

She shared how God had brought me to mind over the past week, and she'd been praying for me. I stood there and wept. He chose Sandy to be a great source of encouragement that day. He knows exactly what I need and when to supply it. I trust Him to provide for me in every situation.

The PowerPoint Presentation

There were points while writing this book that I got so overwhelmed. It was a very challenging experience for me. I woke up one Saturday morning and felt unable to complete the task ahead. I cried out to God and pleaded for help. I just wept and wept. I didn't think I could do it anymore.

I was on my way to the store, and I saw a garage sale sign in my neighborhood. Well, that's right up my alley, so off I went. It was at the home of a local pastor that lived in our neighborhood. He knew of me and said my PowerPoint presentation on purity was one of the best he'd ever seen. I was so deeply touched. I walked away and cried like a baby. God knew I needed encouragement.

I was really struggling with feelings of insecurity that morning. He divinely spoke through that pastor so I'd receive the confidence I'd need to move forward. I hope you are seeking His face in all you do, and that you are seeing Him move in deep and profound ways. That is my prayer for you.

Delight Yourself In The Lord

"Delight yourself in the LORD, *and He will give you the desires of your heart"* (Psalm 37:4).

Some of the synonyms for the word delight are: please, rejoice, satisfy and gratify. May these words express the way you feel about the Savior. May you experience the thrill and excitement of being in a relationship with God. Let your heart take flight as you experience His divine love for you. May His desires be your delight! That's how it works when you live for Christ.

When I was young, I used to wait on the front porch for my father to come home. That was the highlight of my day! I have that same sense of anticipation in the Lord and my relationship with Him. I look forward to seeing what my Savior has in store for me each day. It isn't until you seek Him with your whole heart, that you find yourself and His Will for your life.

Prayer: I want to enjoy our relationship. I want to experience a oneness with You that brings great peace and joy into my life. I want to delight in all that You are to me and all that You have for me. I want to be excited as I walk out each day, knowing that Your faithful hand is moving me along. Help me be aware of Your holy presence in a divine way. I want to be sensitive to what Your Spirit is revealing to me. I want to be confident that You are guiding my steps. Help me understand that I am Your princess and You truly do love me unconditionally.

He Rejoices Over You With Singing

One of the most amazing things I have discovered about God's love is that He always wants to be close to me no matter what has happened in my life. He doesn't keep a record of my wrongs, and he doesn't hold things against me. I've failed so much in my relationship with Him. There have been so many times that I didn't care what He said or how He felt. I was more concerned about myself than building my relationship with God. I allowed so many things to come between us. And yet He has shown mercy and grace throughout my life. I stand in awe of my Savior.

Even though I had turned down the wrong road, He was always watching over me. I can see how He always had His eyes on me by the way He has protected and guided me into ministry. He is so faithful and true. Just like God sent Nathan to King David, He sent messengers to me at pivotal junctures in my life who encouraged me to do the right thing.

There were times that I was given spiritual ultimatums that required me to make a choice for Him. I cried out and He answered, enabling me to obey. As I prayed for direction, He provided ways for me to break free of the past. His divine intervention enabled me to see His Hand moving me away from the worldly lifestyle I'd been caught up in. He literally delivered me out of a cycle of unhealthy relationships. He never gave up on me. Even though I chose to put others first, He never left me alone. He saved me, rescued me and planted my feet on solid ground.

"The LORD your God is in your midst, the Mighty One, will save; He will rejoice over you with gladness, He will quiet you with His love, He will rejoice over you with singing" (Zephaniah 3:17).

When I meditate on this verse, I don't understand it. I don't know how He could rejoice over me. But He does. His love runs so deep. I can picture Him smiling down on me. I feel so undeserving of His love and yet, He pours it over me in abundance. My heart is filled with enthusiasm over His constant love and care. That is Him engulfing me with His presence.

I bought an illustration of Jesus embracing a young girl, and it bears a striking resemblance to me when I was little. I have that drawing close by as reminder that His arms are always wrapped around me. I can rest in the fact that He has a passionate love for me that never fails, no matter what. He is my helper! I must always be mindful that we are one.

A Closer Walk With Thee

I've learned to walk closer to Him and that's allowed me to have more insight into what He's doing each step of the way. He doesn't want me to get ahead of Him. I'm constantly asking for His will to be done in my life. If I'm focused on my own agenda, I'll miss what He is trying to accomplish through me. I won't receive the spiritual blessings that He has for me if I'm focused on myself. I am very mindful that the Holy Spirit wants to use me each day to minister to others. As Jesus is the light in a dark world, I want to be that same example to those around me. May my life bear the love of Christ in everything I do.

He wants to keep us in all our ways. He will direct us on our journey home. He is our front, rear and side guard. He is with you wherever you go. The One who hung the earth in space and causes it to spin on its axis is the One who wants to be in control of what happens to you. He is a God of precision. He can divinely unfold His plan for your life. He will reveal His purposes as you walk with Him each day. He's on your side and wants to work on your behalf. But you must let Him have His way in your heart.

Do you trust Him with your life? Are you willing to surrender to Him? Are you willing to pray for the strength to do things His way? That is the only way to experience true freedom in your life. Some of you have been following your own path, and it's only left you more frustrated and confused. I get it! That's my story, too. I am excited to see How God will move in your life, as you move in His direction.

> "The Lord is my strength and my shield; my heart trusted in Him, and I am helped; Therefore, my heart greatly rejoices, and with my song I will praise Him" (Psalm 28:7).

I praise God for the special relationship that I have with Him. My heart rejoices in His grace and love. I want to give thanks for His faithfulness. I want to sing praises, because I was lost, and He found me. I have battle scars from the rejection I experienced in my life. Because of His love, I finally feel secure. I am safe in His arms!! I finally feel loved!! How wonderful you are, Lord!! You have healed my broken heart!!

He's With Me Wherever I Go

"He knows when you sit down and rise up; He understands your thoughts and is acquainted with all your ways. Such knowledge is too wonderful for me; it is high, and I cannot attain it" (Psalm 139:2-6 paraphrased).

As we spend time in Psalm 139, we discover just how close God is to David. He's holding on to David and He won't let go. He knows that God's divine protection is over him. He's overwhelmed at how intricately God is involved in his life. He is not a fleeting thought to God. God is familiar with every thought that crosses David's mind. No matter where he goes or what he does, God is there to carry him through. That should give us great comfort and hope to know that He will never leave or forsake us. We can always be confident that He is there to help us. We can count on our Savior. When Scriptures talk of God's unfailing love, we can see that played out in the life of David. And it is played out in our lives, too.

God's Promises

We all need to draw closer to God. None of us have arrived until we get to the other side. Is the Holy Spirit tugging at your heart? Do you feel the need to get closer to Him and make Him the priority of your life?

Let Psalm 42:1-2 be your prayer:

"As the deer pants for the water brooks, So pants my soul for You, O God. My soul thirsts for God, for the living God. When shall I come and appear before God?"

You are deeply loved by the Savior. He has a passionate desire for oneness with you. He is your husband, if you've received Christ as Savior and Lord. Remember, you are a cherished possession, a priceless gem, a radiant bride. He wants to meet you right where you are.

He wants you to see yourself for the amazing creation that you are. You are royalty—a child of God and a daughter of the King. There is nothing you won't be able to achieve with Him at the wheel. Where is He going to take you? You're in for an exciting ride!

At the end of each chapter, there are Scripture verses to meditate on. I encourage you to get 3 x 5 index cards and put your choice of Bible verses on them. Carry them with you wherever you go. One of the first Christian counselors I met with gave me this advice. It really helped me learn to apply the Scriptures to my daily life. When you are at a red light, say a prayer. It doesn't have to be formal. Just talk to Him. Even though you might not be used to turning your thoughts toward Him, make a conscious effort to do so. The more you include Him in this process, the more you will see His divine hand working in your life.

I encourage you to start your day by spending time in His Word. Make this a priority. Consider it your spiritual fuel for the day. Don't leave home without filling up your tank. Remember when you were told that it's important to really chew your food. Well, we need to "chew" on His truths so that our souls grow healthy and strong. Ask God to empower you through His Word.

Set your sights on things above. Focus on what's eternal. Ask God to engulf you with His presence. His desire is for you to be filled with thoughts of Him. When distractions come, turn your gaze back in His direction. Don't let anything come between your walk with Him. He wants you to cling to Him and never let go. Don't let anything throw you off course. Be single-minded in your quest for intimacy with the Father.

He has a mission for you. He wants to equip you for the work He has called you to do. You have purpose. He has gifted you with talents and abilities that are designed specifically for the plan He has for your life. How wonderful it is to know that you have a divine calling. What comforting and reassuring thoughts on which to meditate.

Sadly, I've spoken to many women who believe they weren't wired for greatness. Those wrong thoughts will only hinder and impede the movement of the Holy Spirit in your life. Don't accept the negative and discouraging thoughts that enter your mind. The Holy Spirit will reprogram your belief system so that you are confident of your divine purpose and calling.

I can't wait to see what He will reveal to you.

Verses For Meditation

*"I will greatly rejoice in the L*ORD*, my soul shall be joyful in my God; for He has clothed me with the garments of salvation, He has covered me with the robe of righteousness, as a bridegroom decks himself with ornaments, and as a bride adorns herself with her jewels."* ~ Isaiah 61:10

*"For you are a holy people to the L*ORD *your God, and the L*ORD *has chosen you to be a people for Himself, a special treasure above all the peoples who are on the face of the earth."* ~ Deuteronomy 14:2

"When I consider Your heavens, the work of Your fingers, the moon and the stars, which You have ordained, what is man that You are mindful of him, and the son of man that You visit him?" ~ Psalm 8:3-4

*"Let the beauty of the L*ORD *our God be upon us and establish the work of our hands for us; yes, establish the work of our hands."* ~ Psalm 90:17

"Do not let your adornment be merely outward—arranging the hair, wearing gold, or putting on fine apparel—rather let it be the hidden person of the heart, with the incorruptible beauty of a gentle and quiet spirit, which is very precious in the sight of God." ~ 1 Peter 3:3-4

CHAPTER 2

First Things First

*G*od wants you to thirst after Him with every fiber of your being. *"Love the Lord your God with all your heart, soul, mind and strength"* (Mark 12:30 paraphrased).

That is the first commandment! He wants every part of your heart to be totally devoted to Him. He wants you to hunger and thirst for Him. Can you imagine being outdoors for days without water? What would your thoughts be focused on? Water... water... please, I need water. I want to thirst after God with that kind of passion. I want to have a deep desire to experience Him in the most profound way. I want to be so consumed with Him that everything I touch has His fingerprints on it!

I want these words to be at the heart of all I do: Fairest Lord Jesus, you are my soul's delight, the spring in my step, the contentment in my heart, the love of my life, the passion that I live for, the person that I long to make happy, the One who has given me all that I have. I stand in awe of you! I pray that my total being overflows with all that you are to me! I pray that my life ministers to others in mighty and powerful ways. Grant me the ability to mirror your awesome wonder and might to those around me.

"There is none like You, O LORD; You are great, and Your name is great in might" (Jeremiah 10:6).

Proverbs 3:5-6

The key to a life of contentment is establishing a closer, more intimate walk with the Savior! *"We must trust the LORD with all our heart. We can't lean on our own understanding. In all our ways we must acknowledge Him, and He will direct our paths"* (Proverbs 3:5, 6 –paraphrased).

In years past, I stumbled along aimlessly searching for the right way to go! I followed my heart and found myself moving in and out of relationships. I believed that I should move forward in a relationship because certain things fell into place. I thought that if I liked someone and had feelings for him, then it was meant to be.

Because I had accepted Christ as Savior, I assumed He was involved in all the inner workings of my decisions. If something or someone was in front of me, then God must have put it there! I trusted the circumstances without even considering how the enemy might be working through the situation.

Because I didn't know how to determine whether a person was the right one for me, I got into relationships that weren't from God. I made some bad judgment calls. I truly believed that I knew what I was doing, but I was so wrong.

So much of my brokenness was a result of letting unhealthy people into my life. I had developed such a deep lack of trust that it was impossible for me to have a constructive relationship. My fears and insecurities caused me to stay in very toxic situations. I clung to people in a desperate attempt to be loved.

I didn't know that I couldn't become a more loving and forgiving person unless I developed a deeper connection with the Savior. I had no clue that I'd never trust anyone until I learned to let God heal me of the hurts and pains from my past. I was never going to be able to love unconditionally until I allowed Jesus to take control of my heart.

There will be many temptations and challenges that will cross our path each day. The Word of God has all the answers to life's problems. There was a period in my life when I didn't go to God's Word to find the answers to the situations that were in front of me. I never sought Biblical counsel to find out what He said about which way to go. I was an immature Christian and didn't even know it.

Let your heart's desire be to get to know Him intimately through studying His Word. He is so amazing! There aren't enough words in the dictionary to describe how awesome He is.

Hansel and Gretel

Remember the story of Hansel and Gretel? They used breadcrumbs to find their way home! Thank God, you have His Word to direct you on your spiritual journey. If we would only realize how dependent we are on His guidance. That's one thing I wished I'd understood sooner. But it's never too late. Always remember that.

> "My soul waits silently for God alone, for my expectation is from Him. He only is my rock and my salvation. He is my defense; I shall not be moved. In God is my salvation and my glory; the rock of my strength, and my refuge is in God. Trust in Him at all times, you people; pour out your heart before Him; God is a refuge for us" (Psalm 62:5-8).

He is the maker of the universe, and He can work His power in and through you. Don't you want to experience everything that God has planned for you? Don't you want His best for your life? Meditate on the Scriptures below and let them take root in your heart. May you comprehend the power that is available through the Holy Spirit to those who belong to Him.

> "[I pray] that the Father of glory may give you the spirit of wisdom and revelation in the knowledge of Him, the eyes of your understanding being enlightened; that you may know what is the hope of His calling, what are the riches of the glory of His inheritance in the saints, and what is the exceeding greatness of His power toward us who believe" (Ephesians 1:17-19).

May you be confident that He is personally speaking to you through His Word. Trust Him to show you what path to take. Believe that He has a specific purpose for your life and will bring it to pass. He wants you to be a living testimony that enables people to see how intricately He works. He is sovereign and in control. He will make it happen.

Beauty For Ashes

"The Spirit of the Lord GOD is upon Me, because the LORD has anointed Me to preach good tidings to the poor; He has sent Me to heal the broken-hearted, to proclaim liberty to the captives, and the opening of the prison to those who were bound; To proclaim the acceptable year of the LORD, to comfort all who mourn, to console those who mourn in Zion, to give them beauty for ashes, the oil of joy for mourning. The garment of praise for the spirit of heaviness; that they may be called trees of righteousness, the planting of the LORD, that He may be glorified" (Isaiah 61:1-3).

I am a volunteer biblical counselor at the church my husband and I attend. God brought me into that ministry. I'm in awe of the deep spiritual connection I have with each woman that I minister to. Because I've gone through similar experiences, I can relate to her pain. I'm able to share how He's walked me through my brokenness, healed me and set me free. He's using what I've gone through to be a testimony to others.

What you've experienced doesn't have to be in vain. God can create incredible beauty from the ashes. Be encouraged. You can be a ray of hope in the lives of those around you. This is only the beginning for you!

We are His hands and feet. The world needs Jesus. For many people, darkness has led to despair. There are many without hope. It's as if they've fallen into a black hole and can't find their way out. They are lost without the Savior. Their only hope is Christ. May your heart seek out those He's trying to reach through you. Let the words and actions that flow from you be connected to the fountain that springs eternal, our wonderful Savior, Jesus.

Prayer: Please guide and direct me as I seek you, Lord. Open my eyes to see your truths. Help me have confidence in the path you have chosen for me. Help me trust you with my whole heart. Help me believe that the same power exhibited in the lives of countless people throughout the Bible will be revealed in my life, as well. Please give me faith as a grain of mustard seed. Help me to believe and trust in Your Word.

"I say to you, if you have faith as a mustard seed, you will say to this mountain, 'Move from here to there,' and it will move; and nothing will be impossible for you" (Matthew 17:20).

A Gentle Reminder!

Christ wants to be number one in your life! That doesn't come without time and effort. A relationship takes time to build, and it is true with the Savior. We've all had best friends that have known all about us. They're the ones that we are closest to and have the deepest connection with. Jesus wants to be your best friend. He wants to be the One that you confide in about all that's going on in your life.

Ladies, I remember reading a poem about a woman getting ready for work. She rushed around frantically trying to get out the door on time. Jesus wanted her to spend time in His Word. He saw what she was going through and wanted to minister to her. But she was too busy. The daily demands of life were calling her name. She kept thinking that she needed to make her devotions a priority, but it never seemed to work out.

She raced out the door and her day fell apart. It seemed like she went from one problem to the next. She got home and broke down in tears. "Why are things so hard?" she groaned. "Why is life so difficult?" Have you ever had thoughts like that? As she cried out to God, He impressed on her heart that she wasn't going to Him for help and strength throughout the day.

As I was writing the above section, I got convicted. I'd gotten up that morning and jumped right into editing my book. I didn't start my day by spending time in the Word and prayer. I needed to do that. So, I went and had my quiet time with Him. God is so incredibly patient with us, isn't He? He is so gracious in the way He works to bring conviction. He used my own teaching to remind me that I needed to make Him my top priority. His timing is always perfect.

Then came some real challenges. My computer started going crazy and deleting sections of the book. I was already feeling discouraged. This was the last thing I needed. My husband is very computer savvy and quickly came to my rescue. But some of the revisions were lost. I cried out, "Why do things have to be so frustrating?"

Then I remembered the woman who got frazzled because she wasn't including God in her day. How quickly we get discouraged, ladies! How often do we get carried away by our emotions? I prayed and sought His help in the situation. Instead of breaking down, I needed to look up. Ask the Lord for guidance to help you work through life's daily challenges.

I was finally able to import the missing text from another file. All was not lost. There will be struggles that test our patience, faith and trust. But we must not let those difficulties weigh us down. When was the last time something caused you major frustration? How did you approach the problem? Did you seek His guidance to navigate through it?

There have been many times when I have fretted and fumed over circumstances that happened in my life. Sadly, too many times to count. That reaction will not help the situation, and it won't change anything. You must go back and claim God's promises. He says that all things work together for good. And if something doesn't work out, trust that He will see you through it. You can rest assured of that!

I have heard individuals who have taken self-defense courses talk about the importance of staying calm in life-threatening situations. We need to seek God in every circumstance and situation. He can give us the peace that passes understanding. He is the One who can save the day! He is the great miracle worker! He will lead you through those choppy waters. He can calm your storm.

Let each trial and tribulation be a learning experience. Spiritual growth occurs when we allow the Holy Spirit to teach us through our struggles. Frequently ask yourself these questions, "Jesus, what are you trying to show me? How am I supposed to grow closer to you through this? How I am to respond to this situation?"

He is always there with His arms open wide. He wants to have an intimate relationship with you. Don't let the flesh and the enemy have their way. Cry out to Jesus! Ask Him for help. He will intervene. Whatever you are confronting, He wants to walk with you each step of the way to get you safely home. The more you seek Him, the more His power will be revealed in your life. His divine timing will leave you in awe. The way He weaves things together will help build your faith. When you experience the gentle and loving Spirit of the Lord, it will make you love Him more. It's an incredible thing to experience and an awesome thing for others to see!

Who Is The Center Of Your Universe?

If I gave you a pad and paper and asked you to write down every thought that crossed your mind over the next 48 hours, what would you say? How many times would Jesus be named on those pages? How often did you pray to Him, meditate on His Word, give thanks or offer praise? The answer is a good indicator of what your world revolves around.

Our lifestyles are so busy. We have so many things that demand our attention. There was a period in my life when I did not walk closely with Him. It was all about what I wanted. I was doing things my way. But He began wooing me back. I began to pray for an awareness and sensitivity to His presence. I wanted spiritual confirmations, so I'd know He was guiding me along. I was begging Him for direction. I wanted Him to make a clear path for my feet. I was so desperate for His intervention. I was so tired of getting hurt because of the foolish choices that I made.

I soon found myself seeking Him about everything. I started directing all my self-talk to him. I found that the more I focused on His Word, the more I understood how the enemy puts wrong thoughts into my head. Those lies caused me a lot of fear and anxiety. His deceitful ways caused me to open many a trap door.

In fact, the enemy of our souls is constantly saying things to condemn us. He'll continue rattling off our failures. He wants us to have an inferiority complex. His goal is to break us down. He wants us to feel discouraged and disappointed. Then we will feel hopeless and helpless. And we will find it much harder to walk out our faith.

That is never how the Lord works with us. His Words are filled with grace. They are meant to empower you! He would never say condescending things to you. He doesn't want you to feel inadequate and unloved. The Lord is always there to build you up. His ways are designed to produce good things from you. He transforms us so that our lives will reflect the heart and mind of Christ. Whatever He does, it's always from a heart of love.

If you have thoughts that make you feel condemned, they aren't from God. He doesn't taunt us with debilitating thoughts. He doesn't deal with His children like that. And you can be confident of it! Throughout the Scriptures, you see the faithfulness of God towards His people. You see how He is totally sovereign over their lives.

That is exactly how he works in our lives, too. And even when you don't understand what is happening, as you seek His face, He will divinely work in your life. That's why it's so important to delve into the Word and let it permeate your being. Let it transform the way you think and feel. You will gain more confidence in His love for you.

Look at how He deals with those who love Him. He is a good, gracious, patient, longsuffering, kind, compassionate, generous, astonishing, amazing, incredible, awesome and loving God! Wow! I'm blessed beyond belief by a God who knows and loves me. And I want you to feel that same sense of awe-struck wonder in Him.

I tell women that I want to eat, sleep and drink my Savior. I want my universe to revolve around Him. Without His gravitational pull, I'd be all over the place. I want God's power to be what keeps me grounded.

Women ask me how they'll know Christ is their center. Well, here are a few key indicators. They'll care more about what His Word says. They'll include Him in their conversations. They'll want to do things His way! They will make wiser decisions that reflect His awesome and mighty power. They'll say no to the things of this world. They will desire to be pure in mind, body and spirit.

Let Christ Be The CEO Of Your Company

I encourage you to start talking to Him about everything. Start the day by going over your daily agenda with Him. What's on your to-do list? Have you asked him about those things? Let Him be the CEO of your company.

I'm sorry that I didn't let Him run my business years ago. He wants you to talk with Him about everything you are going through. It'd be wise to seek His help on how to lovingly reflect a Christ-like attitude in all that you do. Ask for wisdom and discernment as you face each situation. Talk to Him about your frustrations and disappointments.

Give thanks to Him during the good times and the bad, the happy and the sad. Seek Him when you're feeling overwhelmed. Trust Him when things didn't work out the way you planned. Have faith that He is always with you. Determine to reflect His character no matter what the situation.

"Let your light shine before men, that they may see your good works and glorify your Father in heaven" (Matthew 5:16).

As I walk along each day, I try to make sure that I'm holding His hand. I don't want to get up and walk out the door without inviting Him to be with me wherever I go. I don't want to tackle the cares of this life on my own anymore. I have failed miserably in the past and faced much regret, as a result. God has worked everything together for good in my life. Romans 8:28 is my favorite Scripture verse, because He has used all I've gone through for His glory. He is so faithful. I've learned to trust Him, and it's amazing how incredible the journey is when I'm clinging to Him. He is my constant companion.

"Commit your way to the LORD, trust also in Him, and He shall bring it to pass" (Psalm 37:5).

He Wants Your Whole Heart

Jeremiah 29:11 is a favorite Scripture verse for many people. I've seen it on t-shirts, plaques, and other items. It is a beautiful verse. It is encouraging to know that He cares so deeply for us. He wants to do great things through us. We are a vessel meant to bring Him glory, honor, and praise.

"For I know the thoughts that I think toward you, says the LORD, thoughts of peace and not of evil, to give you a future and a hope. Then you will call upon Me and go and pray to me, and I will listen to you. And you will seek Me and find Me, when you search for me with all of your heart" (Jeremiah 29:11-13).

God does promise believers a future and a hope. But the prophet Jeremiah also wants us to understand that there's more to the story! That's why I was surprised by verses 12-13. The prophet stresses the need to seek after God with our whole heart. Our future doesn't just "pop" into being! We don't just automatically become the person He destined us to be. It is when we relinquish our rights and submit to His will, that we discover where we belong. He is not willing to accept just a sliver. He doesn't want just a portion of the pie. He wants all of it and nothing less.

In my earlier walk as a Christian, I hadn't given Him my whole heart. I believed He was in control, but He wasn't. There were times He intervened so I would make the choice to put Him first. I had to decide who I was going to serve. I could no longer have one foot in the world and one foot in church. I couldn't play church on Sunday, and then go back to the ungodly relationship on Monday.

I couldn't let my emotional and physical needs be met by a guy and the things of this world. I couldn't expect Him to control my destiny when I wasn't surrendering my heart to His sovereign leadership. It's hard to say goodbye to the things we're used to doing. It's hard to walk away from what we consider our "comfort food." Worldly habits and addictions are destructive and will deeply interfere in your walk with the Lord. It will only create a wider gulf between you and God.

In our sinfulness, we can't seek God. We need His grace to lead us back to Him. We need His Spirit to move in our hearts. We don't have eyes to see unless He opens them! I know He loved me even when I wasn't showing much love for Him. He had a future planned for me, even when I chose paths that didn't include Him. He still worked through my bad choices to reveal His purposes in my life.

Prayer: Lord, I have failed so much in seeking after You. I want to set my sights on you continually throughout the day. May I long to seek after you with my whole heart. May my desire be to love you with everything I have.

Follow Him!

It's very difficult to break free of sinful desires because of the major struggle between the flesh, the enemy and the Holy Spirit. Just as Adam and Eve had freedom to choose, we are given that same right. We aren't forced to obey Him. Each day we are at a fork in the road, and we must choose which path we'll take.

You don't have to go to church if you don't feel like it. You don't have to read the Bible if you choose not to. Spiritual growth does not occur by wishing and wanting it to happen. It is only by following Him that your plans will succeed. Think of yourself as a little child and your daddy is telling you to take His Hand. Will you release those things that you're holding onto so you can run into the arms of the one who really loves you?

If you don't allow Him to transform your life, you will stay in bondage to sin. Your life will be filled with disappointment. The only way to experience peace and joy is to live for Him and do things His way! But you must let go of the worldly things that create an obstacle between the two of you. You will not experience oneness with the Savior if you allow the flesh to control you. You don't want to quench what the Holy Spirit longs to do through you.

I remember struggling with sinful patterns in my life and praying for those fleshly desires to go away. Just take them away, Lord, then it'd be easier to do the right thing. Can't you just remove them? I mean, you are God and can do anything. But it wasn't about how I felt; it was about being obedient to Him. It meant saying no to the flesh, even if it hurt and caused deep pain. But that is when your spiritual muscles grow stronger, and you become more like Him. And the blessings that come! Oh sister, what you are missing out on by giving into temptation.

As I put Christ first, I saw Him open and close doors, remove obstacles, break down barriers, protect and provide. I have journals full of how He has been so faithful to me. I yearn for women to understand the closeness they can have with the Savior. Let studying His Word and living for Him be your new obsession. That's the healthiest choice you'll ever make.

A Wrong Turn

When I wasn't living for Him my life was a mess. Everything seemed out of control. When I didn't give Him my full attention, I found myself feeling like I'd fallen into a pit! Even when I took wrong turns, He was still there to deliver me. He is my amazing Savior.

Speaking of wrong turns, I remember heading to a party in an undeveloped part of south Florida years ago. It was late at night, and there were no streetlights. I drove my 1973 Dodge Charger down a very narrow road and got lost. I tried to turn the car around and ended up getting stuck in the dirt. I climbed out of the car and headed down the road.

I saw a trailer and the yard was filled with horses, cows and goats. I had to climb over a tall fence to get help. I was so scared, but I didn't know what else to do. I kept praying, "please help me, Lord." I desperately needed a rescue. I was trembling when I knocked on the door. The guy that lived there had a pick-up truck and chain. It was an answer to prayer. Thank you, Jesus. He led me down the street, hooked up my car and pulled it out of the dirt. Woohoo!! Amazing grace!

After it was over, he wanted to show me something. He took me to where my car had gotten stuck in the dirt and said, "You see just beyond that brush? You were on your way into a canal. Just a few more feet and your car would have slipped into the water. And no one would have ever known."

I stood there in shock and then I began to cry! I had no idea that I was so close to death, but Jesus did! I still look back on that event with thanks and gratitude. It can still move me to tears. He truly does have the hairs of our heads numbered. Even though I wasn't doing things His way, He still had His hand of protection over me. I was the lost sheep that He brought back into the fold. He spared my life to bring me to where I am today.

We don't want to make any more wrong turns. We don't want to do things that cause us to wander into dangerous territory. We want to stay away from those things that will cause trauma and tragedy in our lives. We want to learn and grow from our past experiences.

Do you have a testimony of God's hand of protection over you? As you look back, can't you recall a time that He rescued you? Give Him praise for all He's done! You're alive and that's a precious gift from God. What so many would give for just one more breath of life.

We must seek after Him as if He were a priceless treasure—because He is! We need to thirst for Him because He is the Living Water and the Only One able to quench our parched hearts. We need to hunger for Him, because He is the Bread of Life and only He can satisfy. As we search the Scriptures and fill our minds with thoughts of Him, our hearts will overflow with the love of Christ.

"Now may the Lord direct your hearts into the love of God and into the patience of Christ" (II Thessalonians 3:5).

Seek His Righteousness

Are the choices you're making reflecting His character and priorities? Jesus said to *"Seek first the kingdom of God and His righteousness, and all these things shall be added to you"* (Matthew 6:33).

Some people think that they can live the way they want, and God will answer whenever they cry out to Him. Sometimes we treat Him like a doctor on call. There were times when I wondered why God hadn't answered a prayer request. I'd do things my way, expecting Him to solve my problems.

My sinful lifestyle didn't include Him. I wasn't seeking the things of the Kingdom. At that time, I was not putting Him first. He desires for us to have a passion for righteousness, above all else. That's a pre-requisite that many people miss! There is a four-pronged approach that we must commit our lives to, it is: The Word of God, prayer, church and godly service.

How can you become more Christ-like if you're not doing the things that draw you closer to Him? How can you experience oneness if you are allowing other things to separate you from Him? How can He direct you if you're not letting Him?

I remember when I was living for myself. I'd go out and drink on the weekends, and sometimes during the week. I loved going out with my girlfriends and dancing the night away. We used to say that we weren't hurting anyone, because we were just having fun. I used to justify and rationalize my past ungodly behavior.

But God has shown me how wrong it was. I mean, I surely wasn't setting a godly example. At times, I was a very bad influence. I am so thankful that God has enabled me to forgive myself for the crazy things I did and the way I lived. He's redeemed my past, and used what I've gone through to create the person that I am.

It Could Have Been Me

There were many nights that we drank too much, and I drove home. Thank God, I never got a DUI and was never in an accident that caused bodily harm because of driving while intoxicated. But that could have been my reality.

"There, but for the grace of God, go I" is a quote I love. It's been said time and again. I thought it was a verse in the Bible. When I found out where it came from, I was brought to tears. It was originally said by John Bradford, an English preacher who was burned at the stake for preaching the gospel of Jesus Christ in the 1500s. Bradford made that statement as he saw a group of criminals being led to their execution.

All of us need to be so thankful, because if it weren't for His amazing love, we'd be just like one of those criminals headed to their death. Bradford understood that God had mercifully spared him from the same fate. He knew that eternal life awaited Him. He was confident of where he was going.

Our sin requires a payment. Jesus paid the penalty for our transgressions. We are no longer a criminal awaiting trial. We are no longer in fear of standing before the judge of the world. Our Savior has rescued us from the bondage of sin and death. We have been redeemed through the blood of the lamb. We are counted righteous! We are heirs with Christ. The Scriptures refer to us as saints!!! If that isn't a miracle, I don't know what is.

"Since the children have flesh and blood, he too shared in their humanity so that by his death he might break the power of him who holds the power of death, that is, the devil and free those who all their lives were held in slavery by their fear of death" (Hebrews 2:14-15).

It is idolatry when you put people, places and things above your relationship with Jesus. You will discover that life doesn't have true meaning if God isn't at the center. I learned that I needed to walk away from the idols that were interfering in my walk with Christ. I had to say no to those fleshly desires that were consuming me. They only produced heartache and headaches.

Is the Holy Spirit knocking on the door of your heart? Is there an area of sin that He is revealing to you? That is His incredible grace helping you become more like Him. Let the Good Shepherd be your guide. He will lead you to a place of safety. You will find yourself standing on the Rock.

When I'm seeking after Him, He's right there to unveil the next step for me. But I must be close to Him. Don't you want to experience His divine guidance? Don't you want to know that He is right there by your side? Then let go of the things this world is offering and choose to live for Him.

"He also brought me up out of a horrible pit, out of the miry clay, and set my feet upon a rock, and established my steps. He has put a new song in my mouth—praise to God; many will see it and fear and will trust in the LORD" (Psalm 40:2–3).

Choose Christ!

I recently counseled a precious sister in Christ who desired to put God first in her life. She was currently in an ungodly relationship. I showed her Scriptures that told her to walk away from anything that causes her to sin. She wasn't ready to make the sacrifice. She found it very painful to accept the counsel I gave her. I told her that she was going to miss out on God's best for her life.

God was trying to speak through me. He wants to reveal Himself in personal, intimate ways. But she must make a choice. The boyfriend is an idol in her life and is distracting her from walking with the Lord. If she doesn't turn away, there will be much pain, heartache and regret. God is trying to protect her! But she must submit to His Word so that He can take control of the reins. By saying goodbye to the relationship, she'd be saying yes to the Savior and His will for her life.

I've been in her shoes. I know how she feels. I was told that I wouldn't experience intimacy with the Lord if I didn't give up my worldly relationship. By the grace of God, I listened. It wasn't easy. But I can't thank Christ enough for rescuing me out of a cycle of ungodly relationships. He wanted my complete devotion. He wanted to move me into ministry. It wouldn't have happened if I'd stayed in that unhealthy relationship. I had to make a choice to leave the past behind.

There is only one way that an individual will experience a life of abundance, and that is by placing Christ on the throne of their heart. When I compare my life now to what it used to be, I'm motivated to share the truths that I've learned. God wants to do over and above what you can think or ask, but you must let Him be the leader. You must let Him take charge of your destiny. It's a requirement. I had to learn the hard way. I pray that you'll learn from me.

Say A Prayer

Prayer: How do I put You first? What am I holding onto that's preventing You from becoming Lord of my life? Help me cling to You, Lord. I want my heart to long for You. Give me the grace that enables me to place You first and keep You there! Help me have a passion for You, Lord.

Forgive me for all the times I didn't put You on the throne; for all the times that I didn't seek Your guidance and direction; for the countless times that I longed for worldly things; for all the times that I sought people to fulfill the longings of my heart. Forgive me,

Lord, I stand before You and am truly sorry. Thank You for Your forgiveness, mercy and grace. I'm so in love with you. You are the One that has guided and protected me all the days of my life. You are the One who has always been there for me.

I can't thank you enough. That is why I owe You everything. You have been so very good to me. You are so wonderful to your children. You are truly a God of love! That is His incredible love for you, too.

I know that You rejoice over me with gladness. I'm the apple of Your eye! You are in love with me. You are ever faithful. There is no one else like you. You are so magnificent. Thank you for your mighty Hand of redemption in my life. You rescued me out of a pit of despair. I was so lost, but you found me. I was blind but you enabled me to see. I humbly bow before Your Majesty!

"For by You I can run against a troop; By my God I can leap over a wall.
As for God, His way is perfect; the word of the LORD is proven; He is a
shield to all who trust in Him. For who is God except the LORD? And who

is a rock, except our God? God is my strength and power, and He makes my way perfect. He makes my feet like the feet of a deer and and sets me on high places." (II Samuel 22:30-34).

I'm Very Thrifty!

I love yard sales and thrift stores! I'm always looking for a good deal. I love it when I find a collectible that someone has tossed aside! I recently bought an heirloom quilt for $10 and smiled all the way home. Like they say, one man's trash is another man's treasure.

I recently bought a framed painting, and I came home to find the perfect place for it. I had to put thought into exactly where the nail went. I thought about my past broken relationships and realized that I'd spent more time trying to figure out where that nail went, than trying to evaluate the kind of person I had set my sights on!

I've had many women tell me that they have a grocery list of requirements for the guy they dreamed of marrying. I had a list, too! You know: loving, kind, gentle, sensitive, funny, strong, caring, handsome, a good communicator, and the list goes on and on. Sad to say, I didn't adhere to it!

I allowed my feelings to lower my standards. That's when you see the unhealthy behaviors overflow, but you are determined to tie a knot and hang on for dear life. Maybe if I do this or that, things will get better. That thinking caused me to stay stuck in relationships that didn't go anywhere but in reverse.

Ladies, ask yourself these questions? Were the spiritual requirements at the top of your list in past relationships? I mean, one guy I dated said he was a Christian and his parents went to prayer meetings on Wednesday nights. Well, that sold me! Obviously, he's a believer, right? The relationship was a disaster. Boy, do I regret that one. Along with all the other broken relationships.

A Sure Foundation

We are starting over! We are going to experience a total relationship makeover. You aren't going to be the same person you used to be. And you will see that unfold mightily in your relationships with others. We are demolishing the past requirements that weren't built on Him and reconstructing a new list of specifications.

What are some of the elements needed to build a healthy relationship? We'd quickly list qualities like honesty, trust, faithfulness, and self-control, to name a few. But how many have said, with unwavering clarity, that Jesus is their firm foundation? How many are confident that their house is being built on the Rock, which is salvation in Jesus Christ?

The Scriptures refer to Jesus as the chief cornerstone. In Biblical times, a cornerstone was used as the foundation and standard upon which a building was constructed. Once in place, the rest of the building would conform to the angles and size of the cornerstone. If it was removed, the entire structure would collapse.

"For no one can lay a foundation other than that which is laid, which is Jesus Christ" (I Corinthians 3:11).

There will be many happy and sad times under the roof of your home. It will be where countless memories are reflected upon. So, the building of your home requires much forethought, insight and prayer. We must make sure our home is being built on our faith and trust in Jesus Christ.

We will face many storms in our lives. Frequently, we see stories of lives uprooted by a hurricane or tornado. Watching what the individuals have gone through has been heartbreaking. We can face storms like that, too. They can come in many forms: the loss of a job, loss of health and loss of life. At times, we can feel like we are drowning in a sea of pain. Whatever is happening, pray for the faith to get through it.

As you focus on making Him the priority, your foundation will be rooted in Christ. He can give you the strength and stability to handle these tough situations. He can calm the frazzled nerves and bring tranquility to the heart. You will be able to withstand the harsh winds and rains that will come. He promises to sustain you until the floodwaters recede. Wherever He leads you, His grace will see you through.

The Wise Man

The wise man dug deep and laid his foundation on Jesus. He has an intimate relationship with the Savior. He wants to live for Him and do things His way. Jesus is first in his life, and it's evident by the decisions that he makes. He puts Christ before everything. No matter what the circumstances, he seeks to know what God's Word says about it. The Bible is his road map.

When the floods come and the storms beat against his house, it won't be shaken. His foundation is immovable because he is totally dependent on the One who created the clouds and the rain! He knows that His Savior's hand is sovereign over his affairs. He is confident that he will weather any storm with Christ by his side.

> *"Are not two sparrows sold for a copper coin? And not one of them falls from the ground apart from your Father's will. But the very hairs of your head are all numbered. Do not fear therefore, you are of more value than many sparrows"* (Matthew 10:29-30).

But the foolish man did not heed the Word of God. He built his house on the things of this world: *"The lust of the flesh, the lust of the eyes, and the pride of life"* (1 John 2:16). Foolish people live to please themselves. They are building up their treasures on earth where moth and rust destroy and where thieves break in and steal (Matthew 6:19). A life of obedience to Christ is foolishness to them.

The Scriptures tell us not to build a foundation with temporal things that don't have any eternal value! Only those things done for the Lord will last.

If we are making foolish decisions, it's as if our home is being built on sand. The sinful choices that we make can cause deep fractures to the foundation. The consequences of our unwise decisions can cause a ripple effect in our lives for years to come.

We've seen so many around us, including ourselves, suffer because we followed the sinful desires of our hearts. We can no longer be captivated by the flesh. His Word warns us to avoid anything that influences us to sin.

Pray to be wise women of God. His perfect plan for your life will unfold as you make decisions to live for Him. We don't want to be in a home with someone who isn't building their foundation on the Lord. Remember the foolish man who lost everything because he didn't make Christ the chief cornerstone of his life. He lived for himself and lost it all. Please make sure that your house is built on the Rock.

Divine Protection

There have been times that the Holy Spirit has prodded you. He's brought a Scripture to mind. He's spoken through a pastor, a friend, or a family member. You have heard messages on Christian radio and TV. But you continued to make decisions that caused brokenness in your life. You ignored the wise counsel. Please pray for a keen awareness of the things He is doing and the ways He is speaking truth to you. Ask God to give you an understanding and strong conviction of the sin that is in your heart. What is God saying to you? What is the Holy Spirit showing you? What is He leading you to do?

Prayer: Help me see you in everything that I do. Help me be aware of Your presence. God, show me the way that leads to You. Help me be confident that You are truly guiding my steps. Please let me know that Your sovereign Hand is leading me through the sea that You will part for me. Help me have faith to get through these dark and confusing days. Help me have faith that You still work supernaturally in people's lives. That You are a God who performs miracles. And you want to do a miracle in mine! There is hope!

"Your Word is a lamp to my feet and a light to my path" (Psalm 119:105).

He Still Splits The Seas

God split the Red Sea 3,500 years ago, and He is the same today. The One who spoke the universe into existence is the same one who works through us. He is the one who created every star in the sky. *"He counts the number of the stars; He calls them all by name"* (Psalm 147:4). How much more does He know your name? How much more does He care about you?

Precious sisters, if we only understood the oneness we can experience in Christ. You can be so intertwined in Him, that your steps will be guided by the Holy Spirit. Your footprints can leave an eternal impression on those around you.

We live in the Milky Way Galaxy that consists of 200-400 billion stars. Wow! And the earth is just one planet in that galaxy! And on our planet with almost eight billion people, He zooms in to take care of you and me. And because of Christ's sacrifice on the cross for my sins, I have been adopted into His royal family.

"You did not choose Me, but I chose you and appointed you that you should go and bear fruit" (John 15:16).

It just doesn't get any better than that, my precious sister. This is the same God who wants an intimate relationship with you. Won't you let Him have His way? Won't you surrender to Him?

"One generation shall praise Your works to another and shall declare Your mighty acts. I will meditate on the glorious splendor of Your majesty, and on Your wondrous works. Men shall speak of the might of your awesome acts, and I will declare Your greatness. They shall utter the memory of Your great goodness and shall sing of Your righteousness" (Psalm 145:4-7).

Hallelujah to the King of kings!

Verses For Meditation

"You will keep in perfect peace those whose minds are steadfast, because they trust in you." ~ Isaiah 26:3

"Then Jesus spoke to them again, saying, I am the light of the world. He who follows Me shall not walk in darkness, but have the light of life." ~ John 8:12

"If you love Me, keep My commandments. And I will pray the Father, and He will give you another Helper, that He may abide with you forever—the Spirit of truth, whom the world cannot receive, because it neither sees Him nor knows Him; but you know Him, for he dwells with you and will be in you. I will not leave you orphans; I will come to you." ~ John 14:15-18

"Therefore, let those who suffer according to the will of God commit their souls to Him in doing good, as to a faithful Creator." ~ I Peter 4:19

"For the grace of God that brings salvation has appeared to all men, teaching us that, denying ungodliness and worldly lusts, we should live soberly, righteously, and godly, in the present age, looking for the blessed hope and glorious appearing of our great God and Savior Jesus Christ." ~ Titus 2:11-13

CHAPTER 3

The Armor Of God

*W*hy is life such a struggle? Why do we find ourselves overcome by temptation? Why is the lure of the flesh so appealing to us? Even when we want to do the right thing, we find ourselves falling into the same old trap, and we end up doing what's wrong. Well, we are in very good company. Our brother Paul talked about this in Scripture.

> *"For I know that in me (that is, in my flesh), nothing good dwells; for to will is present with me, but how to perform what is good I do not find. For the good that I will to do, I do not do; but the evil I will not to do, that I practice. Now if I do what I will not to do, it is no longer I who do it, but sin that dwells in me"* (Romans 7:18-20).

There is a fierce battle that goes on between the flesh, the enemy and the Holy Spirit. It is an intense struggle for the heart of man. The question is: Who will the person choose to obey? Will they follow Christ or the sinful desires of their heart?

Our flesh feeds on the depraved things of this world. It dwells on the things that lurk in the darkness. The sinful lifestyle that I was living didn't seem depraved to me, at least not at the time. That's how seared my conscience was towards God. I couldn't hear His "still small voice," because I wasn't listening.

"Therefore, do not let sin reign in your mortal body, that you should obey it in its lusts. And do not present your members as instruments of unrighteousness to sin but present yourselves to God as being alive from the dead, and your members as instruments of righteousness to God" (Romans 6:12-13).

I was not aware that I was in bondage to the things of this world. I had become a slave to the flesh, and it wasn't pretty! I was not looking at my worldly decisions from a spiritual perspective. I wasn't going to the Word of God and prayer to fight the spiritual battle. I wasn't letting the Holy Spirit lead me. I allowed my flesh to take me down a hard, splintered road.

It was all about having fun and gaining acceptance. I listened to the enemy's lies too many times to count. He deceived me the same way he did Eve. I didn't know how much sin dwelt within my heart. I didn't think there was anything wrong with my behavior. And when conviction came, I'd convince myself that things were fine. But they weren't. I didn't understand that the Lord had a path for me that was different from the one I was on. Sadly, I wasn't seeking His Word to find out.

Cry Out To Jesus

I spent a lot of time hanging around people that were not good influences on me. They weren't living a godly lifestyle. In fact, they never talked about spiritual things. They were too busy indulging themselves in the fleeting pleasures of this world. They rarely ever brought up God in a conversation. But I tried to.

One night I was hanging out with friends and asked one of the guys about the cross around his neck. I wanted to see if it held any spiritual significance. The guy said, "Lady, I thought it looked cool." He didn't understand why I asked. I tried to share Jesus with Him, but he scoffed at me.

There were so many times I'd call out to God, because I wasn't happy with my life. I'd find myself yearning for more, but not knowing how to attain it. Even though I wasn't following God's will for my life, I knew that Christ died for me. I knew that He loved me. I never doubted that. I have always known that I belonged to Him. I pray you have that same assurance of His presence in your life. And of your salvation in Jesus Christ.

I often cried on my best friend's shoulder about how miserable I was, and the deep anguish caused by my relationships. She encouraged me to walk away, but I never listened. One piece of advice she'd try to drill into my head was to never accept lying and cheating in a relationship. She'd tell me how I deserved better. She would encourage me to break up with the guy. I needed to set healthy boundaries. I was the only one able to do that. No one could do it for me. If I was going to allow disrespect and neglect in my life, then it would continue.

One day I was so deeply wounded. I had, once again, discovered he was unfaithful. My heart was crushed. I was weeping when I called my friend. I could barely get out what had happened. She was so frustrated with what I was going through. She had lost patience with me! "Again!" she exclaimed! "You're kidding me! Not again!" This wasn't the first or second time.

She was so tired of giving me the same advice. It didn't matter what she said, I didn't hear her. I needed to leave. To walk away. To not look back. And she drew a line in the sand. She didn't want me calling about this type of situation again. I could call her about other things, but not about this.

I felt betrayed. I was so angry. I couldn't believe she wouldn't be there for me in my time of need. Shouldn't she keep listening to me? Shouldn't she always be there? She had already told me again and again what I needed to do. But I was too weak to say goodbye to him.

And she did the right thing. I didn't think so at the time. But she had drawn some tough boundary lines. And she had every right to do that. Sometimes people will love you for it and sometimes they won't. Sadly, my pride didn't hear what she was trying to say. The "I'm doing this for your own good" was perceived as rejection.

At that point, our relationship changed. We no longer were best friends. But I learned that friendships have seasons. Some are short-lived while others will stand the test of time. And that's alright. We can learn and grow from each person that comes into our life. We can try to see where we need to change and grow. I look back and see how I could have tried to understand her frustration. I needed to respect her boundaries and the decision she had made. Should I continue bringing up the toxic situation? Why continue to drag her through it? I needed to respect her decision.

We shouldn't stay with people who continue to hurt us. God doesn't want that for us. And neither did she. Hopefully, the boundary lines individuals draw will cause us to look at things with a fresh, new perspective. She gave me good counsel. Her advice was the right thing to do. I should have listened. I should have realized that she was trying to help me.

But I kept going back into a very destructive situation. It was such a vicious cycle. And it went on for several more years. I was so drained. I believed that there was more to life than what I was going through. I knew that God could help me.

God began to move when I started wanting to make real changes in my life. I cried out to God, telling Him I was finally ready to surrender and do things His way. I wanted to break free and move in His direction. I wanted to experience His best.

At that point, He came alongside and provided in ways that showed His incredible mercy, grace and love. I began to see the movement of His Hand divinely orchestrating events in my life!! As things began to come together in ministry, I knew it was Him doing it!! He will supernaturally infuse us with the strength and help we need to be obedient to His Word.

Because we walk in the flesh, it can be very draining and debilitating. But, because we have His Holy Spirit within us, we can be confident of His working power in our life. *"But if the Spirit of Him who raised Jesus from the dead dwells in you, He who raised Christ from the dead will also give life to your mortal bodies through His Spirit who dwells in you"* (Romans 8:11). God raised Jesus from the dead! That same God dwells within you, if you have come to Him in faith and repentance and invited Jesus Christ into your heart!

You are saved! We aren't helpless and hopeless. We aren't victims of our circumstances. We aren't destined for things to happen a certain way because that's the way it's always been. Because of His death and resurrection, we can live in victory. We don't have to succumb to our foolish desires anymore. We are no longer slaves to sin. We are no longer chained to the past. At least, we don't have to be. We are children of God! We are daughters of the King. He has opened the prison door and set the captives free! Will you walk out of the cell?

Adam And Eve

How did we get into this mess? Well, we can scroll back to the beginning of creation to see where it all began. This is the story of the fall of man. God created man in His image and likeness! He saw that it was not good for man to be alone, so He created Eve, a helpmate for him. He told them to be fruitful and multiply. He gave them access to everything on earth. There was total perfection: no problems, no difficulties, and no sin. Life was pure and clean. There was no pain and heartache. Oh, what a wonderful world it was.

There was only one thing withheld from them, and that was the tree of the knowledge of good and evil. God told them that fruit tree was off-limits. They were warned not to touch or eat it. His counsel was clear and concise.

He gave them a command and set a boundary line they should not cross. It was a message that warned them of danger ahead. God didn't want them to suffer physical and emotional consequences as a result of sin. His desire was to prevent them from experiencing pain and heartache. We expect a loving father to tell his son not to touch the hot stove, or he'll get burned. How much more do we expect our Heavenly Father to do the same for us?

> "And the LORD God commanded the man, saying of every tree of the garden you may freely eat; but of the tree of the knowledge of good and evil you shall not eat, for in the day that you eat of it you shall surely die" (Genesis 2:16–17).

He wanted them to be obedient to His Word. He wanted them to follow Him because they wanted to, not because they had to. Not out of fear, but out of love. He didn't create robots or program them like a computer. He gave them a choice of who they would serve.

Well, the enemy came crawling along at the opportune moment, and was craftier than any other creature God had made. He asked Eve if God really did say they couldn't eat of every tree that was in the garden. He made it sound like God was holding out by not letting them have every piece of fruit. Why couldn't they have it all? Haven't you heard that line before?

The Lies From The Enemy

"Then the serpent said, 'You will not surely die. For God knows that in the day you eat of it your eyes will be opened and you will be like God, knowing good and evil'" (Genesis 3:4-5).

The enemy was causing her to doubt God's command not to bite the fruit. The enemy lied when he told her she wouldn't die. He was busy convincing her that nothing bad would happen to them. In fact, he was telling her that taking the fruit would make them wise, just like God. That it was a good thing! But that was a lie.

He wanted her to disobey the Lord. We will never be satisfied by following the deceptive ways of the enemy. Many have had wilderness experiences by heeding his voice. Our hearts will suffer. We will find that it only leaves a painful path of misery.

She took her eyes off the Lord and put her eyes on the tree. It seemed to be calling her name. *"So, when the woman saw that the tree was good for food, that it was pleasant to the eyes, and a tree desirable to make one wise, she took of its fruit and ate. She gave it to her husband, and he ate. Then the eyes of both were opened, and they knew they were naked"* (Genesis 3:6–7).

The enemy told her all the wonderful things she'd experience if she would just take a bite. It's only a piece of fruit. I can imagine her gaze as she looked intently at the delectable fruit that was good for food, pleasant to the eyes and would make her wise. It looked so harmless. The fleshly feelings and desires were growing, and she couldn't resist. She picked the fruit and shared it with Adam.

Where was Adam's spiritual leadership? Why didn't he tell her it was wrong to bite the fruit? Why didn't he remind Eve of the Lord's command? Adam shouldn't have submitted to Eve. After they ate the fruit, shame and fear flooded their hearts. It was no longer a perfect world; sin had invaded paradise. The enemy didn't warn Eve of the consequences that would be unleashed on mankind as a result of their disobedience.

The enemy's always trying to plant confusing, sinful thoughts in our heads. He focuses on the fleshly, lustful desires of the heart that will draw us away from God and cause us to sin against Him. He tempts us with things that revolve around our pride and selfishness. The enemy tries to convince us that following the flesh is the right thing to do. He is the king of deception.

I believed that I could find happiness in my past worldly relationships. What a lie! I was convinced that the relationships had potential. I didn't look at the lying, cheating and abusive behavior as enough of a reason to leave. The enemy convinced me to hang on, and my flesh was too afraid to let go. It took me years to overcome the insecurities that kept me in bondage to a worldly lifestyle.

Those relationships were not worthy of my time or effort. In fact, they were a waste of energy. God wants to give you the courage to let go of those influences that are preventing you from having a close relationship with the Savior. He wants to be first in your life.

When I finally said goodbye to the guy, it was an incredibly powerful experience for me. I'd always been so dependent on a relationship. I was finally able to put things in their proper spiritual perspective by not having a man in my life. The break-up really did give me a sense of confidence that I hadn't felt before. The Lord was trying to teach me that He was enough.

Relationships were more of a ball and chain for me. They held me back and really did stunt my spiritual and emotional growth in so many ways. The Lord wanted me to take that giant leap of faith. I was so afraid that I'd be lost if I walked away. Little did I know, that's when I'd discover the amazing plans God had for me.

The Disobedient Child

God wants to pour out an abundance of blessings onto His children. I think this little story helps put into perspective the dilemma that God might face when dealing with us. Imagine that you are a mom with a 17-year-old daughter. You've told her that she has a 10 p.m. curfew. She often traipses through the door at 11 p.m. and sometimes midnight. You've told her how irresponsible she is and that you're not going to put up with that behavior. You've told her that she can't go out for a month, and she doesn't care. She acts like she has the right to do whatever she wants. She doesn't want to submit to your authority.

She's angry and thinks you are unfair. She slams doors and talks back to you. She definitely needs an attitude adjustment. Does that sound familiar? Well, imagine that there is so much you want to do for her. You love her so much. You really want to bless her. You have wonderful things planned for her. Would you still shower her with blessings while she is being so defiant and rebellious? I wouldn't! You would be rewarding her bad behavior.

I can't imagine all the times that God wanted to bless me and couldn't because I was talking back or being stubborn, selfish and disobedient. I have never lacked food or shelter, thank God. But He is a just and righteous Father! He won't pour out His blessings while we are being prideful. He wants us to be humble and responsive to His will. Say yes to Christ! Pray for a desire to follow His ways, not the path that leads to brokenness and despair.

"Oh, that men would give thanks to the Lord *for His goodness, and for His wonderful works to the children of men! For He satisfies the longing soul and fills the hungry soul with goodness"* (Ps. 107:8-9).

We are His children, and we can't rise above His Word and act like we are our own god. When people make decisions that don't include Christ, they are stepping outside of His will, and that's not a safe place to be.

There are people who take matters into their own hands to try to maneuver the direction of their lives. We don't have power or control over anything. Even when people think they have control over the future, it's so easy for God to prove them wrong. And, so often, He does. God is sovereign and holds the very breath of our lives in His hands.

"Many are the plans in a person's heart, but it is the Lord's *purpose that prevails"* (Proverbs 19:21).

Don't Be Wise In Your Own Eyes

The story of Adam and Eve is a perfect example of why we can't base decisions on the way things look or how we feel. It didn't seem like eating the fruit would cause any real harm. What's the big deal? God told them the truth, but the enemy played with her head and she believed his lies, again. He played on the desires of her flesh, and she gave in!

We can't allow ourselves to be enamored by the things of this world. Remember how appealing things were to Adam and Eve? The Lord warned them, but they didn't listen. When God says no, we must understand that He is protecting us from danger. If we continue in the wrong direction, we will suffer consequences.

We must be on guard. There were times when we didn't know the enemy was planting thoughts in our heads. We must be critical of the messages that run through our mind. I call this taking "critical thinking" to a new level. Are your thoughts Christ-centered or focused on the flesh? Will your actions produce godly fruit? Is what you're considering doing something you can share with a seasoned Christian? What does the Word of God say about it? Have you searched the Scriptures to find out?

"He who trusts in his own heart is a fool, but whoever walks wisely will be delivered" (Proverbs 28:26).

It's Not From God

I recently counseled a woman who'd been a Christian for several years. She prayed for a relationship, and it wasn't long before one came together. She was confident the Lord had answered her prayers. But they were doing things that were inappropriate.

She believed that her choices were acceptable to God, but he'd never condone a sinful relationship. As much as she trusted He was moving them forward, He wasn't. He isn't going to lead her to sin. He will lead her in the way of righteousness.

So, what happened? She was so confident that God had orchestrated it. He did allow it. Everything is under His control. But He'd never tell her to progress where sin is involved. She should have seen the ungodly conduct as a serious red flag. No matter how perfectly things lined up, there were warning signs that the relationship wasn't from Him.

"But flee from these things, you man of God, and pursue righteousness, godliness, faith, love, perseverance and gentleness" (I Timothy 6:1).

Who do you think told her to progress in that ungodly relationship? The enemy definitely had a hand in it. I can recall times when I was tempted to do things wrong with thoughts like: "It's ok to have another drink. No one knows where you are or what you're doing. It's your life. You can do what you want. Nothing is going to happen. Don't worry!" Remember how he talked to Eve.

We must be able to discern the truth from a lie. The enemy deceives, frustrates, lures, tempts, pressures, prods, pokes and pushes people to sin. When we are weak in the flesh, it's easy to be led astray by our lustful desires. Sometimes without even batting an eyelash. I need to take responsibility for stepping outside of His will and making ungodly decisions. I can't quip, "The devil made me do it!"

Remember, you have a choice of who you will follow. Seek God's truth to know if something isn't from Him. Pray for the Holy Spirit to bring conviction when there are thoughts that will produce sinful actions. What would Jesus do? Will the decision you are making reflect His character?

The Three Temptations

Well, the story of Adam and Eve is at the beginning of creation. Have things really changed? No! There is nothing new under the sun. Let's look at the different tactics the enemy uses to undermine Jesus' authority. And to cause us to sin!

Christ had been fasting in the wilderness for forty days and nights. Famished, He's ready to eat! It was at that moment the enemy swooped in to tempt Jesus. He said, *"If You are the Son of God, command that the stones become bread"* (Matthew 4:3).

Because Jesus was hungry, the enemy figured he'd give into the temptation. He wanted Jesus to use His miraculous power to create food. If you're really the Son of God, then this shouldn't be hard for you. It should be a piece of cake. Why would Christ have to prove who He is? Even though Jesus was in a weakened state, He is God! He responded to the enemy by quoting Scripture. He said, *"It is written, 'Man shall not live by bread alone, but by every word that proceeds from the mouth of God'"* (Matthew 4:4).

Jesus wasn't focused on the bread we eat. He is the Bread of Life. He used the Word of God to combat the enemy. By following Christ's example, we learn that responding with Scripture enables us to resist temptation. The Word is what we use to fight the false accuser. The Word protects us! The Word defends us! The Word empowers us! Are you feeding on His Word?

The enemy returned, encouraging Jesus to cast Himself off the temple so the angels could rescue Him. Doesn't throwing yourself off a temple sound like a crazy thing to do? What kind of foolish suggestion is that? The angels are under His authority and at His beck and call. Jesus could click His fingers and produce a legion of angels.

It was just another scheme of the deceiver. The Lord's response? "You shall not tempt the LORD your God" (Matthew 4:7). Again, he tries to get Jesus to prove who He is. The enemy constantly works on the pride issue. But Jesus isn't proud. He is God almighty. He is the creator of everything. He deserves to have every knee bow before Him. Jesus didn't fall for the temptation, and neither should we.

The enemy will put thoughts in our head to make us feel rejected and unloved. He will use crafty schemes to try and get us to fall into the pride trap! His goal is to make us do things to prove that we are significant. We don't have to convince people of our capabilities and worth. We shouldn't long for the validation of others. We should seek to find our acceptance in Christ.

Remember who you belong to. Remember who died for you. Remember there is no one who loves you more than Jesus. You belong to Him. You are part of His royal family. You were knit together by the creator of the universe. He designed you for a special and specific purpose. That makes you of the highest quality.

The Great "I AM!"

Finally, the enemy offered Jesus the kingdoms of this world, but it was under one condition: *"All of these things I will give You if You fall down and worship me"* (Matthew 4:9). But Jesus resisted the enemy. He responded, *"Away with you, Satan! For it is written, you shall worship the LORD your God, and Him only will you serve"* (Matthew 4:10).

Satan wanted Jesus to bow down and worship Him. Jesus is the ruler over all creation, and that includes every nation. The things of this world didn't appeal to Him. He wasn't going to be deceived by the enemy. He knew that the devil was trying to thwart the plan of salvation for mankind. Jesus knew why he came to the earth. His purpose was to die for man's sin. He wasn't here to achieve success, popularity or power. He wasn't going to be thrown off course. He is resolute! He is the great "I AM!"

After the third temptation, the enemy finally left Him alone. Jesus had won! The truth had prevailed! But, because Jesus was human, it did affect Him. That's when the angels came and ministered to Jesus and brought Him food. He needed to be revived spiritually. We need that too. When we say no to lust and temptation, it can cause us to be emotionally depleted. It can take a lot out of us. But remember that your spirit will be re-energized as you seek Him and do the right thing. He will strengthen you. He will not leave you to handle the struggles on your own! He is with you.

Do you know that there are angels watching over us? Isn't that an amazing thought? We can't see them, but they are with us. They are our constant companions. Praise God. When you are walking with Jesus, you are under the shelter of His wings. I get goose bumps thinking of the ways God has protected me all the days of my life.

"He shall give His angels charge over you, to keep you" (Luke 4:10). If you are a child of the King, you have that same protection over you. There are supernatural beings that are safeguarding you in all your ways. The Lord is with you.

Victory In Jesus!

The enemy wears us down by working on our fleshly thoughts and sinful desires. There are so many that accept whatever is put in front of them without even realizing the enemy had set a trap. They do not see the red flashing lights ahead. And look at what some people will sacrifice for their eternal life.

"For what profit is it to a man if he gains the whole world, and loses his own soul? Or what will a man give in exchange for his soul? For the Son

of Man will come in the glory of His Father with His angels, and then He will reward each according to his work" (Matthew 16:26).

If the enemy tempted Jesus, don't you think he'll tempt you? The answer is yes!! Ladies, there have been times we haven't challenged the adversary's lies. We didn't understand all the ways that he can work. How many have fallen prey to his ways? How many have felt the pain of going through that wrong door? But it looked so right! How many times did we think that? We can't put the car in reverse, but we can be wiser as we drive forward.

The Holy Spirit can help you discern when the enemy's lurking around looking for a crack in your armor. When he is attempting to gain a foothold in your life. Sometimes it only takes a toehold for him to make his way in. So how did the enemy set things up to draw you into sin? What did he say to convince you that a certain behavior was the right thing to do?

In one of my past relationships, I believed we had to stay together because we were in a sexual relationship. I thought that I'd be committing adultery if I left him for someone else. How could I be committing adultery when we weren't even married? But I was committing sexual immorality. That didn't even register in my head at the time. I had a serious lack of spiritual understanding.

Where did those thoughts come from? The enemy planted ideas in my head to keep me bound to the flesh. Because I didn't have much knowledge of Scripture, I wasn't able to contradict the lies. I didn't have enough spiritual strength to fight the ungodly desires of my heart. I didn't know how to achieve victory in Christ. Because we are children of God, we can resist the ploys of the enemy, through the awesome power of the Holy Spirit. We need to let our minds dwell on those truths! The battle belongs to the Lord.

Are You A Babe In Christ?

When we accept Jesus as our Savior, we are considered babes in Christ. We are just starting out on our spiritual walk. You can't expect an infant to make wise decisions. You can't assume that a small child will choose the right path. What's sad is that many people never spiritually grow up. They stay small in their faith, because they don't know how to use the Scriptures and prayer as spiritual tools to grow! They don't understand that they must be intentional in their efforts to seek after God.

> *"Everyone who partakes only of milk is unskilled in the word of righteousness, for he is a babe. But solid food belongs to those who are of full age, that is, those who by reason of use have their senses exercised to discern both good and evil"* (Hebrews 5:13–14).

If you are "unskilled in the word of righteousness" you aren't going to do the right thing. It takes time, prayer and effort to study His Word and understand what it is saying to you. As you meditate on the Scriptures, your eyes will open to His truths. You will desire righteousness and want to live for Him. You will become more aware of the sin in your life and desire change.

The more you feed on His Word, the more spiritually healthy you will become. As your spiritual diet goes from milk to meat, you will find yourself maturing in Christ. You will trust Him no matter what is going on around you. Your desire to make Him the priority of your life will be paramount to everything else.

You'll want to be obedient to Him. You'll understand that it requires sacrifice. You'll no longer want to live for the things of this world. You'll discover that there is no meaning in life without a relationship with Christ. You'll grow up and say no to all those childish and foolish things you used to do.

The apostle Paul said it well: *"When I was a child, I spoke as a child, I understood as a child, I thought as a child; but when I became a man, I put away childish things"* (I Corinthians 13:11). That is how one knows they are no longer a babe in Christ.

I Was Very Immature

I found myself struggling with feelings of fear and insecurity in my early thirties. I got depressed over certain things happening in my life. I had been so bullied as a young girl. I had been so broken from past relationships.

Those wounds had not healed. I couldn't trust anyone. I didn't know if I'd ever trust again. You know the saying, "Fool me once shame on you, fool me twice, shame on me." Well, that was the motto I lived by because of the pain I'd been through.

I accepted Christ at 12, so I'd been a Christian far too long to be experiencing these types of emotions. Where was it all coming from? I finally was ready to humble myself and seek Biblical counseling to help overcome my fears. I surrender! I couldn't do it on my own any longer.

I was at church one Sunday night, and they asked people to come forward for prayer. I felt compelled to respond. I'd always been embarrassed to do that because of my pride. I was so desperate for answers to my insecurities that I bolted out of my seat. The woman I prayed with told me that I needed to meet with her for counseling, and I agreed.

When we met, she asked a lot of questions about my past. She said that I had a lot of unresolved issues. It was evident to her that there was still unforgiveness and anger welled up inside of me. I really didn't know all the emotional baggage I was carrying around. I guess the behavior I was exhibiting should have produced a red flag for me. But sometimes we can ignore what we don't want to see. But it doesn't really go away, does it?

One of the first things the counselor asked about was my relationship with Christ. She wanted to know how much time I spent in prayer and the Word each day. She asked what Scriptures I'd been meditating on to deal with my struggles. She wanted me to show them to her. I quoted some verses, but only knew where a few of them were located.

I didn't have a deep understanding and knowledge of His Word. I really wasn't good at memorizing information. I am more of an audio/visual kind of girl. That was my excuse for not knowing Scripture. "Will God enable you to memorize His Word?" she asked. "Well, sure He is able," I responded.

She called me an immature Christian. Excuse me! I was so offended. How could she say that to me? I was in a relationship with Jesus. Well, just because I'd been a Christian for years, didn't mean I was becoming a mature believer.

She helped me understand that a person growing in their relationship with Jesus will seek His Word for answers to their situation. They trust that the Holy Spirit will guide them into all truth. They are earnestly seeking God to know which way to go. And they are confident that the Good Shepherd will lead them back into the pasture and safe from harm.

I didn't know how to respond to my daily struggles by applying His truth to my circumstances. The counselor gave me verses to meditate on and encouraged me to spend time reflecting on them throughout the day. I needed to take His Word and apply it to my specific situation. She helped me understand that the Word of God has the power to transform my heart and mind, enabling me to become more like Christ.

The Bible is the greatest source of strength, hope and direction for our lives. I needed to let the Word of God soak into my heart and soul. I needed to let the Holy Spirit empower me! I needed for God's truth to wash over me and heal the hurts. I needed a spiritual transformation from within.

When I met with her again, she held me accountable. She really challenged me. She wanted to make sure that I was meditating on Scripture and implementing it as a daily regimen in my life. Her Biblical advice was the best counsel I ever received.

"With my whole heart I have sought You; Oh, let me not wander from your commandments! Your word I have hidden in my heart that I might not sin against you" (Psalm 119:10-11).

A Volcano Erupts

As I began the healing process, a lot of things were surfacing at the same time. Have you ever experienced that in your life? It was as if a volcano had erupted. I had an incredible fear of failure. It was starting to reveal itself in major ways. I was terrified that if I tried something it wouldn't work out. I feared being laughed at and made fun of if I made a mistake.

I'd ask myself: "What if I fail? What if I look stupid? What if I can't do it?" Do any of these comments sound familiar? And then the enemy would tell me that I was right. I had enough doubts of my own. Ugh! The negative thoughts paralyzed me. I'd procrastinate to avoid moving forward.

I discovered that I was too concerned about what others thought. I spent too much time trying to be perfect to avoid criticism. In fact, the counselor said there's only One perfect being, and that is Jesus.

I had to allow myself to fail. I had to accept that I was human. I had to learn and grow from my mistakes. I want to do a good job. I want to get things right. But I can't be so worried about failure that I stay frozen, unable to advance. Have you felt like that before? Have you allowed your fear of failure to prevent you from accomplishing something?

The Scriptures tell me that I am a child of God. He has a plan, and it's all good! I can persevere. He will enable me to achieve the goals He has planned for me. With Him guiding me along, He will help me rise above the struggles that I'm going through. As I've applied His truths to my life, I have learned not to let fear and insecurity plague me.

If you let fear stop you, you'll never achieve the great things God wants to do through you. Step out of the boat and onto the water. Have faith and trust Him!! He can catch you when you fall. Just like He rescued Peter (Matthew 14:18-21). He will rescue you!

"Have I not commanded you; do not be afraid, nor be dismayed, for the Lord your God is with you wherever you go" (Joshua 1:9).

And the enemy still tries to trouble me with debilitating thoughts. I've learned to work through what God has placed in front of me. I have learned to fight the negative thoughts that the enemy throws my way. I've learned to combat his lies! I use the Sword of the Spirit, and it works! His WORD has power!

I have seen His Hand guide me along. I must follow through with what He has given me to do. I must trust Him to help me navigate through this life. If it doesn't work out or I fail, He'll teach me through it. He is sovereign. There is a reason He's allowing things to occur. It's all about trusting Him each step of the way, knowing that He loves me and wants what is best for my life. He will complete the good work He has begun in me.

You must let Him lead, and you must follow. It is a process, ladies. At times, it can be scary. We don't have control of the reins anymore. But look back on your life. We should have surrendered the reins long ago. His ways are so much higher and better than ours. When you release control, He moves and intervenes. Heal our broken hearts, Lord. Restore our faith and trust in You.

"Who among you fears the LORD? Who obeys the voice of His Servant? Who walks in darkness and has not light? Let him trust in the name of the LORD and rely upon his God" (Isaiah 50:10).

The Lord Sustains Me

I used to be so afraid of the dark. I watched too many scary movies while growing up. I'd stay up watching "Creature Feature" on Saturday nights. I was a fan of *The Twilight Zone* and *The Night Gallery*. And still am. I know why they call them thrillers. I spent hours watching those shows with my brother, Carl.

Speaking of brothers, Carl and Greg have been an incredible source of encouragement and support to me. I care so deeply for them. Some of my fondest memories are times spent with my brothers. I remember the countless hours playing board and computer games and going snorkeling with them.

As an adult, I still had dreams that haunted me! There'd be times I'd wake up in a cold sweat. There'd be nights I couldn't sleep, because I feared another nightmare. It was exhausting and so debilitating. I began spending time in the Psalms every night before bed. I would meditate on His Word and remind myself that He is watching over me.

I started planting verses in my heart to overcome the intense anxiety I was struggling with. I used Scripture to fend off the fearful thoughts. I began praising Him because He never sleeps or slumbers. His eyes are always on me. He is in control, and I had to trust His promises. The more I talked to Him and read His Word, the more peaceful my sleep became.

"I lay down and slept; I awoke, for the Lord sustained me" (Psalm 3:5).

The bad dreams got less and less, and it wasn't long before I was sleeping soundly. I am no longer troubled by bad dreams. Praise God, He brought peace to my troubled sleep patterns.

There is good reason why the apostle Paul says to only dwell on thoughts that are good, pure and lovely (Philippians 4:8). Those scary and sinful images can come back to haunt you. And you'll find yourself sleeping with the lights on and checking underneath the bed! Did you do that too? Seek to fill your heart and mind with thoughts of His unconditional love for you.

"When you lie down, you will not be afraid; Yes, you will lie down and your sleep will be sweet" (Proverbs 3:24).

Rahab's Response

Consider the harlot, Rahab, in Joshua chapter two. Joshua is getting ready to invade the land that God had promised the Israelites as an inheritance. In preparation, Joshua sent two spies to scope out the land of Jericho. When the king of Jericho found out about the spies, he sought to capture them. They came to the home of Rahab, where they found safety and were able to escape from the enemy.

Rahab had heard of the amazing miracles that had been performed by God. The incredible stories of the Lord's mighty power were spreading like wildfire, to the point that people were filled with fear. When the spies came, she knew the right thing to do. She defied the king's orders and rescued them. Rahab said, *"For we have heard how the Lord dried up the water of the Red Sea for you when you came out of Egypt, and what you did to the two kings of the Amorites. Neither did there remain any more courage in anyone because of you, for the Lord your God, He is God in heaven above and on earth beneath"* (Joshua 2:10-11).

She had heard of how the Lord's hand parted the Red Sea. How He had miraculously rescued the Israelites from Pharaoh and the Egyptian army. She believed that the same protection would be given to those who put their trust in Him.

She responded in faith, which was the opposite of her fellow countrymen. Rahab could have lost her life by disobeying the king. She was faced with a serious dilemma and chose to stand with those that defend righteousness. I'm sure there was fear in her heart. But her faith in God prevailed.

As a result, Rahab and her family were spared. And that's not the end of the story! She became an Israelite and is listed in the lineage of Jesus Christ. She is an ancestor of our Savior. How awesome is that? Talk about a redemption story. The Lord saw a harlot who had faith and delivered her to greatness. Trusting in the Lord is what produces amazing God stories.

What an incredibly loving and merciful Savior we have. God wants to do awe-inspiring things in your life, but you must make decisions for

Him to receive His greatest blessings. God offers a life of abundance to those who live for Him (John 10:10).

We can't allow our fears to prevent us from receiving God's best! What are you facing today? What thoughts are running through your mind? Are they thoughts of fear or faith? Are they going to produce trust or anxiety? He can help you.

The God that delivered Rahab is the same One that we trust and believe in. He hasn't changed. He wants to reveal Himself mightily in your life. No matter how many times you've fallen, and no matter how many times you've failed, reach out your hand to Him. He will lift you up.

How would you treat your daughter if she came to you crying and asking for help? What if she was afraid to take the next scary step? You'd surely offer grace and mercy to her. But you'd also encourage her to move forward and trust you. That's exactly what you have to do with God. You have to believe that Father knows best. And no matter how challenging the road, He will give you the grace that you need to walk the path He sets before you.

Read the story of Rahab and read it again. Ask God to help you have the same kind of certainty that Rahab exhibited by her brave actions. Tell Him you desire to honor His name above all else. Pray for Him to give you the courage to do what's right! Pray for God to help you stand, even when no one else stands with you. You'll be so glad you did, my precious sister.

I'm Ready For Duty, Sir!

We are Christian soldiers, and we are in a battle against the forces of evil. *"We do not wrestle against flesh and blood, but against principalities, against powers, against the rulers of the darkness of this age, against spiritual hosts of wickedness in the heavenly places"* (Ephesians 6:12-13).

And whether we like it or not, we've been recruited into the Lord's Army. When we accepted Christ, we signed up! We didn't realize all that it entailed, but we are on the battlefield and the war rages on. Jesus said that Satan is a thief who comes *"to kill, to steal and to destroy"* (John 10:10).

We only need to look at the book of Job to see the power this creature can wield. He isn't called a serpent and roaring lion in the Scriptures for nothing. We don't want to underestimate the impact he can have on someone's life.

In fact, when you see someone in a sinful state, you can guarantee the enemy is close behind egging the person on to take the next disobedient step! My husband and I were recently at a restaurant. I was on my way to the restroom, and I saw this large picture of an alligator lurking in the water. I had to stop and take note! His eyes were menacing. It made me think of the way the enemy lurks around, watching and waiting, seeking whom to devour. He will put a thought in someone's head to move them to sin, and they don't even know they're being played like a puppet on a string.

The Enemy Flees

We don't have to fear the enemy, but we must know how he works. He is the master of trickery.

> *"Be sober and vigilant; because your adversary the devil walks about like a roaring lion, seeking whom he may devour. Resist him, steadfast in the faith, knowing that the same sufferings are experienced by your brotherhood in the world"* (I Peter 5:8-9).

God wants us to be watchful and clear-minded, always keenly aware and on the alert. Can you picture a person on the watchtower? He's on the lookout. He knows the enemy is prowling around, waiting for an opportunity to attack. He's not letting his guard down. He has his armor on and weapon in hand. He's ready for battle. He doesn't shrink back! And we don't have to either!

God is more powerful than the enemy and He will help us overcome the spiritual battles that we encounter. As you focus on the Lord and His Word, the enemy will flee from you. He has no place where the authority of Christ reigns.

> *"Therefore, submit to God, resist the devil and he will flee from you"* (James 4:7).

The devil will make attempts, but you must fight against it. Remember how he kept tempting Christ in the wilderness. He was relentless. The enemy dangled worldly temptations in front of Him, in hopes He'd take the bait. But he was in for a surprise. Jesus stood His ground and with His help, we can too.

Don't give up. Say no to temptation and sin. Don't even look at something that causes lustful thoughts to stir within you. That's what Eve should have done. Don't allow your gaze to focus on the things of this world. Don't let your heart be taken in by the lust of the flesh. Remember that those fleshly things are not from God.

Consider the consequences. Look at what happened when Eve bit the fruit. Cry out to God. Ask Him for help. He really does care, and He will give you the victory. The Lord God is mighty to save. Allow the Holy Spirit to empower you! We are more than conquerors in Christ!

I'm In The Lord's Army

The Lord tells us to get suited up, because He's preparing us for the spiritual battle. The apostle Paul is encouraging us to have our armor on before we go onto the battlefield. It's a privilege to serve under God's command. I want to be a good, faithful soldier. I want Him to be proud of me. I want to make sure that I have every piece of spiritual armor on before I go out each day.

Here is our spiritual checklist: *"Stand therefore, having girded your waist with truth, having put on the breastplate of righteousness, and having shod your feet with the preparation of the gospel of peace; above all, taking the shield of faith with which you will be able to quench the fiery darts of the wicked one. And take the helmet of salvation, and the sword of the Spirit, which is the word of God, praying with all prayer and supplication in the spirit"* (Ephesians 6:14-18).

Some don't even understand that we're in a spiritual battle, and that is sad. Many have no clue that the enemy works through our difficulties and challenges to drag us down and defeat us. He's constantly throwing arrows our way. Are we resisting his attacks? Each day we are given an opportunity to follow Christ. If we obey His commands, our faith and trust will grow, and we will be able to quench the fiery darts of the enemy.

Ask God to help you see things from a spiritual perspective. As we take steps of faith, He will be leading the way. Be confident that God is going ahead of you and will fight on your behalf. You can be assured of the Holy Spirit's presence. You have a protector. He is your great defender! He wants you to achieve great things for the sake of righteousness.

"The Lord is the one who goes ahead of you; He will be with you. He will not fail you or forsake you. Do not fear or be dismayed" (Deuteronomy 31:8).

The Great And Mighty Armor Of God

Just as soldiers in ancient Rome wore armor for battle, Christians must be equipped with the armor of God, so we can stand against the wiles of the devil. We don't have to fall prey to his schemes any longer.

We need to have the belt of truth. His absolute truth is the foundation on which we stand. If a believer allows the enemy to plant negative, deceitful thoughts in their head, they will fall prey to all kinds of painful, sinful situations. If we know His Word, it will enable us to discern right from wrong and know how to make Godly choices.

I've counseled women who are struggling in so many areas of their lives. I'll ask them to show me what His Word says about their specific situation. So often they have no idea what Scripture says about it. They really don't know how to seek direction from the Word of God. You must constantly be meditating on Scripture verses to grow in your knowledge and understanding of Him. I used to be unfamiliar with Scripture, too.

I remember being caught off-guard when the counselor asked me to share what the Word said about the difficulties that I was facing. I didn't know where to go. But as you study the Bible, it becomes a part of you. And you will see how naturally His Word comes to mind when you are more acquainted with it. The Holy Spirit will guide you through the learning process.

The Roman soldier's breastplate was made of metal plates and covered the body from neck to waist, and from front to back. When we are obedient to the will of God, a Christian's breastplate gets tougher and more fortified. As we follow His commands, we can imagine it wrapping around our chest, protecting us from harm.

If we make ungodly choices, we are not strengthening our armor. In fact, if we give into temptation, our hearts will grow more vulnerable, weak, and emotionally torn. And this will make us much more susceptible to the enemy's tactics.

We must guard our hearts, ladies, because wrong choices will produce a wealth of negative feelings and consequences. And that's what the enemy wants. His goal is for you to give up so that you will give into temptation. So don't let him win! Pray for a passion to "seek His statutes and obey His laws" (Psalm 105:45). Those right decisions will enable you to stave off the aggressive attacks of the enemy.

When I'm ministering to someone, I want to find out if they are living a sinful lifestyle. Is there something preventing them from a life of victory? Is there something that is making them open to attack? Is there an idol in their life? What changes can they make to strengthen their breastplate? What practices do they need to implement to experience more of Jesus?

The Shield Of Faith

As Christian warriors, we are instructed to always have the shield of faith. The Roman soldier carried a shield that was two by four feet in size, made of wood and covered with tough leather. Before engaging in battle, they'd dip it into water so the flaming arrows of the enemy couldn't penetrate their fireproof shield. It was large enough to protect the soldier's body.

Just as soldiers used shields to protect themselves, our faith works in the same way. It is like a shield that creates a barrier of protection around us. Our trust in the Lord and His Word will extinguish the fiery darts of the enemy. The darts are those thoughts and temptations that get thrown our way each day. It's important to replace what the deceiver whispers in your ear and shouts in your head with what the Word of God says. Imagine those arrows breaking down and disintegrating to dust on the ground. When you trust in His power and promises, your shield of faith will grow. And the enemy's ploys will weaken. And the arrows will fall. And the enemy will be defeated.

Your understanding in Him will grow as you seek His face and learn to understand His divine attributes. You will be able to overcome the doubts and fears, as you learn to trust Him with your life. Your ability to rest in what He's doing will bring assurance of His mighty Hand surrounding you. As you look up, you'll know He's there and you'll feel the love. Your faith will be like a seed that grows and becomes like the mighty oak tree, known for its resilience and strength. You will discover that following Him is the absolute best choice you will ever make. You will be a warrior that will make your daddy in heaven very proud!

"Faith comes by hearing, and hearing by the Word of God" (Romans 10:17).

The Roman soldier wore sandals with hobnails in the soles to give him better footing for battle. As Christians, our feet are shod with the Gospel of peace. The last command Jesus gave was to go into the world and tell others what He'd done for mankind. It was so the lost could be found and those in darkness could experience the light of Christ. We have a message to share. We have hope to bring. We have the greatest news the world will ever hear. Are you ready to share what Jesus has done for you? Do you want to share the message of salvation to a lost and dying world? Then put on your armor! Grab your shield and sword! Let's go! Saddle up and we'll ride out together.

And He said to them, "Go into all the world and preach the gospel to every creature" (Mark 16:15).

Take Every Thought Captive

Over the years, we have had unproductive and negative thoughts that have created strongholds in our minds. It has prevented many from surrendering to the Lord. The false beliefs have severely hindered our spiritual walk and made us unable to hear from God.

Many have believed the fault-finding, negative comments, put-downs and demeaning remarks that were instilled in them while growing up. How many can recall, with amazing clarity, comments like, "You will never amount to anything. You are a failure. Can't you do anything right?

What's wrong with you, anyway? You are hopeless!" Those are just a few of the crippling things you may have heard throughout childhood. If so, they left deep cuts to your soul. You found that you constantly questioned your self-worth.

That is one of the main reasons you have never felt good enough. The negative comments have played again and again in your head. And for some, the tapes are still playing. It's as if someone keeps hitting the repeat button. The criticisms have become your belief system. You bought into the lies. You were brainwashed into believing that you were worthless and not good enough.

What a cruel thing to do to a child or an adult. We are to encourage each other. We aren't to say things that break individuals down. We are to build each other up. They were wrong to say negative things to you. Even if you were disobedient, one should have disciplined and instructed you without making you feel insecure and inadequate.

But some of those people didn't know how to be encouragers, because they never experienced that in their own lives. We must pray to have mercy on those who've hurt us. We must ask God to help us forgive them. Holding a grudge will only impede our spiritual growth. It will end up causing emotional and spiritual harm. It's not worth it!

Well, it is time to say goodbye to the lies told to you over the course of your lifetime. Don't believe them. Meditate on His Word. The Bible will transform your way of thinking. He wants to renew your mind! He wants the messages that flow through your head to be ones that give you faith, hope and love! He wants you overflowing with thoughts of His amazing grace. He wants us to see ourselves as a beautiful creation of God because of what His Spirit is doing in our lives.

You must learn to take those thoughts captive. If you keep listening to those tapes, you will not achieve what He is calling you to do. Break free of the lies, so you can receive His truth! Hit the erase button. If you don't, the thoughts will continue to defeat you! Let your value be determined by who you are in Christ. You will discover that His amazing love will enable you to embrace who He created you to be. I've learned to be at peace with myself by seeking Him and doing His will.

"For the weapons of our warfare are not carnal but mighty in God for the pulling down of strongholds, casting down arguments, and every high

thing that exalts itself against the knowledge of God, bringing every thought into captivity to the obedience of Christ" (II Corinthians 10:4-5).

When negative thoughts enter your head, replace them with the truth of God's Word! Constantly challenge those words with messages of love from our heavenly Father. The Scriptures bring life and hope! Try declaring this—even aloud—when those thoughts come: "I know the Father loves me! I know He has a plan for me! I am valuable and worthy of love! He sacrificed His life for me! He died for my sins! He wants me to trust Him! I'm not a failure! I'm not worthless! I have intrinsic value because of who God is and who He created me to be." Is there anything of more value than God's children? Jesus doesn't think so. And neither do I.

"May your unfailing love be my comfort, according to your promise to your servant" (Psalm 119:76).

"See what great love the Father has lavished on us, that we should be called children of God! And that is what we are!" (I John 3:1).

The Sword Of The Spirit

Take the Sword of the Spirit, which is the Word of God and use it as your defense. It is the most powerful weapon in your arsenal. Mentally take hold of the critical thoughts that enter your mind and examine them against the light of His Word. Would God really say the things that are running through your head? Can you find those things anywhere in Scripture? Where are they?

He does not belittle His children. He never gives you thoughts that would defeat you. He is the great encourager. He is much too loving to be unkind. Let His Words be what run through your mind all day! His joy is your strength (Nehemiah 8:9,10).

There are scriptures in the first chapter that focus on your identity in Christ. Go over them and ask Jesus to help you understand how valuable you are to Him. He loves you so much that He died for you. He wants you to embrace His love. Don't let those debilitating thoughts continue to control your life. Don't focus on the negatives, focus on His Word. Don't focus on what you think, focus on what He declares! You are a child of God! You are a precious daughter of the King. You are deeply loved. You have been redeemed. You have immeasurable value and worth.

Mt. Everest

There will be people and circumstances that will pose Mt. Everest-like obstacles in your life. There will be times of great discouragement and challenge but remember that His ways are always better than your ways. He still works through our pain to create progress. And even though we can't always comprehend the reasons behind the struggle, He is still working in ways that will produce glorious results. Take heart that the Holy Spirit will strengthen you. Be confident of His power that works in you. Seek to draw from the spiritual blessings that are available to every child of God (Ephesians 1:3).

Stay in close communion with the Savior. He has gone through far worse than you ever will. He promises to carry you through. He is guarding your path. He surrounds you and will fight for you. He is your advocate! He is your great defender. He is your mighty redeemer. He can restore the darkest moments of your past. He can create a calling where there seemed to be no purpose. Be encouraged, dear one! I've felt like you, too.

I am rejoicing in God who has turned my life around and set my feet on solid ground.

"Then I said to you, 'Do not be terrified, or afraid of them. The LORD *your God, who goes before you, He will fight for you, according to all He did for you in Egypt before your eyes, and in the wilderness where you saw how the* LORD *your God carried you, as a man carries his son"* (Deuteronomy 1:29- 31). You can be confident that, just as He delivered the Israelites out of slavery, He will deliver you. Your deliverer has come!

"Jesus Christ is the same yesterday, today and forever" (Hebrews 13:8).

I want to have the same kind of assurance of God's power that David exhibited when he stood before Goliath: *"Then David said to the Philistine, 'You come to me with a sword, with a spear, and with a javelin. But I come to you in the name of the Lord of hosts, the God of the armies of Israel, whom you have defied'"* (1 Samuel 17:45).

God is with us and we don't need anything else but Him by our side! He is the sovereign Lord, and everything must submit to His authority. Wow! That's our Heavenly Father, and we are His daughters. How incredible is that?!

We Are Royalty!

I'm so proud to be a daughter of the King. Our brothers are Moses, King David, Abraham, the apostle Paul and a whole host of others. We belong to a royal line. Our family tree can't be compared to anyone else's, no matter how powerful or popular those people are. Our ancestors are of the greatest lineage on the face of the planet. They are your family, too, if you've asked Jesus into your heart.

> *"But you are a chosen generation, a royal priesthood, a holy nation, His own special people, that you may proclaim the praises of Him who called you out of darkness into His marvelous light; who once were not people but are now the people of God, who had not obtained mercy but now have obtained mercy"* (I Peter 2:9–10).

One Of My Favorites

Beth Moore is a good Bible teacher. She has helped me learn to study God's Word in a way that is practical and applicable to my daily life. I have done a number of her Bible studies and have experienced significant growth through every one of them. She is so passionate about studying His Word. I continue to pray for an understanding of Scripture that will help me guide others to the Living Water. I want to have an enthusiasm that is contagious. I want to have so much zeal and passion for the things of God that others will desire to know Him! That is a heartfelt prayer of mine. I hope that it is for you, too.

Proclaim your trust in what He's doing in your life. God wants you focused on the great things He will do, not the past things that can't be changed! He wants you to live in the moment as you walk step-by-step with Him.

He will pave a road for you. He will clear a path that has your special name on it. He will always be there for you. Please believe in Him. Trust His heart, even when you can't see His hand. Let praise, thanksgiving and thoughts that conform to His Word be what you feast on. All day, every day.

"In the day when I cried out, You answered me, and made me bold with strength in my soul" (Psalm 138:3).

Verses For Meditation

"Your ears shall hear a word behind you, saying, 'This is the way, walk in it,' whenever you turn to the right hand or whenever you turn to the left." ~ Isaiah 30:21

"Nevertheless, I am continually with You; You hold me by my right hand. You will guide me with Your counsel, and afterward receive me to glory." ~ Psalm 73:23–24

"I will instruct you and teach you in the way you should go; I will guide you with My eye." ~ Psalm 32:8

"For You are my rock and my fortress; therefore, for Your name's sake, lead me and guide me." ~ Psalm 31:3

"As for God, His way is perfect; the word of the LORD is proven; He is a shield to all who trust in Him." ~ Psalm 18:30

"For the LORD GOD will help Me; therefore, I will not be disgraced; I have set My face like a flint, and I know that I will not be ashamed." ~ Isaiah 50:7

CHAPTER 4

Renewal Begins

I was invited to a local Bible study when I was 12, and that is where I accepted Christ as my Savior and Lord. The pastor at the non-denominational church I attended told us the Good News that salvation is free! He said that God sent His only begotten Son into the world to die on the cross to pay for our sins! He talked of the suffering Jesus went through on our behalf. He shared the sacrifice that He made for you and for me. Jesus bled and died to set us free!

He told us the only way to heaven was by trusting in Christ alone for our salvation. We could never be good enough, no matter how hard we tried. Without Him, it was hopeless. We were helpless. We have all sinned and fallen short of the glory of God. We are in desperate need of Jesus. "I am the way, the truth, and the life. No one comes to the Father except through me" (John 14:6). He is our lifeline to the Father.

He said that we needed to acknowledge our sin and ask Him into our heart. We needed to understand that our transgressions had separated us from God. There was no way back to the Father without realizing our need for the Savior. He said *"Behold, now is the accepted time; behold, now is the day of salvation"* (II Corinthians 6:2).

God was leading me, by His grace, and drawing me to Himself. He was opening my eyes to truth! I was only 12, but I knew I'd done things wrong. I was convicted of my sin and prayed to receive Him that day. I said the sinner's prayer, repented and asked Jesus to come into my life and transform my heart.

I was now a child of God and a daughter of the King. I had been adopted into God's family. Even though I had no inkling of a clue as to what it all meant, I believed! I knew it was true! I had been redeemed! I had been rescued! His seal of protection and love were over me. And He promised to never leave or abandon me.

> *"Now all things are of God, who has reconciled us to Himself through Jesus Christ, and has given us the ministry of reconciliation, that is, God was in Christ reconciling the world to Himself, not imputing their trespasses to them, and has committed to us the word of reconciliation"* (II Corinthians 5:18-19).

When we accept Christ as our Savior, we aren't just receiving eternal life, we are now able to experience an intimate relationship with God. His sacrifice on the cross enables us to become one with the almighty God of the universe. We become an heir with Christ. We've been born again. It is His death and resurrection that gives us new life. God's greatest gift to the world is Jesus. And all we must do is believe and receive! It's a free gift! We can't earn it, and we don't deserve it.

The pastor said that those who haven't received Christ as Savior walk in darkness, and the enemy has them in his grip. He said that when they die, that's it! There are no second chances. He went on to say that without Christ, they're going to hell. I was saddened and burdened by that message. I understood that there was a point when the door shuts! It's over. That made me want to tell people about Jesus. I wanted them to have a relationship with God, too. I didn't want anyone to go to hell. It broke my heart.

The church I attended was a strong, evangelical church that believed it was important to share the faith. They'd give us tracts and we'd head to the mall to share that salvation was in Christ alone. There we were, a group of young teenagers, telling individuals that Jesus is the only way to heaven.

I didn't know how to share the Gospel, but I knew that, without Jesus, people were doomed for all eternity. That is what motivated me to share the message of salvation then, and it's what motivates me to share it today.

I continue to ask people if they know for certain they're going to heaven! It is the most important question you can ask someone. Why? Because their answers reveal what they are trusting in for salvation. And, if the focus isn't on a relationship with Jesus, I want to try and share the Gospel message with them. There are so many ways we can share His love with individuals. I try to invite them to church, offer to pray for them or give them a tract.

The Wrong One

I was involved in church activities three times a week. I really did want to live a life of obedience to Him. I was learning and growing in my relationship with Jesus. However, a few years later, I met a guy. You know where this is headed, right? Sadly, downhill.

I was a young teenager when I met my first boyfriend. I was hanging out with friends, when some guys pulled up on motorcycles. I still remember the initial attraction. He got off the bike and walked over to me. My knees began to buckle, and my heart skipped a beat. He asked me out and I nearly fainted. This is too good to be true. He asked if I wanted to go for a ride later that evening. I couldn't believe it. I ran into the house and jumped for joy. I felt so special. He is so darn cute, and he wants to go out with me.

Now, before I took that motorcycle ride, I should have asked myself a few questions. Do I know anything about him? Why did his last relationship end? Does he go to church? Is he even a believer in Jesus? Sadly, those thoughts never crossed my mind.

I wish I could say things started slow, but the relationship took off. Before I knew it, we were inseparable. Remember the song "Puppy Love" by Donny and Marie Osmond? That was my song! I thought our love would last forever.

The guy became the focus of my world. I lost sight of God. My dad told me that the relationship wasn't good for me, but I didn't listen. He tried to stop me from going out with him. I was warned that he'd break my heart. How could I say no to someone who wanted to spend every waking moment with me? How could I turn away from a person who constantly told me that I was beautiful? I was hungering and thirsting for love.

After a few months, he didn't like me talking to other guys. He was so crazy jealous of me. It seemed like every guy was a threat. I had several platonic male friends, but he made me cut ties with them. In fact, all guys were off limits. I was to have absolutely no connection with the male population. I was told to avoid even simple conversations. Why? Because you never know where they might lead. Little did I know, it was him who was up to no good. But I won't find that out for several months. What seemed so promising ended up creating a pattern of insecurity that became very hard to break.

I should have been concerned when he began telling me what to do. I was flattered that he cared so much about me. I didn't see it as control. I didn't see it as a lack of trust. How foolish was I? It was a very unhealthy relationship that caused me to feel anxious, overwhelmed and depressed. I was a young, immature teenager who believed he really loved me. He was always there for me, so I did what he said. I thought I was supposed to make him happy.

I had been dating him for exactly one year when he broke up with me. Yep! On our one-year anniversary. The words heartless and insensitive come to mind, don't they? He gave me the sorry excuse that he needed to find himself. Was he lost? Sadly, I had no idea just how lost he was.

Well, so much for the promise that he'd never leave me. Now I understood what the phrase "empty promises" really meant. My heart shattered into a million pieces. The tears fell like rain. I just wanted to crawl into a hole and cry. I withdrew from everyone. I wouldn't go out with my friends, and I lost a lot of weight. I dwindled down to a size 0.

I kept asking him to come back, but he didn't care about me anymore. In fact, I'd call him in the middle of the night, and he'd hang up on me. Why did I humiliate myself by reaching out to someone that was rejecting me?

My girlfriends stuck by me. They had my back! They tried to convince me he had been unfaithful, but I didn't believe them. Denial causes severe emotional blindness when you don't want to face the truth.

Until the truth stares you in the face. God knew I needed convincing. I was praying so hard about what I was going through. I didn't understand what was happening to me. I was so confused. The truth was going to come in a very unsuspecting way.

The Truth Hurts

My first job was at Burger King. One day, a man on crutches hobbled up to the counter. I loved the car my ex-boyfriend drove. I wanted one just like it. I asked the man if he knew someone who was selling that model car.

The guy looked surprised. He'd been hitchhiking a few weeks before, when a man driving the same vehicle had picked him up. I couldn't believe it. So, I asked the guy what the car looked like. He described it, right down to the x-boyfriends banged up quarter panel. And then I said, "He's got this color hair and eyes and he's about this tall." The guy almost fell off his crutches. "That's him!" he proclaimed.

"That's the guy that gave me a ride. Do you know him?"

I stood there practically in shock. What were the chances? I had to know! "Was he with someone?" I asked. What he shared broke my heart! It was one of the women my girlfriends had been telling me about. Truth and reality had just converged.

It was incredible what had just happened. I knew God heard my prayer. He heard my cries for help! I needed clarity and the Lord brought it to me. He is faithful. It wasn't a coincidence that the hitchhiker came into Burger King that day. I needed a serious dose of truth, and I had to hear it from some stranger.

But rejection runs deep. The boyfriend had chosen someone else over me. He didn't love me anymore. It was such a painful reality to come to grips with. Why wasn't I good enough? Why didn't he love me? My self-esteem plummeted to the ground.

God Rescued Me

It was so overwhelming that I didn't know what to do. I just wanted the hurt to go away. It felt like a knife had ripped open my heart. The rejection was taking its toll. One night I stumbled into the bathroom, my eyes welling up with tears. I took the bottle of sleeping pills out of my mom and dad's medicine chest. There I stood, broken and in pain. I did not want to die; I really didn't. At this point, all drugs scared me. I just wanted to deaden the pain. I understand why people do things to numb their feelings. Sometimes facing reality can be so unbelievably hard.

I was weeping, asking God to please take the pain away. Please stop this ache that had paralyzed my soul. He heard my pleas and came to my rescue. He is a God who delivers His children. He spoke into my heart. Suddenly, I felt different! There was an immediate transformation. It was as if a light switch had been turned on. My thoughts were, "What's wrong with me? How could he treat me like this? I don't ever want to see him again! He's not worth it! I deserve so much better!" The Holy Spirit was encouraging me in my time of need.

I didn't want to waste another minute on someone who had caused me so much heartache. It was time to move on. The pain had subsided, in a miraculous way. I realized that he really wasn't the one for me, and to think that I ever thought he was.

God was with me, because I couldn't have recovered on my own. That's how I knew God helped me overcome. There was no way I could have had a change of heart and mind so quickly. My cuts ran too deep. I can still get choked up thinking of how much He deeply cares about what I've gone through. I can't imagine the path my feet would have taken without His mighty hand of intervention. That's what leads me to declare His power and awesome works to the world. You are my Savior and Lord! My great Redeemer!

"One generation commends your works to another; they tell of your mighty acts. They speak of the glorious splendor of your majesty – and I will meditate on your wonderful works. They tell of the power of your awesome works—and I will proclaim your great deeds" (Psalm 145:4-6).

I look at this experience as His divine power rescuing me out of a very dark and difficult time. It was as if He touched my eyes so I could see. It was as if He touched my heart and set me free! He worked a divine miracle inside of me! And look at how young and immature I was. He had His hand on me then and He has His Hand on me now! I give Him all the praise, honor, and glory for His faithfulness and love! I bow my knees and lift my hands to You, Oh Lord. For You alone are worthy of my devotion and admiration.

Haven't you seen His miraculous hand deliver you from an awful situation? Can't you recall an occurrence where you knew He was there for you in a major way? He is always with us no matter where we've been or what we've done! Even after we fail Him, He pulls us back up out of the murky pit. Sometimes it takes us getting dirty again, before we finally realize that staying under the shelter of His wings is the only safe place to be.

We've seen it countless times in Scripture. The Israelites cry out to God, and He faithfully delivers them, and then they go right back to their old ways. It's very sad to say that I treated God that way too. But praise God He never gave up on me.

His mighty and powerful Hand lifted me up out of the deep waters. He didn't let me drown. *"For He is the living God, and steadfast forever; His kingdom is the one which shall not be destroyed, and His dominion shall endure to the end. He delivers and rescues, and He works signs and wonders in heaven and on earth"* (Daniel 6:26-27).

I rejoice in His mercy over me!

Mr. Toad's Wild Ride

It was my first relationship. And, sad to say, it wouldn't be my last. You'd think that I wouldn't allow myself to fall into another bad relationship, since I had been so severely wounded the first time around. But we can be led astray by our hearts. Love is blind, as the saying goes. And how true is that ladies?

So began the roller coaster ride of relationships. It was like being on Mr. Toad's Wild Ride, and it wasn't fun. Up and down I went, from one relationship to another. Some would last for several years, but then I'd be off again! I'd strap myself in for another crazy ride! I'd get off the roller coaster dizzy, sometimes broken, and always bruised. It was such a vicious cycle.

How many of you have gotten back on the "hamster wheel?" That's when you make it out of one relationship, only to find yourself trapped in another. Each one had its share of promises, but in the end, we are trying to figure out what went wrong. Ladies, aren't we tired of going around in circles? When will we say enough already?

Excuses, Excuses, Excuses

I had gone through several unhealthy relationships, but there was one I believed would stand the test of time. But it ended up being so toxic. We didn't have trust, and it was obvious by the way we manipulated each other. We were so jealous and insecure that it was hard for us to do things together without getting angry and upset. Now, there was good reason not to trust him. When we first started going out, he'd hang on all the pretty girls. He was a lady's man, for sure.

And, to top it off, his ex-girlfriend was still in the picture. One night, I was driving by his house and caught them in each other's arms. I quickly turned my car around and zoomed back to confront them. She took off, thank goodness. That would have been a messy confrontation. He claimed that she was the one making the advances and blamed it all on her. He pledged his innocence, and I believed him.

Now, do you see any red flags flying here?? How many warning signs do I need? My thoughts were, "He really cares about me. He's adorable. He's worth it. Everyone has a past." I was blinded by his good looks and suave personality. And so many girls wanted to go out with him. I considered myself the "lucky one."

I was very insecure because of past relationships. So, I am not going to handle his flirtatious behavior very well. Instead of considering the emotional danger ahead, I decided to follow my heart. I was so infatuated with him that I ignored all the danger signals.

He wasn't a godly guy, and I got sucked into a very sinful lifestyle. We argued constantly because we didn't meet each other's expectations. It was such an unstable relationship. Around and around we went. The cycle continued for several years. We both had said and done so many hurtful things to each other. How could I ever survive the emotional toll the unfaithfulness and deceit had done to my heart? We argued. We criticized. We condemned. We never gave each other time and space to heal.

And even if we had taken a break or given each other room to breathe, there was so much healing and restoration needed in each of our lives. We both had too many unresolved issues that needed to be addressed and dealt with. Stuffing the pain down didn't make it go away. What was I to do? Should I stay or should I go? Is there hope for this fractured, broken relationship? At times, confusion was my only friend.

I started wanting to go back to church. This yearning for God began to grow. The Lord was putting that hunger and thirst into my heart. There was a little Jewish girl that lived next door to us. I started teaching her Bible stories. She'd come over and I'd spend the afternoon telling her all about Jesus. That was the highlight of my weekend. The Shepherd was luring me back to Him. I was the lost sheep being drawn back into the pen, praise God. *"No one can come to Me unless the Father who sent me draws him"* (John 6:44).

Word Of God Speak

God was doing a new thing. *"Yes, I have loved you with an everlasting love; Therefore, with lovingkindness I have drawn you"* (Jeremiah 31:3). I started reading the Bible. I prayed for His guidance and direction. I searched the Scriptures to find out what it said about our relationship. I discovered that His Word is not silent! God spells out the kind of people He wants us spending time with.

It was very unsettling for me. The Scriptures said that I had to be with someone who walked with Jesus. I couldn't stay with a person that wasn't living for the Savior. I needed to be with an individual who understood the meaning of living a life of purity for the King. I hadn't felt bad

79

about the lifestyle I was in, and when I did, I'd justify and rationalize the guilty feelings away, sad to say. But that was beginning to change.

"Therefore, let us cast off the works of darkness, and let us put on the armor of light. Let us walk properly, as in the day, not in revelry or drunkenness, not in lewdness and lust, not in strife and envy. But put on the Lord Jesus Christ, and make no provision for the flesh, to fulfill its lusts" (Romans 13:12-13).

It seemed like every time I opened the Bible, my eyes focused on verses relating to promiscuity. I couldn't escape what God was telling me to do. How many times have you experienced something like that?

I started meditating on I Corinthians 7:2: *"Nevertheless, because of sexual immorality, let each woman have her own husband."* That was troubling to me because we weren't married. I couldn't be in a sexual relationship with a person that wasn't my husband. How could I have allowed such depth of intimacy with someone who wasn't my spouse? I really didn't understand; I really didn't get it. God was lifting the veil of truth, revealing the sinful life I'd been living. Not to condemn me but to set me free.

My Bible had markers at I Corinthians 6:15-21 and I Thessalonians 3:4-8. It was clear: God's will for my life was to abstain from sexual immorality. The Scriptures say that *"He who is joined to the Lord is one spirit with Him"* (I Corinthians 6:17). I was blown away by that verse. The physical relationship had interfered in my experiencing oneness with Christ. The sexual immorality had caused me to sin against my own body. My body is a temple where the Holy Spirit dwells.

The Word was telling me that my body belonged to Jesus Christ. He made a huge sacrifice so I could be free from the bondage of sin. I am not my own. I belong to Him. He ransomed my life from the grave. He rescued me from destruction. I was bought at a price that took His life! Because He overcame death and sin, we can too! He calls us to glorify Him in body and spirit.

There were many reasons why I had stayed in the relationship. But I could no longer be with someone because I was too afraid to be alone. I couldn't let the worries of the future keep me stuck in the past. I couldn't allow my insecurities to rob me of the amazing things God wanted to do in my life.

I had to take that step of faith. I had to trust what His Word was telling me to do, knowing that blessings come to those who live in obedience to Him. I had to believe the promises were meant for me. That His plan was grander than anything I could ever imagine. And if I was to marry, it would be with a person who understood the spiritual transformation that was happening to me. The guy I was with had no clue.

Because he wasn't my husband, I was taking something that didn't belong to me. As much as I believed that the physical made the relationship more meaningful, it did the exact opposite. It caused a void in my heart that left me feeling empty. It caused a false sense of intimacy that left me feeling insecure. It never made me feel complete. I really didn't understand the value of a sexual relationship within the confines of marriage.

Now I understood why God tells us to wait until marriage. Now I understood why we are to be with someone that's willing to make a lifelong commitment. Would God really want His children to have these types of relationships and then move onto another person? A sexual relationship isn't supposed to be thrown away. Sadly, it's thrown away every day. God is trying to preserve our lives and protect our hearts.

I began experiencing a deep conviction over my sinful behavior. I was sorrowful over the relationship and the ungodly path I'd taken. I was grieved over the choices that I had made. My heart was heavy over how long the tangled relationship had dragged on. I was burdened by all the sin I'd been living in. God's Word was reaching down into my soul and revealing the neglect, the neediness, the longing, the rejection, the fear, and so many other things that had kept me in bondage.

I wasn't happy with myself. I no longer felt comfortable with the ways of the flesh. I no longer wanted the sinful desires to rule my life. I began worrying about the consequences of my actions.

I started drawing serious boundary lines between us. I began telling him we couldn't be physical. I didn't believe the behavior was acceptable or appropriate. The Holy Spirit was empowering me to make radical changes in my life. There was such a dramatic change of heart, that the guy couldn't comprehend what was happening to me. I wanted to be obedient to the Word of God. I wanted to live for Jesus. I wanted to do things His way. I decided it was time to move out. He begged me to stay, but I refused.

I went back home at just the right time. My mother was having some serious health issues, and I needed to be there for her. She had to have a knee replacement and could barely walk. My dad still worked full-time, so they really needed my help and support. I never thought I'd go back to my parent's home. But amazing things happen when we submit to the will of God. I am in awe of His awesome and perfect timing.

Still Hanging On

I struggled with what to do. I was so confused. Even though there had been so much water under the bridge, I still wasn't ready to break up. I still wanted things to work out. You know, we'd been together so long. We'd gone through so much. And I'm a creature of habit. Change terrifies me!

So began my quest to bring Him to Jesus. I decided that the boyfriend needed to get saved! I was on a mission. I tried to help him understand that Christianity isn't a religion; it's a relationship with Jesus. God was transforming me into His image. I started seeing His power exhibited in mighty ways. He was bringing godly friends to encourage me! I was experiencing so many blessings. There were so many amazing things happening to me. I was experiencing miracles in my life. I could see evidence of God's Hand over me. I found myself in awe of His love. I found myself wanting more of Him.

I shared all the incredible things God was doing in my life. I had so many stories to tell. I wanted him to capture the excitement of living for the Savior. I prayed that my enthusiasm for the things of God would rub off on him.

They had a new member's orientation at the church I had started attending. I marked my interest in the nursing home ministry and an outreach to children from single-parent homes. And then, just a few months later, God divinely orchestrated a meeting with the leader of both those ministries. There began His confirmation of my involvement in them. I had these desires to serve, and He was guiding me to them. God was using me to reach others for Him. It felt so good to be serving the King.

But I was still hanging onto the relationship. I convinced myself it was ok because we weren't sleeping or living together anymore. I wasn't supposed to abandon him, right? If I lead him to the Lord, that will make everything alright. That was another lie from the enemy.

I told him that he needed to live for God. I'd talk to him about Jesus, and he'd act interested in what I was saying. I told him that he needed to put Christ first! But he never brought up God on his own. Ever!! He never picked up the Bible. Not even once.

He was still partying and living a worldly lifestyle. His friends had always been first in his life, and they still were. He didn't want to lose me, so he'd promise to go to church. But he never did! It was all lip service just to please me, and that is the wrong reason for a boyfriend to walk with Christ.

I asked God to show me if this person was the right one for me. I did see some positive changes in his behavior, so I was confused. He was complying with some of my many requests. I had gotten to a point of desperation. I remember praying, "Lord, please show me what to do. Please let me know whether this is your will for my life. I don't want to marry this person if he isn't the one You have for me."

Then God did a wonderful thing and answered my prayers. Just a few days after my cries for help, I ran into a pastor who asked how I was doing. I described my confusion about the relationship, and my need to know God's will for my life. He invited me into his office and told me God's Word had the answer. And that I could get clarity today.

Wow! That was fast, Lord! He doesn't waste any time! He is faithful. The pastor said it was important to know if this was a Christ-centered relationship and if it was glorifying to God. Gulp....

The Four Questions

He told me that there is a way to evaluate if someone really is the right person. Then he proceeded to ask me four questions that literally changed my life:

1) Does the guy love Jesus?
2) Does he love the Word of God?
3) Does he lead in prayer? Does he even pray?
4) Does he go to church? Does he care about ministry, and have a desire to serve? Does he have a heart for the lost?

Wow! The guy got all the answers wrong. I told the pastor that the boyfriend believed in God, but he said that wasn't enough. He said God wanted me with someone who loved Him and was a godly leader. He said the Scriptures required me to be with someone that pursued righteousness. God didn't want me being the leader in our relationship. He said I had a choice to make! If I didn't choose God, I'd be putting the boyfriend first. He urged me not to continue in an idolatrous relationship.

Do The Right Thing

He said I'd miss out on all the wonderful things that God had in store for me if I didn't walk away. He said there'd be negative consequences if I didn't obey God's Word by ending the relationship. He was firm and resolute. I could no longer live a life of disobedience. He talked to me about King David and the consequences he suffered. He wasn't saying that would happen. But he wanted me to understand God disciplines those He loves.

God had been very patient with me. He was rescuing me. God sent Pastor Jim to tell me it was time to go. He is so good, merciful, and gracious. He wants what's best for me, and it wasn't an ungodly relationship. He didn't want me to be unequally yoked! "So, he isn't the one?" I asked. I was surprised.

Just because the boyfriend let me read Scripture to him and pray, didn't mean that things were moving in the right direction. I'd been deceived. Oh no! I began to cry, and then I began to weep! He encouraged me to trust in God, because He has a better plan! He said I needed to be with someone that encouraged me to be obedient to the Lord. Someone who would encourage me to surrender my life to Him. Someone who would encourage me to be more like Christ, not less. He really gave me hope. I sensed that if marriage was in my future, He'd bring me a spiritual leader.

The Security Blanket

One of the main reasons that I clung to the relationship was so I wouldn't be alone. The guy was my security blanket. I felt comfort knowing that someone was there. Even though it was so broken and imperfect. It's scary when there is no relationship to fall back on, especially when that's been the pattern in past years. What's heartbreaking is we stay in unhealthy relationships, even when we know they aren't good for us.

Remember, we have a natural desire for a companion. But the only thing that will ever make you feel whole and complete is a close relationship with Christ. A human being is not capable of giving you the acceptance and approval you long for. *"The fear of man brings a snare, but whoever trusts in the Lord shall be safe"* (Proverbs 29:25).

I remember thinking, "What do I do?" I was scared, but I knew that God had sent me a messenger. There was no denying it. *"For God has not given us a spirit of fear, but of power and of love and of a sound mind"* (II Timothy 1:7). I didn't know what would happen, but I didn't want to be disobedient. I was experiencing a revival in my heart. I didn't want to put the boyfriend before God any longer. It was time to make the break, as painful as it would be. My spiritual eyes were opening to His ways. I finally understood that he wasn't the one for me.

I've had countless women ask me how I made the break! It wasn't easy. I told the pastor that I couldn't break-up, because he'd beg me to stay. I didn't want to hurt him. I really cared about his feelings. I was so perplexed. The pastor told me to send a letter if I couldn't face him. Ahhhhh! You're kidding me. I don't think so. Isn't that a heartless and cruel thing to do?! Well, the pastor told me that I needed to be more concerned about God's feelings. And no matter how I ended the relationship, it was going to hurt and cause pain. I dreaded it! Which would I choose? A face-to-face confrontation or a letter? Yikes!!

The Good-bye Letter

The pastor prayed with me and encouraged me to write the letter. *"I can do all things through Christ who strengthens me"* (Philippians 4:13). I spent hours pondering what I should say to him. And how I would say it. I knew that God had opened a door, and I had to go through it. But I was scared.

I finally finished and brought the letter in for the pastor to review. I had written that there was still hope for us. I told him that I couldn't make any promises, but you never know what the future may hold. I just didn't want to say goodbye. I just couldn't let go.

The pastor said I needed to take out all the references on getting back together again. He said it was unfair to mislead him. He wasn't God's choice for me, and I had to walk away. He wasn't a godly man or a spiritual leader. He told me that I needed to stop acting like his savior. My missionary dating had come to an end.

I can't tell you the number of tears that were shed in his office. In fact, the pastor said he didn't care if I cried, and that made me cry even more. If his guidance helped me break off an ungodly relationship, then it was worth my tears. He was so right. I was so afraid to let go, but I knew that God had brought me to that point, and I trusted the pastor's counsel. And I trusted the Lord's divine timing.

I removed all the hopeful references and mailed the letter. Well, he came looking for me. He sent me cards and flowers. It was overwhelming. He'd call me at work and beg me to come back. It was so painful. My boss threatened to fire me if I couldn't get control of the situation. I finally had to stop taking his calls. It was over, and I couldn't go back. God was already doing so much in my life. He was opening so many doors, and I didn't want to do anything to hinder my relationship with Him.

It was time to start a new chapter in my life. I was so excited about the positive changes that were happening to me. I'd spent years with some-one, and it wasn't productive, at least not from a spiritual standpoint. And that's what really matters in a Christian's life.

But, praise God, all those sinful things I've done have been redeemed. God has used it for His glory, because here I am writing about how He delivered me. And, just as Moses praised God for delivering the Israelites out of the hands of Pharaoh, I will praise Him for rescuing me out of an ungodly, unfruitful relationship. He had bigger things in store for me.

How To Disconnect

Women ask me how to break up with someone if they are in an ungodly relationship or he isn't the right one for them. If it is safe to tell them it's over, then nicely and politely tell them that it's not meant to be.

Here are some things to consider:
- God is moving you in another direction.
- You're not the one for me.
- This is an unhealthy relationship.
- You can't live in a sinful relationship any longer.
- You can't be disobedient to your Savior anymore.
- You read a book called *Guard Your Heart!*
- The person has become an idol in your life.
- You must say no to sexual immorality.
- You desire to live a life of obedience to Christ.

You can say those kinds of things. It's OK to tell people that you're making decisions for the sake of Christ! If you've told him goodbye and he keeps coming back or calling, then it'd be wise not to respond to his many social media advances. I'd encourage you to disconnect from him. You aren't being rude by not responding to his attempts to get back together or reconnect. He's trying to lure you back into an unhealthy relationship. He's trying to pressure you, and that's not from God. And you are trying to leave the past behind, where it belongs. I'm so glad I left the relationship to follow Christ.

Oftentimes, we don't want to say goodbye because we are hoping that things will work out. You still might have strong feelings for him. And considering not being with him can make your heart feel like it's splitting in two. But, you won't receive all that God has for you if you remain in an ungodly relationship. God requires us to make sacrifices for Him. And, leaving behind a person who is not walking with Jesus is one of them. The benefits will, by far, outweigh the risks. Your list of pros will far exceed the list of cons. His way is always better! His way is always safer! His way will lead you on a path of righteousness! On a journey of freedom and deliverance. On a path to make you whole.

I was urged to walk away and I'm issuing the same plea to you. You don't want to be with someone who does not put Christ first in his life, no matter how great a person he seems to be. The relationship must revolve around the Savior. No relationship is perfect, but you want someone who is seeking to live for God. You want a person who desires to be obedient to His Word.

The pastor loved me enough to tell me the truth, as painful as it was to hear. I love you enough to want God's best for you. You are making the break for Christ. It's time to begin again.

"That you may walk worthy of the Lord, fully pleasing Him, being fruitful in every good work and increasing in the knowledge of God; strengthened with all might, according to His glorious power, for all patience and long-suffering with joy; giving thanks to the Father who has qualified us to be partakers of the inheritance of the saints in light" (Colossians 1:10-12).

God Is Amazing!

I began to desire a man of God. I had manipulated that area of my life for years, and I finally relinquished control. It was a matter of trust and faith! I didn't want to be led astray again. I had made so many bad choices in the past. I finally understood that He could help me. I didn't have to continue floundering around trying to figure this relationship thing out. I discovered that He gives wisdom and discernment. The Holy Spirit can reveal when something isn't from Him. He can open and close doors. He can intervene in amazing ways. I learned that I could trust Him with my life.

"Being confident of this very thing, that He who has begun a good work in you will complete it until the day of Jesus Christ" (Philippians 1:6).

Looking back, I wondered why I stayed in unhealthy relationships for as long as I did. I see now how I had decided to do things my way.

I made decisions based on what I wanted and believed was right. I followed my heart. I thought God was involved in the process, but I really didn't include Him. The person was my choice. I thought that I had God's approval, but I was wrong! Whatever made me think that the relationship was acceptable to God? Whatever made me think He would be happy about the sinful choices that I made? I was ignorant of His Word.

I was the one who had turned away from Him. I was the prodigal who had taken the wrong road. I was the one who had left home to find the happiness that I longed for. I was the one who ended up in the thicket! He was ready to rescue me, but I wasn't ready to be rescued. As soon as I turned my gaze towards Him, He was right there! When I began to ask Him for help, He answered. It was amazing how quickly things began to move when I started seeking after Him. There was no doubt He was pruning away the ungodly things from my life. There was no doubt that He was intervening to bring me back to Him.

"Who redeems your life from destruction, who crowns you with loving-kindness and tender mercies, who satisfies your mouth with good things, so that your youth is renewed like the eagle's" (Psalm 103:4-5).

The Lover Of Our Souls

He is the Good Shepherd, and we are His sheep! He leads the sheep to food and water. He protects them from getting devoured by wild animals. He rescues them and guides them to safety. You are not a little speck in the universe to Him. You are His child, and He has a deep and abiding love for you. It's as if you are walking through this life and He is unfurling a personal path for you, step-by-step, day-by-day.

As you submit to His Word, He'll mold and shape you into the person He wants you to become. You'll be a person that can love more completely because of the transformation He's making in your life. He'll empower you to forgive. He'll help you to become selfless and humble. He'll enable you to reflect the fruit of the Spirit in all you do. He'll give you a heart of love and compassion for people. It's a serious learning process. But one that brings great spiritual growth into your life.

God has taken me on a journey to understand why I experienced such brokenness in past relationships. He's helped me understand why things failed so miserably, and He really wants me to share those truths with you. No matter what's happened in your life or how many failed relationships there've been, He can redeem what you've gone through. Never fear, Christ is here!

He is our Super-Hero! God can do anything and everything. And He wants to liberate you! Set your eyes on Him. Let Him save the day! Let Him save your life!

Jesus, the Living Water

Beth Moore has an illustration in which she describes how we attempt to let the things of this world satisfy us. She began rolling up pieces of paper towels and stuffing them into a vase. Each piece represented money, a job, people, men, power, fame, fortune and beauty. There are so many people who have all these things and still feel empty and alone. Then she poured water into the vase and it covered all the empty spaces.

The Living Water, which is Christ, was reaching places and ministering to spaces that all those worldly things can't fill. The things of this world will never make you happy. They will only make you long for more. Living for Jesus and focusing on His will for your life will enable you to live a life of contentment.

> *"I am the bread of life. He who comes to Me shall never hunger, and he who believes in Me shall never thirst"* (John 6:35).

I pray for God to minister to your heart with His comfort, strength and love. Let your heart's desire be to meditate on His truths, His commands, His righteousness, His holiness, His power, His grace, His strength, His comfort, His faithfulness, His justice, His mercy, and His perfection. May you desire Him more than silver and gold, and may you find that His truths are sweeter than the sweetest honey. May you understand that the only hope for freedom is to follow the Savior and be obedient to His Word.

> *"Out of my distress I called on the LORD; the LORD answered me and set me free"* (Psalm 118:5).

Verses for Meditation

"Call upon Me in the day of trouble; I will deliver you, and you shall glorify Me." ~ Psalm 50:15

"But I will sing of Your power; Yes, I will sing aloud of Your mercy in the morning; For You have been my defense and refuge in the day of my trouble. To You, O my strength, I will sing praises; For God is my defense, My God of mercy." ~ Psalm 59:16

"And this I pray, that your love may abound still more and more in knowledge and all discernment, that you may approve the things that are excellent, that you may be sincere and without offense till the day of Christ." ~ Philippians 1:9

"Therefore, whether you eat or drink or whatever you do, do all to the glory of God. Give no offense, either to the Jews or to the Greeks or the church of God." ~ I Corinthians 10:31

"I have chosen the way of truth; I have set my heart on your laws. I hold fast to your statutes, O LORD; do not let me be put to shame. I run in the path of your commands, for you have set my heart free." ~ Psalm 119:30-32

CHAPTER 5

Friends First

*W*hat is a friend? It is someone that will always be there for you. That is a true friend, and His name is Jesus. He is faithful and will always be by your side. He will be with you through thick and thin. He will never fail you. Jesus is the only one able to heal the heart, right the wrong, set the captive free, enable someone to forgive, deliver us from evil, cleanse the mind, and restore the soul.

We must seek Him for everything we need. He is our supplier and provider. We can always put our trust in Him, because He will never disappoint. That is who we must depend on!

You've heard of Old Faithful, the geyser in Yellowstone National Park. Well, our Savior is even more dependable than that. He can be trusted one hundred percent of the time! I think that's a pretty impressive track record, if you ask me.

Perfect Love

The kind of love that Jesus exhibits is selfless. He laid down His life for us. His sacrificial love is seen by His death on the cross. I Corinthians 13:4-8

is a section of Scripture that is frequently used in marriage ceremonies and sets forth the model of Christian love we are to emulate. These verses help us understand the true meaning of God's love. It is unconditional. It is quite challenging to love someone no matter what they've done to us. But we are called to love like He does. The Holy Spirit will enable us to follow in His footsteps. As children of God, we must love and forgive.

> *"Love suffers long and is kind, love does not envy; love does not parade itself, it is not puffed up, does not behave rudely, does not seek its own, is not provoked, thinks no evil, does not rejoice in iniquity, but rejoices in the truth; bears all things, believes all things, hopes all things, endures all things. Love never fails"* (I Corinthians 13:4-8).

Agape Love

Love that suffers long describes Christ's continuous love towards us. I have done so many hurtful things to my Savior, and He has drawn me back to Himself. He has suffered long in our relationship. I used to be so selfish and rebellious. And yet, His eyes were on me and He had a plan of redemption for my life.

God has continued to weave me into the image of His Son. He never gave up on me. He always believed I was worth fighting for. I am His child and He wasn't going to leave me to my own devices. He loved me too much to do that. That makes me cry. I pray that your heart will receive the love He has for you. And that you will embrace the many ways He's revealed His hands of grace.

Love doesn't envy what others have. It's not focused on taking something that doesn't belong to it. Love isn't boastful and proud. It's not haughty and vain. It isn't unkind and selfish! It's not crude or rude. It's not going to be mean or hostile. It doesn't have ulterior motives. It's not going to run over people to get what it wants. Its purpose isn't to push people out of the way to get to the front of the line.

It's not easily upset. Its buttons aren't easily pushed. Those tender spots have healed, and they are no longer sensitive to the touch. Its heart isn't bent on evil. It looks for the good in everything. It focuses on purity and holiness. Its desire is for truth to prevail. It never, ever fails! It always forgives, and never gives up. It believes when there doesn't seem to be any hope.

It endures the darkest pain and the deepest wounds, and yet, never stops loving. That is Christ's perfect love for you and me. And He can empower us to love with that same selfless compassion He has shown toward us.

Because the Word of God tells us to exhibit unconditional love towards everyone, many think they're obligated to accept an individual's ungodly antics, no matter how sinful they may be. God's Word instructs us to draw healthy boundary lines in our relationships. Do you know how many Scriptures tell us to avoid unhealthy habits? Isn't that refreshing to hear? He seeks to protect us from those destructive influences that can lay waste to a life and create an ineffective witness for the Lord.

It's OK To Walk Away

Women who stay with men that aren't following the Lord are choosing the relationship over intimacy with God. The Lord's voice will be muffled because of the direction they have taken. They will not be able to get a clear signal. He wants your full attention. He doesn't like competition.

I have been called judgmental for saying goodbye to the guy I was dating. Some thought I should have forgiven his sinful ways. You know, take him back. They felt that I should have given him more chances. That was the problem. I gave him too many chances, and the bad behavior continued.

We weren't centering our relationship on Jesus. I suffered from a serious case of the "I-syndrome." Have you ever struggled with that before? You know, it's all about me and my happiness.

We shouldn't be with individuals that are hindering our walk with the Lord. It's not going to be spiritually beneficial to hang out with people who draw you away from Christ. You will end up getting deeply wounded. There were many harmful situations that occurred in my past relationships, and I chose to stay, instead of walking, no, running away.

You might be in a relationship where you aren't ready to say goodbye. God cares about what you are going through, and He sympathizes with your pain. But He is more concerned about your obedience to Him. And, that you are listening to His voice over the flesh and the enemy.

Here are some questions to ask yourself. Are you being influenced to sin in any way? Is there drinking and sexual immorality in your relationship? Does the person focus on themselves instead of God and others? Are they so caught up in the world that they have lost sight of God? Do they think you are old-fashioned and out-of-touch because of your love for the Lord and His commandments?

And, what if the person is a believer, but isn't putting Christ first? Well, if you are friends with a brother or sister that is living an ungodly lifestyle, the apostle Paul instructs us to limit our time with that person (I Corinthians 5:9-11). There are several reasons why we must draw a boundary line.

First, if I hang around someone who is blatantly sinning, it could harm my reputation. Second, I need to make sure that I'm not tempted by their bad behavior. My main priority is to glorify God by living a holy lifestyle that honors the King. And, when I do spend time with those individuals, I want to be wise in my interactions. I want to pray for opportunities to share the Gospel and be a light for Christ in their life.

When you evaluate the conduct of those closest to you, are they helping you mature in Christ? Is their behavior affecting your ability to focus on Jesus?

To Tell The Truth

Some people, out of fear they'll offend, won't confront the sin in their friend's life. Wouldn't it be wise to tell someone why you need to draw boundary lines? It's so important to be open and honest with people. That is one of the bedrocks of a healthy relationship. So, you should be able to lovingly discuss your concerns with a brother or sister in Christ. It's unwise to turn a blind eye to worldly conduct.

A woman shared how her friend was always in control. She was very selfish. It was always about what her friend wanted to do. It didn't matter what the woman wanted, the friend always got her way. Sadly, the woman never said she felt it was unfair. That there needed to be more of a give and take. That there needed to be more of a balance in their friendship.

One day the woman decided she was tired of being "miss nice gal." She wanted to go to Olive Garden and there was no if, ands or buts about it. The friend refused and a blow-up ensued. I wish I could say that they remained friends, but that wasn't the case.

Months and months of bullying had caused the volcano to explode and lava spewed everywhere. I pray they have made peace with each other. But she should have drawn a boundary line much sooner. In building a friendship, make sure the concrete you're pouring creates a foundation that's filled with truthfulness and candor. It will have a much better chance of surviving an earthquake.

"As iron sharpens iron, so one person sharpens another" (Proverbs 27:17 NIV).

And if you aren't close to the individual, please pray for God to confirm that you're the one to bring correction. Always pray for God's perfect timing. And go with Scripture in hand. Your opinion, as great as it might be, isn't going to change their life. As the Holy Spirit leads us to share His truths, dramatic spiritual change can happen. It's God's Word telling them what to do. We are an Ambassador for Christ. A spokesperson who speaks on behalf of the Lord. If you're the one, He'll open that door.

"Him we preach, warning every man and teaching every man in all wisdom, that we may present every man perfect in Christ Jesus. To this end I also labor, striving according to His working which works in me mightily" (Colossians 1:28–29).

And even if they reject your words, it doesn't mean you were wrong to share. Love speaks the truth. Just make sure you have the right attitude and are peaceful in your approach. Are you going to the person because you are deeply concerned about their spiritual walk? What is your motivation? Are you trying to change them? Are you frustrated with their behavior? Is anger simmering below the surface?

There are times we must have these hard conversations, but are you going to speak in an edifying and encouraging way? That's why we must be driven by love. Our goal is to build each other up in a way that brings spiritual growth, through the power of the Holy Spirit.

"I planted the seed, Apollos watered it, but God has been making it grow" (I Corinthians 3:6 NIV).

In chapter six, I share the story of a woman who confronted me about my wardrobe. What she shared was painful to hear. She told me the truth in a very kind and caring way! Ouch! And the Holy Spirit spoke through her. She was right! Conviction came that brought change!

If you've got sin issues in your life, the person will consider you a hypocrite. You'll hear comments like, "Why is she preaching to me? Look at her own life? Who is she to judge?" So be prayerful about removing the log from your own eye before you try taking the speck out of your friend's eye.

"You hypocrite, first take the plank out of your own eye and then you will see clearly to remove the speck from your brother's eye" (Matthew 7:5).

It's easy to focus on changing someone else, isn't it? But are you being transformed into the image of Christ? Are you seeing godly changes in your own life? Your spiritual walk is the focus, not the other person. It's about your relationship with Jesus. It's important to frequently take a spiritual self-examination to insure you aren't judging the imperfections of others while being totally unaware of your own sinful flaws.

I think of how God wants us to imitate Christ in everything we do. He wants our lives to give off a sweet fragrance that leaves a wonderful scent in the air. He wants your actions to be a powerful example of the love of Christ. When people look at you, what do they see? What kind of aroma do they smell? Do they think you are loving and kind? Does your example reflect that of the Savior?

"Therefore, be imitators of God as dear children. And walk in love, as Christ also has loved us and given Himself for us, an offering and a sacrifice to God for a sweet-smelling aroma" (Ephesians 5:1-2).

You're My Brother, You're My Sister

We are to treat each other like brothers and sisters in Christ, with all purity (I Timothy 5:1-2). When God looks at us, He sees sons and daughters. We are His family. He wants us to have the highest level of respect for each other.

We should look at the Christian men in our life as brothers. That's how God sees them. You shouldn't get physical with your brother. It's not appropriate. I know! There have been times I've taught classes and when this came up, some women didn't like considering that concept.

I didn't write the Book!! Those are His words. I am just the messenger. He wants there to be purity in our friendships. Pray that God would enable you to see the guys in your life as godly men who are meant to be positive influences. They understand that you are a daughter of the King and they must answer to God for how they treat you. They will protect you. They won't do things to cause you harm. And sex outside of marriage will do that.

There is nothing wrong with having guy friends. But, God doesn't want our friendships to look like that of the world. We are supposed to be different. We should be able to show restraint. We should be able to exhibit willpower. We can't depend on them to do the right thing. We must protect ourselves. You can't leave it up to the guy. Too many women have done that and been deeply saddened by how things turned out.

We need to set up a dividing line that will protect us from getting physical. We must implement godly standards and draw spiritual boundary lines to insure we don't inflict physical and/or emotional trauma on ourselves and others.

God cares deeply about your purity. He doesn't want someone coming along trying to take it from you. There are many who will not think twice about doing that. It is a precious gift from God. Consider locking it up in a treasure box. And only giving the key to the man you will marry.

As difficult as it is to accomplish, the Holy Spirit will enable you to exhibit self-control. The question is, do you want to let righteousness rule in your relationship? Or is the flesh going to win? I know there are some of you reading this book that have crossed boundary lines. You don't have to continue down that road any longer.

You can make a U-turn. It's not too late to cry out for a heart of holiness. I did that. I sought after God and asked Him to cleanse me of the relationships that had left stains to my soul. I earnestly prayed for a washing that would bring renewal. I cried out for the feelings of being used and abused to be removed. As I hung on His Words, He began to enable me to see my value in Him. I began to truly believe that I can start over again.

So, determine to be friends with people who aren't tempting you to sin against God. You want to hang around individuals who really do want to live a righteous lifestyle. Their lives reflect true repentance. They have grown to understand that living for Christ requires obedience to His Word. And, they have come to the place where surrender is a part of their vocabulary.

Pray for God to direct you to individuals that reflect His goodness and grace. We will connect with a lot of people in our lifetime. I encourage you to spend time with those who will spur you on to run the race for Christ. Make sure that those running alongside aren't preventing you from reaching the finish line.

"You were running a good race. Who cut in on you to keep you from obeying the truth?" (Galatians 5:7).

Will He Protect Your Purity?

I was so impressed with a story about Billy Graham. He always kept his office door open when he met with a woman. He'd never allow any signs of impropriety. He'd do everything to avoid giving sin an opportunity to present itself. His conduct was above reproach. That's the kind of behavior you want the guy to exhibit in his relationship with you. You want someone who values you and wants to protect your purity. A brother should have your back. He won't play with your head and he definitely won't do things that can cause deep, emotional turmoil in your life.

"And whatever you do in word or deed, do all in the name of the Lord Jesus, giving thanks to God the Father through Him." (Colossians 3:17). Are you glorifying God in your behavior towards each other?

We want to say no to those things that even look like we're doing something wrong. God wants us to care about the example that we set before others. He wants us to be a godly role model to those around us. We are to avoid even *"the appearance of evil"* (I Thessalonians 5:22). You want someone that is concerned about the way the behavior looks. If it has a tinge of impropriety, he's not going to hang around. You don't have to tell him to leave.

He's steps ahead of you. He's a leader and you see it in his behavior. He doesn't want to hurt you, himself, and most importantly, his relationship with Christ. His reputation matters. He wants to be known as a man of integrity and honor. And he doesn't want to do anything to negatively affect the way people look at you. He's a good brother that is protecting your reputation from being tarnished.

There have been many women that have said they were first to bring up the "no sex before marriage" conversation. Why tell someone that you can't get physical? Why bring up that topic? You shouldn't need to. Obviously, feelings are being stirred.

And then she is baffled when he starts getting physical. She couldn't understand why he was making sexual advances. It's because staying pure was on her radar screen, but it wasn't on his. The woman drew the boundary line, he just went along to win her over.

Many of my precious sisters have been so disappointed. They truly believed the guy was waiting until marriage. They felt so deceived. It has been disheartening for many of them.

When abstinence was brought up, he might have agreed with you. But that didn't mean he was truly living a holy lifestyle. You don't know what someone does behind closed doors. That's why he must be the one that starts this discussion. The conversation needs to be initiated by him. The boundary line needs to be drawn and he should be the first to do it. That way there's no doubt it's something he truly cares about.

So, when establishing friendships, there shouldn't be a dialogue about sex. This should come up as things are getting more serious. And if it is, he should be the one that sets the standard by saying, "I am a Christian and my desire is to date in a Biblical way by treating you as my dear sister in Christ, with all purity (II Tim 2:22).

We are doing this relationship God's way. I honor Him first, and then you, in that order. I am sorry but, sex before marriage is off the table. I do not believe in test driving the car before the purchase. We must have a license to drive! And that is the bottom line. And how refreshing would that be?

Guard Your Feelings

Everyone agrees that living a life of purity and holiness is quite the challenge. It is very hard in the current culture we are in. The closer you get to someone, the more feelings you have for him. It's wise to limit the time you spend together. If both of you have suffered from inappropriate relationships, don't go places and do things that will cause you to fall into another trap. There needs to be rigid barriers set up or things will happen. Are you the only one setting the spiritual boundaries in the relationship? Are you the one that is telling him to back off? Are you the one saying that you can't get physical? These are important questions to ask yourself.

For me, I should have told numerous guys no when they asked me out, and I shouldn't have been alone with them. I should have avoided places where there was no accountability. Most of the time I wasn't trying to stop something from happening, I was actually hoping something would occur. I let my fleshly feelings lead me down a dangerous road. I'm encouraging my precious sisters in Christ not to make the same foolish choices that I did.

And don't believe the lie that nothing will happen. I said that in my first relationship. I really did! When my father said he was concerned about the time spent alone with my first boyfriend, I told him not to worry because everything was under control. I had no clue. I was very foolish. He was right because something did happen. And then began a lifestyle pattern that got me on the "hamster wheel."

No More Counterfeits

It's not easy to draw a line in the sand. I understand. We must combat the fleshly desires to do things our way. We have been drawn into physical relationships time and time again. It has been a devastating cycle for many of us. We are crying out to God for help to do it His way.

We don't want to forge ahead into another counterfeit relationship. Counterfeit relationships are not the real deal. They can look and feel genuine, but you will discover that the level of spiritual and emotional maturity is very low. You will start to realize that the relationship is focused on the flesh.

God can give you the grace and strength to do the right thing. His sacrifice on the cross was painful and our sacrifice for Him will be challenging too. If you make the decision to do life His way, you will experience Him moving, guiding, and providing in unbelievable ways. You don't want to miss out on all the benefits and blessings that He has in store for you.

If you are to be married, He wants you with a spiritual leader. A pastor told me that, and I met my husband seven years later. I know. It sounds like a very long time. For some, an eternity. But it was so worth the wait. Food for thought: If I had it to do over again, I wouldn't go out with any of the guys that I dated. And that's the truth. Hindsight is always 20/20.

I've learned that He really does have a glorious plan for my life. But it doesn't just materialize. I had to choose to follow Him. I had to turn away from the idols that I clung to. I had to say no to those worldly influences that prevented me from experiencing intimacy with the Savior. I had to stop being I-focused, and start being Christ-centered.

As I drew near, He revealed Himself more and more. To experience harmony with Christ, we must move in His direction. Don't you want your journey with Him to sound like a beautiful melody? His arms are always waiting to receive you. God is a Father who truly does love His children unconditionally.

A Game Of Limbo

You need to set the bar high, because some guys will treat your relationship like a game of Limbo. They'll test you to see if the bar can be lowered. And sometimes they'll try to jump over it!! If you've placed the bar at a high level, they'll know your standards. You'll be known as a woman of purity. And if they don't respect that, they aren't the one for you. This is not an area open for compromise. This is a deal-breaker.

And people that have the same heartfelt commitment to purity will be drawn to you. Don't allow someone to cause you to drop your standards. This is an important rule to remember: God doesn't want you advancing in any kind of relationship that leads you to sin in thought, word or deed. Question: Where is your bar set? Can it be lowered?

Establishing Healthy Friendships

Establishing a friendship enables you to get to know him. When we get physical, it tends to thwart the development of a healthy relationship. If you spend time together without connecting on a sexual level, you'll find out more about each other. This is a good test for your relationship.

What do you do when you are together? What are the topics of conversation? How do you get along? Is the spiritual connection something you spend time talking about? At the beginning of a relationship, it's important to keep it on a platonic level.

At the early stages of the relationship, it seemed like the two of you were made for each other. Everything seemed perfect. You started out so strong, but as the months went by, it seemed as if the person was wearing a mask. He was not the same person that you started going out with. You began seeing some unhealthy behaviors emerge. You are in shock. You can't believe how drastically things have changed.

Sound familiar? This is one of the main reasons why you want to keep things on a friendship level. The closer you get to each other, the harder it is to break free. And the more emotionally attached you will be. Please guard your heart against doing anything inappropriate.

You don't want to be in another relationship with someone who is focused on the physical. You want to make sure that he is a man of honor and respect. You want to be accepted for the complete person that you are, in mind, body and spirit. It doesn't mean there can't be an attraction for each other. That's natural but are the two of you able to control your emotions? It's important to avoid being alone together because the water can quickly go from calm to a boiling point. Keep that thermostat on cold.

It's good if he understands the need to develop a strong friendship, while avoiding tempting situations. This way, you are getting to know the whole person instead of just giving into the lustful feelings that can be brewing underneath the surface. When temptation sets in, it hinders the building of a healthy relationship. Determine to focus on developing good communication and a strong foundation that is built on Jesus Christ.

"But thou, O man of God, flee these things; and follow after righteousness, godliness, faith, love, patience, meekness" (I Timothy 6:11).

It's good to be prayerful and cautious, as you wait on the Lord to confirm if He is bringing the two of you together. There shouldn't be a rush to judgment. God can reveal if he's the one. It's important to establish the friendship under the church's protective covering.

This will enable you to:

- see if he truly does have a relationship with Christ.
- see if he seeks Him for guidance and direction.
- learn to communicate with each other while you find out about your differences, likes and dislikes.
- see how he responds to different situations.
- see how he interacts with friends and family.
- get confirmations from others about his spiritual walk.
- find out if he truly does serve in ministry.
- make sure that the two of you exhibit Christlikeness in your relationship.
- find out if he has a clean, honorable reputation.
- seek accountability and guidance from counselors and leaders in the church.

Consider the above and the importance of each element when establishing a godly relationship. How many of these questions can you answer yes to? These principles were not a pre-requisite in my prior relationships, but they needed to be. Pray about these things. Do you want to make sure that your friendships have the best possible chance of survival? If so, keep Jesus at the heart of all you do. If that is your deep and abiding prayer, it will come true.

It is possible to have fun and fellowship with the opposite sex. A woman from the class told me that she went out with a group of twenty Christian guys and gals and they had so much fun together. She was encouraged by the fellowship.

She said it was refreshing to get to know the opposite sex in groups. She said there were a few nice guys, but she determined not to get too close to them. She realized how having others around provided account-ability and protection. She is being very cautious. And that's wisdom on her part. She has been deeply hurt in numerous past relationships. She is determined to establish a friendship first!

Ask God to help you have healthy relationships with your brothers in Christ. Ask Him to bring you Christian friends that will be a source of encouragement in your daily walk with Him. You want individuals that have had their faith tried and tested and are confident of God's love for them. They know God's faithfulness because He's proven Himself time and time again. They have learned to seek Him, and through good and bad, they are firm in their commitment. They are living a life of submission to the King.

> "Let love be without hypocrisy. Abhor what is evil, cling to what is good. Be kindly affectionate to one another with brotherly love, in honor giving preference to one another; not lagging in diligence, fervent in spirit, serving the Lord; rejoicing in hope, patient in tribulation, continuing steadfastly in prayer; distributing to the needs of the saints, given to hospitality" (Romans 12:9-13).

Ask the Lord for friends that have a passion for the Savior and will encourage you to put Him first. It's good to have individuals that don't just say they believe in Jesus but are vivid examples of His amazing grace. Their testimonies reflect His mighty power.

You want people that will direct you to God's Word. They no longer trust their own opinion. I spent too much time around people who gave me bad advice. I had friends that told me to stay in ungodly relationships, and that advice caused great pain in my life.

I recently had a precious sister-in-Christ tell me she'd been encour-aged to go out with a guy she barely knew. She didn't feel a connection and really didn't want to go. Her friends kept trying to convince her to spend time with him. They kept insisting he was a good fit for her.

When she talked to me, I asked her a few questions. Did her friends say anything about his spiritual walk? Did they know if he was truly a believer in Jesus? Is he putting Christ first? Well, her friends weren't sure of his relationship with the Lord. The friends kept saying, "He's such a nice guy!" Yeah!! How many times have you gone out with a nice guy and regretted it? She ended up refusing the date. I was so proud of her.

Do we really want to get to know someone and then find out he's not the one? When we pray for answers to the spiritual questions, the Holy Spirit can give us discernment in how to move forward. Are you really looking for a godly leader for your home? Do you really want a man who will lead in devotions and prayer?

Her friends meant well. But they were not providing Godly advice. We want friends that base decisions on what the Bible has to say. We want individuals that will interpret what's going on from a spiritual perspective. Not on feelings and emotions. Not on the outward appearance. That's when you know if your friends truly are wise.

"He who walks with the wise grows wise, but a companion of fools suffers harm" (Proverbs 13:20 NASB).

No Pressure

A friend is someone who won't pressure you and make you feel bad if you don't do what they want. They don't lay a guilt trip on you to get their way. They aren't manipulative. They treat you with great care and respect. You can be yourself. You don't have to perform for a true friend. You don't have to be someone you're not. You don't have to worry that they will reject you. You know they will be there for you, no matter what.

"But let none of you suffer as a murderer, a thief, an evildoer, or as a busybody in other people's matters. Yet if anyone suffers as a Christian let him not be ashamed, but glorify God in this matter" (I Peter 4:15-16).

A woman recently told me that she wasn't looking for a serious relationship, because she needed to grow in her walk with the Lord. She didn't want to start spending too much time with someone, because she didn't want to be distracted. There was a guy calling every day, trying to lure her into a relationship. She only wanted to be friends, but he kept insisting they were supposed to go out with each other.

She felt so much pressure. She prayed for direction on how to deal with the situation, and God brought me into her life.

I helped her see that his constant calls and texts were serious signs of infatuation. Friends don't manipulate and control each other. A person who cares about your feelings will respect when you say no. If something is the Lord's will, they will trust Him to bring the relationship together. They try to understand how you feel. They might not agree, but they will honor your boundaries. They hear you. You don't have to keep repeating yourself with a true friend.

She received the counsel with enthusiasm. It was an answer to prayer! She is polite when she sees him at church. But she doesn't hang around him, because she doesn't want to encourage or lead him on.

Don't Wear Your Heart On Your Sleeve

I'd encourage you not to wear your heart on your sleeve. Don't tell him everything about yourself in the early stages of a relationship. The deep, dark secrets from the past need to stay hidden, at least for now. You shouldn't talk about all the pain and heartache you've been through. I know this is tempting to do, but you are establishing an emotional bond.

It's so easy to start sharing everything about yourself, especially when you desire a close relationship. I've had so many women share how quickly they got attached, and they never got physical. Ladies, this is intimacy and that type of bonding needs to be saved for the relationship that's moving forward towards marriage.

It's not good to establish relationships that cause you to be dependent on someone. Women tell me how they spent countless hours on the phone with their boyfriend. They were texting each other numerous times a day. They are consumed with thoughts of each other. And this is at the very early points of the relationship.

Guard yourself against getting too close to someone without an understanding of what stage your relationship is in. We have gotten emotionally intimate and suffered immensely for it. People have made so many promises they couldn't keep. We've been shattered by the emotional break-ups that have occurred.

There shouldn't be discussions about love, marriage and kids without a commitment. Many women have told me that they should have held the guy accountable for the ways he led them on, but they were too afraid that the confrontation would turn him off. It's so hard to draw a boundary line because of the strong feelings you have for him. The magnetic pull seems to be too hard to resist.

Christ must be your focus. Jesus wants to be the One you have a deep connection with. He doesn't want the guy to be the one you seek constant comfort and reassurance from. How many have opened their heart in this way, and been so disheartened and dejected, as a result? We've all been there and done that, haven't we ladies? But do you really want to experience that pain and heartache again?

It's not wrong to share things about yourself, but please proceed with caution. You should be more dependent on Christ than your boyfriend. In fact, are you talking to God about everything that is going on in your life? Remember to make sure you are developing intimacy with Christ, and that no one is causing distance to occur between the two of you.

He's Not Your Girlfriend

We can look back over our lives and see how we treated some guys like they were our girlfriends. They became our confidant. We shared everything with them, and we shouldn't have. You must be careful when sharing intimate details about your life. Some women share that they have more male friends because of the complexities that can arise in female relationships. Many women have told me that it's easier to get along with their male friends. For some, they feel there is less friction and conflict.

But often those relationships ended on a sour note. We started liking them or they developed romantic feelings for us. We lost many friendships because boundary lines were crossed. And so many times with much regret.

It has happened to me more than once. There was one guy who was such a good friend. I went to him about all the struggles I was facing in a relationship. I poured my aching heart out to him. He was such a good listener. He finally drew a boundary line and told me not to share those things with him anymore. I was heartbroken. I felt so close to him. But it was a lesson learned. I saw the importance of having a godly girlfriend.

Again, it's not wrong to have male friends! And fellowshipping with them is a very good thing. But I don't think it's wise if the guy is your best friend. There are just too many risks involved. Let Jesus be the one that you share all your problems with.

It's taken me a long time, but I've learned to seek His counsel first. I go to Him about everything. He is faithful to work the situation out, give me peace or move me in a certain direction. It's so wonderful when you allow Him to guide your steps. And He truly does. That is why I'm able to say that no one ministers to my heart like Jesus. Seek Him and His righteousness and let Him be the One that takes care of you. Let Him be the One who brings hope and healing to your heart.

Questions to ask yourself: "Do you have healthy relationships with your guy friends? Have boundary lines been crossed? Is it time to take a few steps back?" Pray about it. Let the Holy Spirit show you what to do.

Not Too Close

When it comes to counseling the opposite sex, I don't recommend it. If a guy comes to you with his problems, direct him to a spiritual leader. It is good for the person to get advice from someone he can better relate to. Who would be more equipped than a wise guy? You know what I mean. And, you are trying to prevent him from being dependent on you for direction. Let this be another one of your required rules in relationships.

Now, what about seeking counsel from a guy about your problems? I know that you will want to share your heart struggles with the individual you are interested in. He should direct you to a godly woman that will give you Biblical counsel. The same rule that applies to the man, also applies to the woman. Why wouldn't you seek advice from a woman who has experienced some of the things you've been through?

One of the things I commonly here in Guard Your Heart classes are, "You sound just like me. You understand what I've gone through. You've been there and done that." Yes, and that goes a long way in touching someone's heart. I believe it is so important to validate a person's feelings. Don't we want to be heard and understood?

It's not wrong to have conversations and to fellowship with men, but it's not good to form a bond that revolves around discussing your personal problems with them. That is how dependency on an individual can begin.

Now, what questions should you ask yourself. Do I go to him to discuss my problems? How often? Am I starting to depend on him for advice?

As you pray through your difficulties, ask God if the guy is becoming an impediment in your relationship with the Savior. And, why, you might ask, would he ever be an impediment? Because you are seeking His counsel over God's. The guy is the one you depend on. You are talking to the person more than the Savior. Are you really spending quality time with Jesus about your situations?

I've Given Advice

Now, have I ever counseled a man? I've had several come for clarification about the counsel I gave their girlfriend. One guy called me because his girlfriend broke up with him after one of the classes. I had to be honest. I couldn't have been happier for her. It wasn't a Christ-centered relationship, and she began to understand that truth. She was being led by the Holy Spirit to end their relationship. To say the guy was upset is an understatement.

I shared what God's Word said about their inappropriate relationship. I tried to be gentle because I knew he was hurting. How dare I imply their relationship was wrong. He felt I was being very judgmental. He took offense and hung up the phone!

I don't feel comfortable ministering to men. God has divinely brought me individuals and I've spoken truth into their lives. I can still give words of edification. But my goal is to connect them to a pastor or biblical counselor at their local church.

I won't be the one following up with him. I am going to avoid developing close friendships with the opposite sex. The less personal information we share with each other, the safer we will be. I always err on the side of caution. It's never wrong to avoid getting too close to someone, especially when there is a deep attraction and lustful feelings involved.

A Leader's Guidance

Now, I must clarify something. I have received direction from many a male counselor and pastor in my years as a Christian. My husband and I were counseled individually and collectively by the pastor who married us, and we benefitted greatly because of his spiritual knowledge and expertise. He currently runs a counseling center.

But one must be discerning. Ask these questions about the person you are meeting with. Is there something uncomfortable about our conversations? Do I feel safe? Are feelings starting to develop for him? It's not wise to meet with someone you are emotionally and physically drawn to. Guard Your Heart!!

Is She A Wise Woman?

I encourage women to have a mentor that is mature in her walk with the Lord. You want someone that will direct you to the Savior and His Word. She will build you up as you walk out your faith. She will help you understand how to draw closer to Jesus. She will tell you what God says about specific situations. She has walked many of the roads you have travelled and will be a great source of help as you grow in the Lord. You will value and appreciate her Biblical guidance and support in your life.

"Ointment and perfume delight the heart, and the sweetness of a man's friend gives delight by hearty counsel" (Proverbs 27:9).

Check with the Women's ministry at your church to find out if they have a mentoring or discipleship program. Many churches have small group Bible studies available. Pray for opportunities to serve at your church. This is a great way to get to know your fellow sisters-in-Christ. Where will you meet a godly woman if not in the church? How can you be encouraged in your walk with the Lord, if you aren't fellowshipping with other Christians?

Ladies, Watch What You Wear

Ladies, we need to be careful not to wear clothes that cause men to stumble. This is a sensitive area, I know. I get it. Prior to starting back to church, I was living a worldly lifestyle. And a section of my wardrobe reflected that look.

After one of my Sunday school classes, a child's mother pulled me to the side and said we needed to talk. She said the conversation might hurt my feelings. I didn't know who was more uncomfortable, her or me?

She did not pull any punches when she confronted me. She said I wore clothes that were a distraction to the opposite sex. She said there were things that weren't "fitting" for church. Or anywhere else for that matter. She lovingly told me to pray about it. I was so offended. I almost broke down in tears.

In my younger days, I did wear things that were too sexy. But I thought I'd ditched all those immodest pieces that were in my wardrobe. I wanted the Holy Spirit to reveal if there was truth to what she said. I began praying and going through my closet. And, voila! I pulled out some things that were inappropriate.

Now ladies, we don't have to wear burlap sacks. But neither should we wear *burlesque* either. Just kidding!! It's ok to look pretty. We can dress up. There's nothing wrong with that. It's good to wear attire that makes you smile. You know how a nice outfit can make you feel.

Here are some suggestions you might consider:
- I always wear something solid underneath see-through clothes. Someone shouldn't be able to describe what your bra looks like.
- I always wear a camisole under low-cut blouses. Too much cleavage, is well, too much.
- I try not to wear things that fit like a glove, unless I have a shirt/jacket over it.
- I never wear skirts that are too short. The middle of the thigh is way too high. You better have a book strapped to your lap when you sit down. And please don't bend over.

I remember thinking that I looked good. I wasn't trying to impress anyone. But I knew that some outfits caused heads to turn. I liked the attention. That had started young. We don't want to reveal too much of ourselves, if you know what I mean. If you were going on a date with Jesus, would you really wear that outfit?

If your clothes are too revealing, it might attract a guy that is interested in you for the wrong reasons. Why is he wanting to talk to you? Is it because you are so intelligent? Is it because you are so kind and compassionate? Is he drawn to your personality? Or is it your outfit?

Guys are visual. If you are just meeting someone or getting to know him, what is he attracted to? Is it your mind, body or spirit? This is a good question to ask yourself. We are human, and this is a struggle. But we want to do all we can to dress modestly in this crazy world. Chivalry isn't dead and gentlemen do exist. There are many out there. But wolves are lurking in sheep's clothing. Be protective of your space and the guys that are in it.

PS: This is something that God will have to show you, so let Him bring conviction if there's something you shouldn't wear. Boy, did He do that for me. And it was a good thing. I didn't even realize it until a godly sister brought it to my attention. It hurt, but she did the right thing.

Watch The Language

Ladies, what comes out of the mouth comes from the heart. If the heart is filled with a love for Jesus, then good things will flow from that person. If the heart is focused on the flesh, then worldly things will flow out of him.

> *"For those things which proceed out of the mouth come from the heart, and they defile a man. For out of the heart proceed evil thoughts, murders, adulteries, fornications, thefts, false witness, blasphemies"* (Matthew 15:18-19).

We must be wise to examine what people say and do. We aren't being judgmental by evaluating their behavior. What they say is a good indicator of what's going on in their head. It reveals a lot about an individual.

> *"Neither filthiness, nor foolish talking, nor coarse jesting which are not fitting, but rather the giving of thanks"* (Ephesians 5:4).

If their jokes are crude and rude, if their language is foul, if they use the Lord's name in vain, if their conversations are unedifying, and if their discussions revolve around themselves, we must limit our conversations with them. We can't have close fellowship with people that are exhibiting unclean lifestyle traits. God is concerned about those people, places and things that are negatively influencing you.

You are His daughter, and He doesn't want you corrupted by people who aren't living for Him. God wants our focus to be on giving thanks and praises to the King. He doesn't want us polluting each other's minds by saying things that are filthy, vile and unedifying.

I've had women tell me about guys whose conversations were filled with sexual innuendos. The foul language that proceeded out of their mouths was disgusting. I couldn't believe the way some women have allowed guys to demean and demoralize them. It's made me sad.

There have been women exposed to unwholesome material by the guys they dated. This individual is revealing a lust for the flesh, and he's letting you know it. These are serious early warning signs. It's not good to fellowship with someone who's outwardly exhibiting such a lack of care and respect for you. And for God!

A godly man isn't going to take advantage of you. There are many immature Christians who are trying to do the right thing, but they haven't broken free of their worldly behavioral patterns. We still must avoid close fellowship with those individuals. It's important that their behavior doesn't influence us to sin. Or desensitize us to their sin. And that can happen! Be on guard!

"The heart is deceitful above all things, and desperately wicked; who can know it?" (Jeremiah 17:9)

What Media Outlets Are You Tuned Into?

Movies and television shows with inappropriate content are things we've all been exposed to. We have seen this stuff all around us while growing up. Many of the messages that have been poured into our minds are not designed to produce godly character. They are not written with holiness in mind.

Advertising matters! That's why companies spend huge budgets to develop media campaigns. If you see that Reese Cup commercial enough, you'll speed to the store to buy one, or maybe two. And individuals don't think that negative messages create belief systems and thought patterns within us? They can and they do.

"And whatever things are pure, whatever things are lovely, whatever things are of good report, if there is any virtue and if there is anything praiseworthy meditate on these things" (Philippians 4:8).

God wants our thoughts to be filled with those things that make us more like Him. He doesn't want unholy images and messages planted in our heads. He doesn't want the things we see to be filthy and dirty. We live in a sex-saturated culture, so we must be very careful and on the alert. Seek to avoid material that doesn't leave a pure imprint.

What do you spend time thinking about and doing each day? The answers will reveal whether you desire spiritual influences, or the worldly things still might have a strong appeal. We've all fallen prey and been swayed by those influences.

It reminds me of the little boy who sees a monster for the very first time. He's afraid, but the more he sees the scary creature, the less fearful he is. That's the way it works when you watch and listen to unhealthy, sinful material. At first, it might have been uncomfortable to watch sex and violence on a television show. But the more you did it, the less it bothered you.

That's how we've grown to accept things that aren't godly. Do you see how that happened? He wants our media consumption to honor Him. He wants the messages we take in throughout the day to be ones that reflect biblical standards. He wants the material we meditate on to encourage us to walk like Christ.

If we are spending a lot of time feeding on ungodly material, we will find ourselves condoning inappropriate behavior. The enemy tries to brainwash us so we aren't upset or annoyed when we see sin in a situation. God wants our focus to be on spiritual things. Make sure your camera only takes pictures of things that bring a smile to your face. And a smile to your Savior.

"Let the message of Christ dwell among you richly as you teach and admonish one another with all wisdom through psalms, hymns, and songs from the Spirit, singing to God with gratitude in your hearts" (Colossians 3:16 NIV).

He wants us to spend time with people that will reinforce a holy and uplifting outlook on life. Do the people you hang around focus on secular things? Are the latest movies, television shows, album releases and sports teams what matter most to them? Is that all they talk about?

The Good Doesn't Outweigh The Bad

It's not wrong to have a favorite sports team, go to the movies or have a favorite television show. I love *Shark Tank*. I have watched the *Lord of the Rings* trilogy so many times. I used to love *King of Queens* and *Everybody Loves Raymond*! But does he talk about these things more than the Savior? We must be discerning on how much time is spent feeding on worldly things.

Ladies, I used to talk about this stuff a lot, too! In one of my past relationships, we went to countless secular concerts. We constantly talked about the movies we watched, or the funny things that happened in our favorite television show.

In fact, it was as if my life revolved around those things. I understand. I lived a worldly lifestyle, too. We all have things we are escaping to or trying to run from. With me it was television sitcoms. I'd often find myself watching those shows to get some comic relief. But shouldn't I be going to God to calm my spirit and appease my soul?

Again, it's not wrong to enjoy television shows and movies. But, we need to draw a boundary line when the material is offensive and obscene. We can't ignore the bad behavior because the show might have a few redemptive qualities. That is another way the enemy works to get believers to go along with sinful behavior. It's a ploy he uses to get us to accept the things of this world. It's just a movie, one might say. But whether it's art or real-life, we shouldn't go along with things that aren't right.

The Lord wants you to focus on the spiritual things that will build you up. Don't you think the Lord would rather you invest your time on things that will strengthen your Christian character? Don't you think He'd rather you dwell on things that will bring nourishment to your soul?

The Holy Spirit began convicting me of the things I'd fill my mind with. I realized that those influences weren't profitable to my spiritual walk. God had to transform my way of thinking, so the focus was on holiness and righteous living. It is a process, and you must start somewhere. What better time to start than now?

What's On The Cover?

I used to buy *Glamour* and *Mademoiselle* magazines. I loved to read about fashion, style and makeup. It's fun to see the latest styles and trends. But almost every cover talks about how to experience a more active sex life. Why would their focus be on that? It's a woman's magazine.

Who's writing the content? Is that what women talk about in conversations? I hope not.

They're promoting promiscuity. They often don't tell you about the brokenness and/or abuse that can come from unhealthy relationships. They're not advising you on the dangers of moving in and out of them. They're not giving statistics on sexually transmitted diseases, single-parenting and abortion.

That's the reality, but they aren't going there. They're not seeking to do that. Their goal is to make money. And behind the scenes the enemy is working to spread his filthy agenda of brokenness and despair.

I realized that the Lord wouldn't want me spending money that way. I still read magazines, but I am sure to carefully examine the cover and content. Ask yourself, "Could you read this article or show this image to Jesus? Would He buy this magazine for you?"

I don't want you to be discouraged. It's not easy. When you stumble, get back up and start over again. When I taught Sunday school, one of my favorite mottos was "Never give up! Don't quit! Never give up! Don't quit!" I'm sure some of my former students still play that motto in their head. Let it be your motto, too.

A Mountain Out Of A Molehill

I used to watch soap operas. Yes, I did! In the early years of our marriage, my husband took issue with me watching them. What? I'd been tuning in since I was 12. He said it wasn't good for me and I shouldn't do it. I didn't think it'd influence me to do anything wrong. I thought he was making a mountain out of a molehill. I told him that it wasn't a big deal! But he told me that it was.

He asked me to pray about it. As I began lifting it up to Jesus, I became more uncomfortable. I started disagreeing with the behavior that was shown on the television show. I had to acknowledge that a lot of the material focused on sexual behavior. Everything seemed to hinge on making each other happy, and generally without consequences. Hey! Isn't that what the enemy did to convince Eve to sin?

My soap opera went off the air, and I'm thankful for that. The show mocked the sanctity of marriage and the beauty of abstaining from sex until a couple becomes man and wife.

They don't show consequences for sinful behavior. It is all about satisfying desires and fulfilling the lust of the flesh. And we wonder why Christians are so desensitized by the world? I understand. I was one of them. I'm thankful that God gave me a husband that helped me see the error of my ways.

I'm more sensitive to the Holy Spirit in discerning worldly influences. Pray for the wisdom and understanding to know when there isn't a spiritual focus. Ask the Holy Spirit to give you a heightened awareness so those things matter to you. Ask Him to make you uncomfortable when you see things that aren't pleasing to Him. Pray for a conviction of the heart. He'll give it to you.

Friendship With The World

Some Christians still have worldly friends. That is a cause for concern. Here's why: *"Do you not know that friendship with the world is enmity with God"* (James 4:4)? I was only a teenager when the lure of the world began. I started hanging around friends who were lots of fun! But, as I got to know them, they were more concerned about living it up than doing well in school.

It was like every girl had a boyfriend. Everyone seemed to be falling in and out of relationships. Looking back, it was sad to see the unhealthy behavioral patterns that were beginning for so many.

I wasn't evaluating their lifestyle to insure I wouldn't take the wrong path. Sad to say, I didn't see anything wrong with drinking and partying! It seemed like everybody was doing it.

There was pressure to go along with the bunch. That's what I did. We all want to fit in, don't we? Sadly, I didn't consider the consequences or the negative scenarios that I might live out. Wisdom is considering the impact your choices will have on your life and the future.

When a person is training for a sporting event, they must incorporate strict disciplines into their life. They can't eat what they want, stay up late and not exercise. If they are trying to win a race, they must put in the time and effort needed to become a good athlete. If the people they hang around with have unhealthy lifestyle habits, it will be harder for them to achieve their goals. And they might never win the race. Yes, they might have a lot fun! But their life would have been so much richer and more meaningful if they had followed the ways of the Lord. What's amazing is that it's never too late to re-enter the race. So, on your mark, get set, go!!

A Hard Pill To Swallow

I had finished speaking at a local church, and a young guy wanted to talk to me. He had taken serious issue with my teaching on II Timothy 2:22,

"Flee also youthful lusts; but pursue righteousness, faith, love, peace with those who call on the Lord out of a pure heart." He told me I shouldn't tell people not to hang around their worldly friends. God's Word says to only have close fellowship with those that are truly seeking after holiness. If they are unbelievers and/or they aren't living for Christ, then we must draw a line in the sand. You can't be their close friends. The Holy Spirit had convicted this guy's heart. I'm sorry but those are His words not mine. I told him that the struggle was between him and the Lord. That was a tough pill for him to swallow.

There are people that will influence you to go places and do things that are against the Word of God. And friendships like these can cause you to sin against the Savior. I didn't think those ungodly influences would lead me down the wrong path, but they did for many years.

I've had so many questions from others about this topic. There are many people in the church that struggle with this Biblical principle. It's hard to think we can't hang around certain people. But our inner circle should consist of those pursuing purity and righteousness.

Question: Are your friends following Christ? Do they want to live a life of purity? Are they seeking peace and pursuing it? Are they seeking to be pure in heart? He doesn't want you compromising your beliefs for anyone.

"Bad company does corrupt good morals" (I Corinthians 15:33 NASB).

Time To Say Goodbye

When I started going back to church, God began a restoration process in my heart. I was starting to get involved in different ministries, and God was bringing me Christian friends. I started hanging around people that were involved in the Lord's work. I was being spurred on by the body of Christ. A radical change was taking place in my heart.

In my early 20's, I had a best friend and we did everything together. We were inseparable. When I started going back to church, I began spending less time with her. She still tried to get me to go to our local hangouts. I didn't feel comfortable so I wouldn't go.

I told her about my new life in Christ, and the different ministries I was involved in. I shared some of the incredible ways God was moving in my life. On occasion, I'd still go to the beach with her. It was hard listening to the conversations that went on between her and the others. There was such a focus on men, bars and having fun!

One Saturday afternoon, we were soaking up some serious rays. I was offered a beer by one of the guys, and I declined. Then I started talking about my spiritual change of heart. I wanted to tell them about Jesus. He made fun of me and asked why I was hanging out with them? I smiled. But left and wondered that myself.

My spirit wasn't edified during our time together. It was all about planning for their next worldly adventure. I found myself very unsettled and so out of place. I did not belong in that group anymore.

I stopped going and she stopped calling. I was never unkind or mean to her. I tried to explain the incredible work that God was doing in and through me. But we were moving in different directions, and there was a definite disconnect. It was time to move on. She was living a worldly lifestyle and I couldn't live that way anymore. My focus was on pleasing the Savior. I was no longer the same person.

> *"That he no longer should live the rest of his time in the flesh for the lusts of men, but for the will of God. For we have spent enough of our past life-time in doing the will of the Gentiles— when we walked in lewdness, lusts, drunkenness, revelries, drinking parties, and abominable idolatries. In regard to these, they think it strange that you do not run with them in the same flood of dissipation, speaking evil of you. They will give an account to Him who is ready to judge the living and the dead"* (I Peter 4:2-5).

And it doesn't mean that you can't talk to those individuals. Are you encouraging them to go to church? Have you witnessed to them? Are you a light in their life? Are they still trying to lure you back into the world? Is the relationship a negative influence? No matter what, if they are living a sinful lifestyle, boundaries must be set up in the relationship.

Mom Says No

If your daughter came home and told you that she was hanging around people that skip school, would you condone that behavior? What if she said they were smoking and drinking? How about if they're known to lie and have a reputation around the neighborhood? What if they're known for being unkind? I would not allow my daughter to hang around individuals like that. Why not? The reason is they will influence her to do the wrong thing.

I know, I know. She'll lead them to Christ. I said it, too! But if your mom doesn't want you hanging around those types of individuals, how do you think your Heavenly Father feels about it?

"Let the words of my mouth and the meditation of my heart be acceptable in your sight, O Lord, my strength and my Redeemer" (Psalm 19:14).

Is He A Believer?

When I was younger, I didn't understand that I wasn't supposed to be in a close relationship with an unbeliever. One guy I dated told me he was a Christian and had been raised in the church. Well, that was good enough for me. It is important when developing bonds to make sure the person is a true believer. This is a commandment from the Lord. God wants you with someone who is moving in the same spiritual direction that you are.

When asking a woman if the guy they are dating has accepted Christ as Savior, some will say that he believes in God and goes to church. What does that mean? A lot of people believe in God, but their god isn't the One who created the universe. Most religions believe in a god, but you want to make sure that he is worshipping the God who sent His one and only Son to die on the cross for you and me.

Do Not Be Unequally Yoked!

"Do not be unequally yoked together with unbelievers. For what fellowship has righteousness with lawlessness? And what communion has light with darkness? And what accord has Christ with Belial? What part has a believer with an unbeliever? And what agreement has the temple of God with idols? You are a temple of the living God. God has said, 'I will dwell in them and walk among them. I will be their God; and they shall be My people. Come out from among them and be separate,' says the Lord. 'Do not touch what is unclean, and I will receive you. I will be a Father to you, and you shall be My sons and daughters,' says the LORD Almighty" (II Corinthians 6:14-18).

Let's examine what the Scriptures say. First, look at the contrast between the believer and the unbeliever, between trust in Christ and disbelief. The difference is like comparing night and day and apples to oranges.

Believer	*Unbeliever*
Righteousness	Unrighteousness
Light	Darkness
Christ	Belial (Satan)
Belief	Unbelief
Temple of God	Idols

The apostle Paul is telling us that we can't be yoked together with someone who is not a believer in Christ. The yoke fits around two oxen's neck as they plow the field! It steers them in the same direction, enabling them to get more work accomplished. When you yoke two different animals together, that will slow them down and they won't be as effective.

An unbeliever will deeply affect the believer's ability to achieve their true calling. They will be a hindrance to what God is doing in their life. God wants you with a spiritual leader, and this person is far from that if he isn't even a Christian.

So many women have asked me why they can't have a relationship with an unbeliever. It's because God's Word is lovingly seeking to protect them from a life of heartache. The unbeliever is in darkness. He can't see the light, because he doesn't know Christ. He doesn't have the conviction of the Holy Spirit. He's not seeking to live for God, because he's living for himself. He doesn't have spiritual eyes to see, because he is blind to God's truth!

He might even sound spiritual, but it isn't true Christ-centered spirituality. He might have a lot of good qualities, but being a born-again, Bible-believing, Christ loving person is a major requirement in God's Book. He doesn't fit the bill if he isn't even a believer in Jesus. He wants you with someone who will help you grow in your walk with the Savior. Don't let the seeds planted in your heart turn into weeds. People who aren't living for Jesus will cause great damage to your flower bed. This rule of not dating unbelievers also applies to same-sex friendships, as well.

Draw A Line In The Sand

God says to separate from unbelievers and come out from among them! I was teaching a Bible study when one of the ladies said she'd started communicating with an unbeliever. They were texting each other and she said it was all in fun.

After we discussed the above section of Scripture and God's heart on the matter, she decided it wasn't wise to keep conversing with him. God's timing is perfect. I was able to encourage her not to develop a friendship with the young man. These relationships can start so innocently and end so tragically.

You know the saying in the board game Monopoly, "Do not pass go!" I have heard many testimonies of the pain and heartache women have gone through because they married an unbeliever. They are living the I Corinthians 7:10-16 life! They have united with an unbeliever! The Scriptures say the woman is to stay in the marriage if the man is willing to live with her.

Here are the Scriptures:

"But to the rest I, not the Lord, say; If any brother has a wife who does not believe, and she is willing to live with him, let him not divorce her. And a woman who has a husband who does not believe, if he is willing to live with her let her not divorce him. For the unbelieving husband is sanctified by the wife, and the unbelieving wife is sanctified by the husband; otherwise your children would be unclean, but now they are holy. But if the unbeliever departs, let him depart; a brother or a sister is not under bondage in such cases. But God has called us to peace" (I Corinthians 7:12-15).

God can work all things together for good. If you are in that type of situation, you must trust He will bring good out of it. I have heard many testimonies of God working through the prayers and faithfulness of the believing wife. I've listened to stories of husbands that have received Christ. There is always hope! If you are married to an unbeliever, I'd highly recommend seeking godly counsel from the women's ministry/pastoral staff at your church for guidance and direction on the situation. You need spiritual support and encouragement.

God Saves

What if he gets saved? Well, it is not your responsibility to lead Him to a saving knowledge of Jesus Christ. It is God's! One of the reasons you're trying to get him involved in the church is so he will get saved, but there's no guarantee that will happen.

There have been women who've told me that God was going to save their boyfriend. They were convinced it was meant to be. They trusted that God was going to do it.

God's Word says to not be closely associated with an unbeliever, so it wasn't God telling them he would accept Christ. This is a very significant thing to point out. When God says no, He'd never confuse the situation by telling you it's a maybe or a yes. When His Word says no, it is definitive. There is no gray area in God's Book. It is NO!

And it is for your own good. Again, He's always trying to look out for His daughters and protect them from harm. That is our Father. He is a loving dad. If you are living for Jesus, and the guy isn't a born-again Christian, there can't be a close friendship with him, no matter what. Pray for God to protect you from getting romantically involved with someone who has not accepted Christ as Savior.

Remember the campaign, "Just say no to drugs?" Let "Just say no to dating unbelievers" be your motto. Pray over the above Scriptures. Please ask Him for wisdom and discernment so you know if the person truly has a relationship with Christ. Pray for the strength to walk away from an unbeliever. Don't let the enemy tell you that it's ok to stay! Make a commitment to God that you will only marry someone who loves Jesus. That is God's desire for you.

Beginning Again

We are starting over in our quest to do things His way. Many are feeling overwhelmed because you were involved in ungodly relationships and were deeply wounded by them. For some of you, the memories still cause pain.

Like me, you didn't follow the path of God during a season in your life. We don't want to live in the past. We don't want to continue to dredge up all the ways that we have failed. That will get us nowhere. The only way reflecting on the past will help is by seeing how you can do things differently as you progress into the future. There is wisdom in deciding not to repeat bad behavior.

I like this quote attributed to George Santayana: "Those who do not learn from history are doomed to repeat it." We've all made foolish decisions. Let's learn and grow from the sinful mistakes that have occurred in our life. God is telling us to forget those things that have happened. He doesn't want us dwelling on them any longer. He doesn't want us to continue looking in the rearview mirror. Don't keep looking back and remembering those things from the past. It's time to embrace the changes that Christ is doing in your life. The Living Water is creating a new spring of life. Don't you see it happening? He is doing a new thing.

"Do not remember the former things, nor consider the things of old. Behold, I will do a new thing, now it shall spring forth; shall you not know it? I will even make a road in the wilderness and rivers in the desert" (Isaiah 43:18, 19).

He will mend and heal your wounds. He will wash you of the painful memories and restore your joy. He will enable you to start anew. With Christ, the future looks bright! Life-sustaining transformation is on its way.

"Jesus Christ is able to untangle all the snarls in my soul, to banish all my complexes, and to transform even my fixed habit patterns, no matter how deeply they are etched in my subconscious." —Corrie Ten Boom.

You can be confident that God's promises are waiting to be received. He has not condemned you to a life of misery. On the contrary, God is in the business of redemption and restoration. And, just like the oyster whose grain of sand creates a precious pearl, our lives will produce beauty of incredible and immeasurable worth.

"I will restore to you the years that the swarming locusts have eaten" (Joel 2:25).

He keeps His promises. I'm a testimony of that!

Verses For Meditation

"And just as you want men to do to you, you also do to them likewise." ~ Luke 6:31

"I have been crucified with Christ, it is no longer I who live, but Christ lives in me; and the life which I now live in the flesh, I live by faith in the Son of God, who loved me and gave Himself for me." ~ Galatians 2:20

"Make no friendship with an angry man, and with a furious man do not go, lest you learn his ways and set a snare for your soul." ~ Proverbs 22:24, 25

"Can two walk together, unless they agree?" ~ Amos 3:3

"He has shown you, O man, what is good; and what does the Lord require of you but to do justly, to love mercy, and to walk humbly with your God." ~ Micah 6:8

CHAPTER 6

There Is A Love Worth Waiting For

*M*any reading this book have wondered if it's possible to have a healthy, Christ-centered relationship with the opposite sex. Is it possible to find a godly man who really does put Jesus first? Where are you? You're tired of throwing yourself into relationships, only to discover that he's not the one. That's why *Guard Your Heart* caught your eye.

We don't want to continue on a quest to find the right one, Jesus is the One we want to live for. He is the One who will fulfill us and make us whole! He is the One we need to yearn for! He is our heart's desire. Jesus is the only one that can satisfy. We've had too many counterfeits in the past! Only He can provide the unconditional love that we long for.

And, if you are to be married, you want Jesus to be your "composer." You want Him to receive the glory for bringing all the elements of your relationship together. He will bring the relationship to pass. Let it be His divine timing. He does a better job of writing the lyrics than you do. Before I gave him the pen, the music had so many sour notes. Let Christ get the credit for being the orchestrator of your love song.

A Guard Your Heart course attendee shared an exciting testimony with me, and I want to share it with you. She came to the place where she didn't believe there were any godly men left out there! She had been so hurt in past relationships that she'd practically given up hope on finding a spiritual leader.

The emphasis of the GYH class is to make Jesus the priority, create a new identity in the Lord, develop healthy, Christ-centered relationships and learn how to do things His way. As she went through the class, she was inspired and left hopeful that maybe God does have someone special for her. She made a commitment to live a life of holiness and to do relationships God's way. She started putting into practice the Biblical principles that are in this book.

A few months later, she met a godly man who treated her with great care and respect. He led by spiritual example. They were both living a life of purity before Him. Together, they determined to build a strong, Christ-centered relationship. When he asked for her hand in marriage, she was ecstatic.

She shared her wedding photos with me, and they brought tears to my eyes. It is another love story written by our Savior. She now encourages women to make the sacrifice to live for Christ and to say no to ungodly relationships. She can attest to the blessings she has received because she chose to be obedient to Him. She encourages others to trust Him to work things out in the relationship department. He is able! But she learned a vital lesson in the GYH class: One must apply His truths to receive His best.

How To Test And Evaluate Relationships

Is there a way to test and evaluate relationships? Praise God, there is! The Word of God is filled with directives on how to do relationships His way. I never knew how many Scriptures talked about the kind of relationships we are to have! It's sad that we have been so deceived by the enemy and our flesh into believing that we have things figured out.

I look back and realize that, had I known and followed the guidance in God's Word, all my past relationships would have ended within a few weeks—and some, within a few days! In years past, I put others before Him. It never would have been God's will for me to move forward in those toxic situations. His Word is like a compass that brings clarity through the confusion, so you know which way to go. It tells you precisely how to proceed in relationships.

I'm encouraging you to seek His Word for guidance in every area of your life. Just as Jesus was one with the Father, we want to experience that same intimacy and communion with God. We want to follow in the footsteps of our Savior. And that begins with having a good working knowledge of Scripture.

His Word:

- tells us who to be in close fellowship with.
- tells us how to treat each other.
- tells us to live a life of purity.
- tells us how and when to draw boundary lines.
- issues standards to ensure that relationships exhibit His grace, mercy and love.
- tells us to be Christ-like in all we do.
- teaches us what unconditional love really looks like.
- teaches us how to love and forgive like He does.
- teaches us how to disciple others.
- empowers us to preach the Word of God to every creature.

The Word enables us to know what God's heart says about developing healthy relationships. Scripture tells us the kind of gentleman God wants His daughter to marry. No one is perfect, but the Word of God tells us who we shouldn't get tangled up with. I am amazed at how unhealthy my past relationships were. I believed they were right for me, even with all the bad behavior that existed in them. But I saw the light, and it was Christ! He revealed the truth to me! And I hope that His light is shining bright for you!

Because God loves you so much, He'd never want you with someone who would cause you physical and emotional harm. He doesn't want you with someone who is broken and takes their pain out on you. And that can work both ways. You should feel so loved knowing that God wants to protect you from getting caught up with someone that isn't good for you. His pick for you is so much better than any choice you'll ever make. Let Him make the decision for you.

Does He Want To Do Relationships God's Way?

It's important to make sure that the guy has a strong spiritual connection with the Lord before you move forward. The questions below can help you evaluate if they are walking with Jesus. Pray for the Holy Spirit to show you if he is genuinely seeking after God. What level of passion does he have for the Lord? Is it cold, lukewarm or hot? How about you? Go down the checklist and honestly answer the questions.

Does the person:

- talk about Him in an intimate way?
- tell you that he needs to pray about things?
- talk about the importance of going to His Word for direction?
- ever quote Scripture in relation to what's going on in his life?
- tell you that He doesn't want to do a relationship unless Christ is at the center?
- get convicted when he does something wrong?
- desire to live a life of purity and holiness before God?
- care about hurting you and leading you on?
- trust the Lord to confirm if you are the one for him?
- want to be a good spiritual leader for his family?
- care about pleasing God? Is that his ultimate desire?
- know that he can't do life without Christ?

If you answered yes to many of these questions, then all I can say is, "Wow!" That person sounds perfect. Of course, only Jesus can fill all the above requirements. That said, you do want someone whose identity is getting stronger in the Lord and who is growing in their walk with Him. A man who is young in the faith will exhibit a lot more immaturity than a person who is making Christ their priority. You want someone who is no longer a baby in their spiritual walk. Consider how young children can behave. They can be very selfish and stubborn. Can you see one of the reasons why God can refer to new believers as "babes in Christ?" It's important that the individual is growing in their understanding of the fundamentals of the Christian faith.

If you don't implement basic Christian principles in your life, then you won't require that of others. For example: If you don't spend time in the Word, why would you expect him to? If it's not a priority to go to church and serve the body of Christ, why would you desire that of him? If you aren't praying about the things going on in your life, why would you make that a pre-requisite in your relationships? If you never talk about Jesus, it won't matter if he doesn't.

So, the development of a close relationship with Jesus begins with you. If you've recently received Christ or haven't spent much time getting to know Him, you will be spiritually immature. And that's not a criticism. We've all been there. And, understanding your desperate need for more of Him is key to the transformation of your heart.

You aren't going to focus on the things of God until you start experiencing more intimacy with the Savior. Developing spiritual disciplines in your life will take time and effort. You need to be diligent in your pursuit. Pray for a desire to experience oneness with Him. Ask Him to show you the areas that need strengthening so there is more intimacy between the two of you. Make sure that you are doing the spiritual things necessary to get closer to Him.

Make developing a relationship with Jesus your primary focus. The more connected you are to the Lord, the more wisdom and discernment you will have. He'll give you the spiritual eyes to see things from His perspective. And then you will love like He does and want what He desires. When you start seeing how rich and fulfilling your life becomes when you have a deep connection with Jesus, you'll never want to return to your old ways. When you begin to see all the many ways He shows up in your life, you'll understand why nothing compares to Him.

Is He A Man Of Faith?

Are you praying for someone who has strong godly qualities? Are you looking for a man of faith? Is that what's most important to you?

When examining the lives of the disciples, there is a faith that resonates within them. Many of them left behind everything to follow Jesus. Why did they turn their backs on the things of this world? Because the Lord offered them something much richer. A life filled with goodness, grace and love. A hope for the future. A purpose and a calling. A reason for living. A love everlasting.

That life is available to each of us. These examples of faith in the Bible aren't just bedtime stories to read to your children. They are spiritual food for the nourishment of our souls. The testimonies of these godly men will strengthen and encourage us as we seek to understand the way God works out His plans through the hearts of His people.

God wants His precious daughters with men who understand the meaning of the word faith. You don't want guys who are wishy-washy in their spiritual walk. Who won't, like some of the disgruntled disciples referred to in John 6:53-69, walk away from Jesus because they didn't like the things He says.

Remember the faith of the 11 disciples who stuck by Jesus' side. They stayed close to Him, because, as Peter said, *"You have the words of eternal life. Also, we have come to believe and know that You are the Christ, the Son of the living God"* (John 6:68-69).

You want a man who will follow Christ, no matter the cost. Have there been challenges in his life? How has he responded to them? In faith or in fear? Has he learned to trust Jesus through the trials? Have you? We've all experienced difficulties in our lives. But the more you walk with Jesus, the more your faith in Him will blossom. What are some amazing God stories in your life? How has He revealed Himself to you recently?

Is God going to bring you someone who has no faith or trust in Him? Or who has no clue what a personal relationship with Jesus really does look like? Is God going to confuse you by bringing someone that sounds spiritual but isn't the real deal? Does He want your head to constantly be spinning around in circles?

The Lord God doesn't give you different doors to choose from. Is it door number 1 or door number 2--or door number 27? What about this person or that person? Hey, how about Him? We're not playing a game of Let's Make a Deal! This isn't a game of Mystery Date. There are many who treat dating relationships just like that game by Milton Bradley. There are too many people going through the wrong door and are missing God's richest blessings in their life.

How about believing that God has one door for you to go through? How about believing that there will be a big reveal and the choice will become crystal clear.

Don't make the desire to have a relationship what you live for. Take a heart check! What's at the root of your passion? What drives your desires? Is it a passion for Jesus or a relationship with the opposite sex? It's natural to want companionship. I understand. But, until that person is in clear view and close proximity, adjust your camera setting so that the focus is on the Savior and His Word.

"For God is not the author of confusion but of peace" (I Corinthians 14:33).

God Will Give Confirmations

If He loves Jesus, you won't have to play a guessing game to figure out where he stands with the Lord. It is obvious by the way he acts and the things he says.

And people that know him can confirm that he is a godly man. I remember when my husband and I became friends. Several people told me that he really loved the Lord and was committed to Him. There were two women who encouraged me to pursue a relationship with him. But I didn't want to show an interest until he started to move in my direction. I did not want to seek him out. I did not want to manipulate circumstances. He had to be purposeful in his quest for a relationship. I wanted to make sure that he was interested in me.

And even then, I needed to know that He was living for Christ and in service to the King. Because serving the Lord was important to me, that was a requirement. Because I was in several ministries, I needed someone who could share that with me. It didn't have to be the same ministries. But it ended up being that way. Praise God!

God doesn't play with your head. He doesn't work like that. He is methodical in all that He does. He is a God of order and structure. The God that watches over you is the same God that made the sun, moon and the stars. He put them in their celestial order and set them on a path of precision. If every element of creation has been perfectly placed by our Creator, don't you think He will move and work with the same kind of precision in your life? He's not going to leave you groping and stumbling around in the dark. He'll move you in a certain direction.

But we still must contend with the enemy and the flesh. So, things can get very confusing. But God will cut away the vines that are growing up in front of you. His plan will unfold as you live for Him. The closer you are to Jesus, the more you'll understand His will for your life. When you are sold-out for the King, He will plant desires and direction in your heart. The Holy Spirit will light the way. You are more precious and valuable than a shining star! In God's eyes, you are a star! A light that brightly radiates the love of Christ.

When my husband and I got engaged, a few issues cropped up that we had to address. We remained pure in our relationship and sought godly counsel as we prayerfully moved forward. We asked God to separate us if we weren't supposed to be together, and God continued to move us closer to the altar. It was hard for me to lift that prayer up to the Lord. And, at times, it caused extreme fear and anxiety. But I wanted God's best for my life, even though my heart yearned to be married. Even though I really didn't want to consider my life without him.

The Lord gave us confirmations that helped us know we were supposed to press on. I truly believe He will do that for you. It was His will for us to be man and wife. He had His hands all over our relationship, and if you're supposed to be married, His fingerprints will be all over yours. It's a matter of trusting Him to guide your steps, knowing that He will divinely show you the way. He will not lead you astray! He will come through for you! He is faithful! He is in love with you! He is your God!

Focus on Your Heart

We have a flesh that we must battle with. The enemy is always trying to undermine the work God is doing in our lives. There can be a lot of underlying fears and insecurities that hinder individuals from having a successful relationship. There can be sinful behaviors that are deeply affecting the couple's ability to build a strong foundation.

Are there negative personality traits that need to be uprooted in your life? We all have issues that need to be addressed. It's as if we've been wired to do and say certain things. And those behavioral patterns can cause serious problems in our relationships. As we get closer to Jesus, He reveals our need for a personality transformation.

So, how well do you get along? Do the two of you argue a lot? Is there constant conflict? Is it an unhealthy relationship? We will discover that our unresolved issues can ruin relationships that might have survived if we'd been emotionally and spiritually healthy. It's important to prayerfully look within to see if there are areas that still need divine healing. The Holy Spirit can reveal those things that are still sensitive to the touch. Let Him show you what needs spiritual restoration.

Here are a few questions to ask yourself:

- Do I still have chambers in my heart that need healing?
- Do I constantly bring up the past?
- Do I have a hard time forgiving?
- Am I an angry and bitter person?
- Am I selfish and self-consumed?

These are just some of the areas that need to be evaluated. It isn't to condemn you. It's to help strengthen your spiritual walk. God wants you to be emotionally and spiritually healthy. All the above questions were a yes at one time in my life. And many of those issues came to light after I got married.

The Biblical counseling that I received enabled me to understand how to seek God and His Word to experience healing. It wasn't a quick fix! There is no "magic bullet." But as I drew closer, He began to heal my deep wounds. I took His Word to heart, and it changed my life. It restored my soul. It enabled me to forgive, love and trust again. He renewed my spirit and gave me a passion for Him. And a passion for the things of God.

If you are struggling with unresolved hurts, it's important to seek the Word of God and wise counsel to help you interpret the cause of your emotional pain. What is the underlying motivation for the things you do?

"Plans fail for lack of counsel; but with many advisors they succeed" (Proverbs 15:22 NIV).

It Wasn't Meant To Be

How will you know if God is bringing someone into your life? That's not always clear. Sometimes people can be a good choice, but not God's choice. We must be very prayerful as we work through the evaluation process. As you spend time with Him, He will give you the discernment to know whether to move forward or withdraw. As you seek His face for direction, He will enable you to know what to do.

There was a time when I thought the Lord had brought a godly man into my life. I had spent so much time praying for a strong, spiritual leader. I really believed the Lord had brought us together. We had the same heart for ministry. We had so many things in common. Our relationship seemed to be moving in the right direction.

The guy seemed really interested in me, but never enough to move beyond the friendship stage. We spent quite a bit of time together outside of the ministry. He said things that made me think he wanted more than a friendship. My heart was constantly warmed by the kind and uplifting things he said and by all the time he wanted to spend with me.

I began having feelings for him. I wondered why our relationship had not developed into something more serious. He never said we were dating or referred to me as his girlfriend. I just kept waiting and hoping he'd make the first move. But he never ventured into that territory.

So, I was receiving many mixed signals and getting very frustrated. I had to know if there was a potential future for us. After one of our ministry events, I said we needed to talk. I confronted him to see if the relationship was moving to the next level. "Why do you think that?" he asked, looking puzzled. "You say and do things that make me think you want to be more than friends," I said, as my voice began to quiver.

I shared how he was always pouring on the compliments. He thought it was important to be a supportive brother in Christ. I questioned him about all the time we spent together outside of the ministry. He said that he was just having fun and enjoying my company. I was so confused by his reaction. It looked like I had egg on my face. I wish there had been a rock close by to crawl under. I would have shriveled up and slithered away.

How Will You Know?

That was a humiliating experience, to say the least. He said we were just friends. That was it! He had nothing more than platonic feelings for me. I wish I could have eliminated platonic from the dictionary. When that happened, I should have taken a huge step backwards. But I still wanted to be more than friends.

I was still hopeful that things might change. I should have listened when he said that the relationship was not moving forward, and he had no feelings for me. It wasn't wise to continue spending time with him outside of the ministry, especially since I desired a more serious relationship. I should have put up some clear boundary lines. I should not have fellowshipped with him beyond our service to the King. I should have rejected his advances to just hang out. It would have prevented a lot of sleepless nights and a wealth of hurt feelings. I should have focused on Christ and asked Him to help me *Guard My Heart*.

I'm so grateful that he didn't pursue a serious relationship with me. He wasn't supposed to be my husband. Just because we had many spiritual connections, didn't mean that it was God's choice for me. Just because things seemed right didn't mean he was the right one. He wasn't.

I've had countless women ask me how they'll know if someone's interested in them. That question reveals that he's not showing enough of an interest. You don't want to waste countless hours of time and energy wondering when something will happen between the two of you. If he's interested in you, you won't have to read between the lines.

You'll know it. He'll be trying to develop a relationship with you. Let him pursue you with more than winks and smiles. Is he wanting to get to know you? Does he want to develop a healthy friendship? If he isn't, then don't continue to dwell on the hope that things might work out. You don't want to keep waiting for him to come around. Remember, you want a leader who is going to take the initiative.

These are questions that should be scrolling through your mind: What kind of history does he have with the ladies? How did his last relationship end? Has he asked you out? Is he taking you to the next relationship level? Is he leading you on? Does he say one thing and then do another, leaving you confused about his intentions?

And if things aren't moving forward, ask God to remove the feelings. There have been times that women have struggled for months, and even years, with a desire for a certain person and it didn't work out. I had feelings for several years and nothing ever materialized beyond a platonic friendship. I wasted a lot of time on the hopes that things would progress.

Our thoughts and feelings can really deceive us. And those desires can negatively impact your relationship with Christ. Because there is such passion for an individual, the fire for Jesus can smolder and even go out. That's why it's important to evaluate where your passion lies. Are you really seeking to know Jesus and His will for your life? Are you really falling in love with the Savior?

Women have shared how hard it's been to get over someone. Seek to pray and meditate on His Word, as you work through the emotional struggle. It takes time to heal after a break-up. There's no doubt that it's a painful process. There can be so many restless nights and buckets of tears. But God will heal your heart and help you to carry on. The focus is always on filling yourself up with Him. It's important to dwell on the things that draw you closer to Him. He is able to restore and mend your wounded heart. He is able to breathe new life into your broken soul.

Don't Waste Your Time

A man of God should come to the place where he wants a committed relationship and is open to marriage. And that shouldn't take years to figure out. You should look at the first year as a good indicator of where the relationship is going. And then, if you are in the second year, are you in the courting stage? Is there any hope that it's moving in that direction? How much time does he need? If there is no promise for the future, then hit the escape button and just remain friends.

I am encouraging you not to let someone toy with your emotions. A guy may like you but not enough to get married. He might love your company but a walk down the aisle is not in his future. And that means it's not in yours either. Be friends but limit your time together. And let's make sure that you are remaining pure. The temptation grows as the friendship deepens. It becomes much more challenging to say no to fleshly desires. It's very important that the physical boundary lines are not crossed. Because if they are, it becomes so much harder to walk away. And so much more painful to get over. Protect your heart! Protect your purity! Protect your walk with the Lord!

If this is God's choice for you, it will work out. If you are asking the Lord for direction, He will pave the way. The Lord is the greatest navigator the world has ever seen. He is the only one who knows where the two of you are and how to bring you together. Don't you want to make sure that He is the one who caused the divine connection? And that He will bring clarity and confirmation.

If you are wanting to do it God's way, He's going to let you know. If your desire is to please the Savior in your relationships, He has more than an opinion on your situation. He has a plan. Let Him work out the details as you continue to engulf yourself in service to the Lord.

May your hours be spent being a blessing to others. May you desire to bring hope to the forlorn and torn. May you desire to be that ray of sunshine that someone needs in their life. May your heart ache for those who are hurting. May you deeply care about their need for salvation. May your love for them overcome any obstacle that Satan puts in the way. Like our dear brother, the apostle Paul, who was willing to lay down his life so that others could hear the only message that really matters, salvation is in the Lord, Jesus Christ.

If you are seeking to enrich other people's lives, you will find the Lord rekindling your joy. You will see the Holy Spirit moving you in a divine direction. You will see the inspiring connections as God's hand of intervention. His power goes with you. Don't let the enemy rain down on you and put that fire out! Let the Lord's passion for people and their lack of Him move you to care enough to share the love of Jesus. God has placed a divine purpose in you that He wants to reveal. Blessings come through being used by the Lord.

God will guide you through the waiting process. I do understand what a challenging time this is. I do empathize with you, my sweet sister. Until God brings someone into your life, set your sights on the Lord. Commit yourself to serving the Savior. The path will become smooth. The fog will lift. The sea will split, and God's answer will be revealed.

Is He Truly A Spiritual Leader?

Don't you want someone who will commit, love, and be faithful till death do you part? Don't you want a man who will be the leader of your home? There are many who married a man and thought he'd go to church, lead in devotions and seek God for guidance and direction on the daily issues of life.

They were deeply saddened when they realized that he really didn't have a close relationship with the Lord, and it was reflected in his lack of commitment to spiritual things. It is important that you see strong spiritual qualities exhibited before you get married.

You don't want to tell a guy that he needs to go to church, read the Bible, pray and be in service to the King. A lot of women feel that they need to encourage their boyfriends to be a spiritual leader. As women, we tend to be very aware of their problem areas and what needs to be corrected. So, you lovingly try to tell them how they should live.

You are their coach! I had a whistle around my neck in most of my past relationships. You are telling them that changes need to be made. I know you think that's helping him, but God says that's not your job. He doesn't want you being the Holy Spirit in his life. He doesn't want you taking on the responsibility of making him more like Jesus. God doesn't want him accountable to you.

It's confusing when you encourage him to stop the negative behaviors, and he starts complying with your requests. Then you move forward because you believe the changes were permanent. But how long did it last? For some it was a few weeks, and for others it was a few months.

I've heard testimony after testimony from women who required certain changes from their boyfriends before they got married. But after the wedding bells rang, he went back to his old ways, much to their dismay. There were many who had much regret because the guy's sinful behavior continued.

If there is a genuine transformation, you'll see behavioral patterns that reflect positive spiritual growth. If they are still doing the same things, that reflects who they really are. Don't try to manipulate them so they conform to your standards. Don't try to control what they do. Don't try to insist that they change for you. Can you accept the person and his negative behaviors? Are you willing to marry him, knowing that after the "I do's" he might not change? Are you willing to love him unconditionally?

The Wise Approach

I'd highly recommend not telling a guy what to do and see how he behaves. If they don't know what your spiritual expectations are, they're not going to know if something offends you. If they are living a worldly life-style, those behaviors will eventually surface, and you want to see them. They are going to behave based on who they are, not what you want. You are looking for the genuine person. Don't you want to see if he is in a serious relationship with Christ?

If you're diligently seeking the Lord in this process, God will enable you to discern if the person isn't living for the Savior. And, if you're not close to God, you will have a higher tolerance level to his sinful ways. This is where you can be excusing his bad behavior, instead of rejecting it! The closer you are to Jesus, the more you'll be aware when things are spiritually out-of-focus.

You want to see leadership qualities in your potential husband. You want him living for Christ because he has a desire to seek after God, not because you told him to follow Jesus.

Remember, God doesn't want him submitting to you. If he's growing in Christ, you won't have to tell him what to do. He doesn't have to be poked and prodded to do things God's way! He doesn't have to be persuaded to seek Christ. You shouldn't have to leave spiritual messages on post-it notes to encourage him to do the right thing. It shouldn't be your voice that He listens to! He should be seeking God's voice for direction. That's someone who gets what it means to be in a relationship with the Savior.

"That the older men be sober, reverent, temperate, sound in faith, in love, in patience; the older women likewise, that they be reverent in behavior, not slanderers, not given to much wine, teacher of good things—that they

admonish the young women to love their husbands, to love their children, to be discreet, chaste, homemakers, good, obedient to their own husbands, that the Word of God may not be blasphemed. Likewise, exhort the young men to be sober-minded in all things showing yourself to be in a pattern of good works; in doctrine showing integrity, reverence, incorruptibility, sound speech that cannot be condemned, that one who is an opponent may be ashamed, having nothing evil to say of you" (Titus 2:2-8).

Is The Guy Controlling You?

There have been many women who were very disappointed when they discovered that the guy wasn't a godly leader. Ladies, don't you want someone who encourages you to walk closely with the Lord? Now that doesn't mean the guy is supposed to lord over you. It doesn't mean he's supposed to tell you what to do and how to do it. He shouldn't be doing that. After you get married, things do change. God has given the man a major responsibility to be the leader of his family. But he still shouldn't be lording over the wife. He still shouldn't abuse and take advantage of that leadership position.

That's why it's so important to evaluate whether you see ANY signs of control and jealousy before you take that walk down the aisle. These are warning signs that can cause serious problems in your relationship. Keep your eyes and heart wide open to what God is revealing to you about a person's actions.

The person has no authority over you before marriage. And that includes the engagement period. There are guys who use engagements to try and get control. He'll try to convince her to submit to his authority. She is not required to do that. God doesn't want a woman controlled and manipulated by her boyfriend or fiancé. If this is what's happening before the I do's, imagine what it will be like after the wedding bells ring?

The man you consider marrying should have an unconditional love for you. He should love you like he does his own body. He wouldn't mistreat his own flesh. And he shouldn't mistreat yours. God's Word gives a clear mandate on how a husband should care for and minister to his wife.

That's why it's wise to discern the guy's leadership style. Has he grown in his walk with Jesus enough to lead in a loving way? And it doesn't mean he'll do that perfectly.

"In the same way husbands should love their wives as their own bodies. He who loves his wife loves himself. For no one ever hated his own flesh, but nourishes and cherishes it, just as Christ does the church, because we are members of his body" (Ephesians 5:28-30).

"Likewise, husbands, live with your wives in an understanding way, showing honor to the woman as the weaker vessel since they are heirs with you of the grace of life, so that your prayers may not be hindered" (I Peter 3:7).

In your dating relationship, who seems to take control? Who is the one that gets angry when they don't get their way? Who is the stubborn one? Is it both of you? You should be looking very intently at how you interact together prior to marriage. The ways you engage and behave towards each other will give you some idea of what to expect as you move forward. This helps discern if you should advance in the relationship.

Ask yourself these important questions. Would you consider him a peacemaker? How about you? Are you both willing to compromise? Do you have freedom to share? Does he? How do you seek to resolve conflict? Are you both willing to seek counseling to work things out? Are you both seeking to bring healing to the relationship? It isn't about winning an argument; it's about pursuing peace and restoration in your relationship.

What Can I Say?

There have been many women who have asked questions about the topic of submission. Questions like: Can't I challenge him? Can't I ask questions? Can't we debate? Can't I disagree with him? You have every right to your own feelings and opinions. There are times when they won't agree with us, and we won't agree with them. You should be able to discuss and hash things out. You should be able to work through things that will bring conclusions and resolutions.

We are human. We aren't perfect. We will get upset. We won't see eye-to-eye. We won't understand our husbands and they won't understand us.

We can find it very frustrating. We can feel like we are speaking a foreign language. We are very different. So, what happens when the two of you disagree? Well, we can't make our husbands do what we want them to or what we think is right.

We are called to respect our husbands. We aren't supposed to quarrel, argue, use the silent treatment, withdrawal, or a host of other things to get our way. We aren't supposed to stomp our feet and throw a hissy-fit. I've been famous for many of those in our early marriage. I have failed miserably at this in the past.

You know the saying, "You can catch more flies with honey than vinegar." In God's book, it's true! Love is what covers a multitude of sins. Love is what can transform the hard heart. When Jesus became flesh and walked the earth, He showed us how to live. He showed us how to love. He showed us how to be gracious and kind. He taught us how to sacrifice for others. He taught us how to be selfless. His example is what we must follow. *"Above all, keep loving one another earnestly, since love covers a multitude of sins"* (I Peter 4:8).

We are called to encourage each other. The Holy Spirit can work through us in ways that will produce positive growth in those around us. But we are always supposed to do that in love. Whether a family member, a friend, a boyfriend or a husband, God always wants our actions to exhibit that same gentleness that Christ extends to us. Even when we must be direct in our confrontations, we are to be humble and compassionate in our approach.

When you do lose your temper and fly off the handle, when you do get frustrated and annoyed, and when you do say foolish and unwise things, you need to apologize. And he should, too. But you can't control what someone else does. You can only control your actions. We'll address the issue of forgiveness in chapter 8.

In a past relationship, I was so jealous and insecure, that I tried to tell him where to go and who he could talk to. He shouldn't have allowed me to do that to him. It was wrong. It was unfair. If you let someone be themselves and they end up flirting and doing things that are inappropriate, you need to know that. You both need to have the freedom to be your genuine self. This way, it might not be a match made in heaven. And you might realize that, early on, you are seeing behavior that doesn't align with your Christian values. Not every attraction and connection are meant to be.

It's unwise to try and control people to protect yourself. It doesn't work. Healthy relationships are built on trust. How many couples have sabotaged their relationship by trying to control it to the point of suffocation? I had no idea how severely crippled my past relationships were. I share this because the woman can be the one who is controlling and manipulative. In my case, it was both of us.

I like the saying, "Trust and verify." What does that mean? You can't take someone at face value. You need to let someone prove that they can be trusted. It doesn't mean that you should be cynical. It just means that you are prayerful and cautious. It's not wise to give away your heart and tell them your secrets when you aren't sure the kind of person he is.

How many have trusted and wished they would have taken more time to verify? This process can cause bewilderment to the soul. But unrighteous actions will eventually surface. Negative behavioral patterns will be revealed. When you are living for Jesus, He will disclose the areas of concern. He will open up the dark places that reveal the sinful spaces. Let Him lead! Let His Holy Spirit show you truth! Trust that He will help you verify what is genuine from what is false. You need His help! You are dependent on it! I hope and pray you realize just how much!

The Love Triangle

I use this triangle illustration to help explain the different pace that individuals grow in their relationship with the Lord. And to give you a better understanding of the differences in a couple's spiritual journey.

At the top of the triangle is the King of kings and Lord of lords, our Savior Jesus Christ. You and the prospective boyfriend are below, at opposite corners of the triangle.

As you grow closer to the Lord, it is evident that you are maturing in your walk with Him. We each have our own personal relationship with Jesus, and everyone moves at a different pace throughout the process of sanctification. We must keep looking up and focusing on Jesus for our relationship with Christ to be healthy and whole. The more time you spend with Him, the more you discover He has all the answers.

If you are thirsting for Jesus and he isn't, the two of you won't be on the same spiritual page. You'll quickly discover that the things of God aren't a major concern for him. You want to study the Word of God, but he doesn't have time. You want to go to church, but he has season tickets to the Dolphin games. It's so hard to understand why your spiritual paths are so different.

Why do things seem so imbalanced? It's because the two of you are at different points on the triangle. You've taken off and are making your way up the spiritual mountain. Nothing is going to hold you back. You are like a deer thirsting after the Living Water. You are filled with a passion to know Him. As you seek after Him, you sense a deeper intimacy with the Lord.

He's not as close to the Lord, so he's lagging behind. He's content in just going to church on Sunday or he might not even do that. A young woman shared how the guy she was interested in didn't go to church because it wasn't his thing. But, he didn't discourage her from attending. Wow, how sweet! God's not impressed with his kindness. In fact, His Word says that this person isn't the right one for her. Hmmm. Will she listen to God?

Remember, just because people say they attend church and believe in God doesn't mean they are experiencing true spiritual maturity. There are many who claim to be spiritual, but don't even know that Jesus is the Savior of the world. Have they really committed their life to Christ?

As you evaluate the guy's spiritual walk, is he still stuck on the corner of the triangle? How long has he been there? Has he started moving up the spiritual mountain, in search of a deeper relationship with Christ? Can he give testimony of how God's transformed his walk? Is he able to give God the glory for his changed life?

The Table Of Contents

You know the saying, "You can't tell a book by its cover." Well, it's true. I tell women that the cover can look so appealing, but the pages can be filled with all kinds of troubling behavior. You might find that you regret ever picking up that book.

What kind of things are inside the book you are about to read? What is being revealed as you turn the pages? What kind of personality does he have? Do you see negative behavioral patterns emerging? Are red lights starting to flash? Are there warning signs ahead?

THERE IS A LOVE WORTH WAITING FOR

What is listed in his "table of contents?" Is he:
- Controlling and jealous? You shouldn't allow anyone to tell you where to go, what to do or who to be with. He has no authority over you. It's unhealthy to be in a relationship with someone who acts like he owns you. Is he jealous to the point that he won't let you talk to members of the opposite sex? Does he check your phone and computer for guy's numbers? Is he constantly interrogating you?
- Possessive? You shouldn't be with him 24 hours a day. Does it feel like he has a leash on you, so he knows your every move? Or, are you like a leech on him—constantly with him?
- Selfish and stubborn? Is it all about him? If things don't work out his way, how does he react? Does he care about your feelings?
- Easily angered and has a bad temper? Does he get upset easily? Does he yell? Does he call you names? Does he act like he'd ever get physical with you? Has he ever threatened you? Has he ever hit you?
- Unforgiving? Does he bring up past offenses? Does he hold a grudge? Does he act bitter? Is it hard for him to say, "I'm sorry or forgive me?"
- Flirting and leading the ladies on? Is he a smooth talker? How did the two of you meet? How did he treat you at the beginning of your relationship?
- Focused primarily on his job, money and acquiring things? Is he consumed with being successful? Does his life revolve around money? Is he determined to prove that he is someone by the possessions that he owns?
- Wanting to get physical in your relationship? Is he crossing physical boundary lines? Is he trying to get you alone? Does he talk about a sexual relationship? Is he pressuring you to do something inappropriate? Does he make you feel guilty if you don't do what he wants in this area? Does he try to brainwash you into believing that this is acceptable behavior?
- Known for his reputation? How is he known around town? Does he have a history of broken relationships?

Have you seen any of the above characteristics surface in past relationships? What about the one you are currently in? These behaviors are very destructive to relationships and reflect serious emotional immaturity. We must look at these negative qualities as major issues. They can be exhibited in our lives too. It's important to take a good look within to see where change is needed. We need to evaluate our attitudes and behaviors to make sure that we are being healed and emotionally restored, through the amazing power of the Holy Spirit.

There are lines that must be drawn when these types of abusive behaviors arise in our relationships. Just because you have strong feelings for someone doesn't mean he is the one. You can't let your heart move you closer to someone that God is trying to protect you from. God's Word speaks loudly concerning ungodly behavior. People that drag us down and interfere in our Christian walk are not heaven sent! These types of relationships end up causing much more harm than good.

We all have sinful patterns that God will continue to eradicate from our lives until we reach the other side. We all do and say things that hurt each other's feelings. The emotional differences between men and women can be a very difficult thing to work through. And sometimes impossible to do. At times, it can mean that the two are just incompatible. And because of their unresolved issues, they just can't get along.

I love this saying. I have repeated it countless times: Man's rejection is God's protection. Don't you just love that? Always believe that God's Hand is in control of your life. If it was meant to be, then it would have happened. Especially if you were praying and trusting Him through the evaluation process. And, no matter the reason it failed, He can always bring healing and restoration out of the heartbreak.

No One Is Perfect

No one is perfect. Remember, we all start out as a babe in Christ. There are many who've done some or all that's listed in the table of contents. We've all been childish and immature. And some still are. We are all being refined as we draw closer to Him. As we seek His face, He will reveal the sin in our heart. We will begin to change and be transformed into His image.

We're all at different stages on our spiritual road of discovery. Change doesn't occur overnight. So, you can't expect the person you're interested in to never say or do anything wrong. If that's what you think, then you will be thoroughly disappointed. I'm a sinner and you're a sinner. We marry a sinner.

What happens when there is an offense? What happens when there is sinful behavior? How did you respond? What did he do? Our attitude should be one of repentance when something isn't right.

There are times that women will try and hold the guy accountable. They will tell him where he has failed. They will demand change. And the guy will succumb to their requests. When there is an offense, he needs to repent because he sinned against the Lord, not because you told him he was wrong. He needs to experience conviction because he cares about His relationship with God.

It's not because he's afraid that you will leave. It's because he has a conscience that causes conviction. As we experience a deeper oneness with Christ, we will have faith instead of fear, self-control instead of lust, forgiveness instead of bitterness, and humbleness instead of pride.

We are putting off the old man and his corrupt ways. We are saying no to temptation. The ways of the world no longer appeal to us. We are learning to turn from all those sinful practices that are a part of our old nature. We are rejecting the ways of the flesh! We don't want to be in bondage to sin any longer. There is true change occurring within us.

When we are living for Jesus, our lives will mirror His reflection. It won't be hard to see Christ in someone, when the Holy Spirit is moving. It should be evident that there is spiritual growth happening. The transformation of a soul brings hope. The relationship with Christ brings new life! It is like a flower in bloom. The bud is opening, and the beauty is breathtaking.

"But now you yourselves are to put off all these: anger, wrath, malice, blasphemy, filthy language out of your mouth. Do not lie to one another, since you have put off the old man with his deeds, and have put on the new man who is renewed in knowledge according to the image of Him who created him" (Colossians 3:8-10).

The Fruit Tree

I like to use this fruit tree illustration when describing the changes Jesus makes in our lives. Before we accepted Christ, we had a tree filled with fleshly fruit. It was overflowing with our corrupt and immoral desires. We had characteristics that were very unseemly and unbecoming. There were times we felt great shame and disgrace over choices that were made. We acted in ways that reflected very selfish attitudes.

It all came down to our happiness. The focus was on self. It was all about me and what I wanted. That's what drove the decisions that I made. And that's the opposite to a life devoted to Jesus. He wants us to be Christ-focused and selfless! He desires for us to think of Him first, others second and ourselves last! In that order.

As we thirst after Him and His Word, our tree begins to burst forth with the fruit of the Spirit. You are learning to exalt Christ to the leadership position that He so rightfully deserves. As you seek to imitate Him, your personality begins to change. The attributes that used to define you no longer do. We begin to reflect godly characteristics that shine for Him. You are looking less and less like the bloodline you were born into and more and more like the line of royalty you now belong to.

You want to share the incredible ways that God has worked in your life. You want others to experience the same hope and confidence the Lord has given to you. The more you experience the love of God, the more your heart will overflow with spiritual fruit. Praise God! What a Savior!

"But the fruit of the Spirit is love, joy, peace, longsuffering, kindness, goodness, faithfulness, gentleness and self-control" (Galatians 5:22-23).

Well, We Are Sisters!

We can't focus and obsess over the negative situations that occurred in past relationships. There were so many heartbreaking and painful moments for each of us. The enemy loves bringing back those awful memories of things the guy said and did that caused trauma. But ladies, we weren't perfect either. We have exhibited some really bad behavior ourselves. We aren't to judge.

> *"Judge not, that you be not judged. For with what judgment you judge, you will be judged; and with the measure you use, it will be measured back to you"* (Matthew 7:1-2).

We can't change what's happened. It's best to forgive and let go so that bitterness doesn't take root in our soul. Don't let the hurtful things that occurred keep you in bondage. Don't let the emotional chains prevent you from experiencing freedom and deliverance.

I was sharing some of my past sinful behaviors during a GYH class, and one of the ladies said that I must be her twin. She couldn't believe how much we had in common. She thought it was uncanny. I said, "Well, we are sisters."

There were so many women that could relate to what I was sharing. They acknowledged how controlling, jealous and unforgiving they'd been in past relationships. We shared how we made demands and required things of the men in our lives and were wrong to do so.

We all admitted to exhibiting some form of abusive behavior. There were some that had been downright mean and cruel. We had lied and been unfaithful; we showed a serious lack of respect for them, and we weren't always caring and compassionate. Almost every woman could relate, in one way or another, to the table of contents list. See why we can't point a finger at them? There are four pointing back at us.

If some of those negative characteristics are still evident in your life, you need to seek His Word, a small group Bible study, and godly counsel. You don't want to continue in these destructive cycles of behavior any longer. You don't want the negative patterns to control you anymore. You don't want to allow triggers to constantly set you off! You don't want for the past to be your present. It isn't a gift! It's more like a weight! And it doesn't get lighter! Don't you want to be free?

If there are unresolved issues and you don't find out what's causing the pain, your relationships will be negatively impacted by those hurts. You will see how the wounds from your past will continue to hinder your ability to have healthy relationships.

You want friendships that will be a blessing, not a burden. Now, we all have complaints about our relationships. Our personalities can rub each other like sandpaper. We must work through our differences. And love each other unconditionally.

But boundary lines can be drawn when things are unhealthy. When sin is involved. When relationships are draining and causing serious pain. When behaviors never change, and things don't get better. When there is more heartbreak than happiness. When there is a serious lack of trust! Be a light for Christ! But be careful not to let anyone darken that light so it no longer shines bright!

And They're Off

I've had women tell me that they had feelings of fear and insecurity about the relationship they were in, but they forged ahead. I use a horse race as an illustration. You're the jockey, and you're in a race; the finish line is marriage. And you're off!!

Serious obstacles arose, but you jumped over them. Another major problem cropped up and you continued to run the race. It's as if you had blinders on. There were red flags and warning signs, but the thought was, "I'm not getting any younger. My biological clock is ticking, and this might be my last chance." You made it to the finish line and got married. Whew! Victory! But it wasn't long before serious problems began to reveal themselves.

What's sad is that there were issues that needed to be dealt with before you headed to the chapel. If there are signs of physical or emotional abuse, God would never want His daughters subjected to that unhealthy conduct. You do not want to be with someone who breaks you down. You shouldn't be with anyone that would put their hands on you (Proverbs 24:25). Your daddy says not to associate with a person who is easily angered and has a hot temper.

He loves you too much to want that for you. He'd never want you to experience such brokenness. That is not love. He desires that you be cherished by the man He has chosen for you. Marriage is a wonderful thing, but don't move ahead when you know there is behavior that needs to be evaluated and processed. Don't ignore the warning signs! That's why they are there: to warn you that there is impending danger ahead. Be wise and heed the yellow flashing light! A train might be coming!

Breaking Up Is Hard To Do

Why was it so hard for me to break free of harmful relationships? What caused me to be so possessive and jealous? Well, to begin with, I never questioned or accused the first boyfriend of anything. I never doubted his word, and I always believed what he said. I never thought he'd cheat or lie. When he left, I was in shock. That break-up really did rock my world.

It caused a deep sense of insecurity to arise within me. I no longer felt confident in relationships. I became cynical and wondered if I could ever trust a man. That's not a healthy thought process to have. But I see how the brokenness and sin from that first relationship caused me to erect walls around my heart. I no longer trusted anyone. My faith in relationships was broken.

I found myself fearful of being hurt again. I felt this underlying sense of mistrust that seemed to taint everything. I thought that I needed to protect myself by requiring the boyfriend adhere to certain strict standards. If I knew where he was and what he was doing, it would prevent something bad from happening ... again. I was very selfish and immature by trying to control the relationship. When I thought he was being dishonest, I started interrogating him. I felt like an attorney. I became anxious when I started seeing similar behavioral patterns that had occurred in my first relationship. Oh no! Here I go again. The cycle continues. But instead of removing myself from the toxic situation, I stayed, determined to make it work.

I had blatant sin in my past relationships, but I rationalized and justified the behavior. That's when we try to downplay the seriousness of what's going on. We pretend everything is fine. We tend to make excuses for what's happening. I had thoughts like, "Aren't we obligated to stay together through thick and thin? Isn't that the definition of real love?"

Wisdom: If you have been deeply wounded in a past relationship and you haven't healed from the hurts, the next person that you are in a relationship with will feel your pain.

There Is Potential

As women, we often see the problems in a relationship. But we've spent too much time trying to make things work to throw in the towel.

I saw things wrong, but my thoughts were, "he'll change, it will get better, and I'm wrong, too." One of my favorite sayings was "Our relationship has potential." So many women laugh when I share that line in class. They can relate to having those same thoughts. That belief caused me to hang on to hope that things would change. I figured that you had to take the good with the bad, because no one can do everything right.

"Set a guard, O LORD, over my mouth; keep watch over the door of my lips. Do not incline my heart to any evil thing, to practice wicked works with men who work iniquity; and do not let me eat of their delicacies" (Psalm 141:3-4).

But the good doesn't outweigh the bad. We aren't to continue in destructive, unhealthy relationships. God tells us to move away from every evil thing. He wants us to turn away from ungodly, inappropriate behavior. We must pray to be sensitive to sin. We don't want to make excuses or allow evil behavior to become an acceptable practice in our lives. We don't want to do things that feed the flesh while starving the spirit. We don't want to fill our hearts with worldly desires that only leave a huge vacuum in our hearts. That is being disobedient to our Father, and we must look at it in those terms.

We must remember that He always wants us to make the sacrifice to put Him first and live for Him.

There are consequences for making the wrong choice. One story that teaches us about the ramifications of sin is that of King David. He is one of my favorite Bible characters. He committed adultery with Bathsheba and had her husband murdered to cover it up! It's a very tragic story.

After David's fall, he was in denial for about a year. He hadn't repented of his egregious sin. He wasn't trying to make things right with the Lord. He believed the cover-up had been successful. And he was going on with his life.

God was not going to allow David to continue in his callousness, so He sent the prophet, Nathan, to confront David about his sinful actions. He told David the consequences that he would face because of his disobedience against the Lord. Nathan was clear and direct. David's heart ached as a result of his foolishness. He repented and penned Psalm 51, one of the most beautiful psalms in the Bible. He followed God the rest of his days. But the time with Bathsheba surely wasn't worth the pain that followed. Go check out II Samuel 11 and 12 to find out what happened to King David and the great love and mercy that God bestowed upon him.

Just Say No

Let's learn from King David. Because of his sinful choices, he suffered serious consequences. Let us choose to live a life of obedience to our King.

I'm here to help others draw close to Him so they will experience God's best for their lives. I'm here to tell you to say no to the ungodly relationship. Resist those individuals that will create pain and cause a crippling effect in your life. Life is complicated enough without their help. Walk away from the things that are luring you to sin. Don't stay around people that are only looking to satisfy self. Don't give into the deplorable ways of the flesh. Run, run, run!! As fast as you can. Into the arms of Jesus! Into the embrace of Your Savior! Into His safety net! He wants to protect you!

Don't go to that bar anymore. Don't even travel down that street. Stay away from the things that remind you of the places you used to go. On those nights, make plans to do something else. The drugs and alcohol will not heal the pain. It'll numb the hurt for a little while, and then the guilt, shame and regret will return, and you'll feel worse about yourself.

Pray for an accountability partner. That's someone you can call when things get challenging. That's someone you can trust when things get tough. But don't become too dependent on them. Remember, you need to always be running back to the Savior. Let His strength be what pulls you up. Let His power be what lifts you high (Isaiah 40:31).

You must work through the spiritual struggles. You must say no and turn from the sinful things that are impairing your spiritual, emotional and physical health. As you seek after God, your spiritual muscles will be strengthened. As you surrender to Him, you will find your true value and worth. You will discover that a relationship with Jesus changes everything.

Celebrate Recovery is a wonderful Christian ministry that helps individuals experience true freedom in their walk with God. Pray for the Lord to direct you to a Christ-centered program if you're finding it difficult to break away from a sinful lifestyle. He'll give you the help you need.

There are many individuals who are deeply wounded by what's happened in their lives. There are churches that offer programs like Divorce Care and Grief Share, as well as many others. There are women who struggle after an abortion. Check with your church or local pregnancy center to find out where post-abortion Bible studies are taking place. There are ministries that help those who have experienced sexual trauma.

Be very prayerful as you move forward. He can give you direction. His divine timing can guide you through this painful process. There were so many times that I needed to experience breakthroughs, and He divinely orchestrated meetings with counselors and leaders that set me on a path of freedom. And I want that for you.

Someone does care, and His name is Jesus. He understands. He loves you. Choose Christ! If you have not already done so, receive Him into your heart today! He can free you from all those things that are holding you back. He can enable you to cast off the burdens that are preventing you from experiencing peace. Release your hurts to Him today! Surrender your heart to Him right now! There is a better way, and it is acknowledging Him in all that you do.

> "Stand fast therefore in the liberty by which Christ has made us free, and do not be entangled again with a yoke of bondage" (Galatians 5:1).

> "If the Son makes you free, you shall be free indeed" (John 8:36).

It is so comforting to know that during those times of sin and disobedience, He never left me. He is faithful, and I am so grateful! He can't deny me because I am His child. He is my daddy. And I feel the love. And even though I know how imperfect I am, His love never fails!

"If we endure, we shall also reign with Him. If we deny Him, He also will deny us. If we are faithless, He remains faithful; He cannot deny Himself" (II Timothy 2:12-13).

We are one and He can't separate Himself from me! I am a part of Him, and He is a part of me. I am a daughter of the King, and I belong to Him. And that leaves His little girl in awestruck wonder!

Verses for Meditation

"So then, my beloved brethren, let every man be swift to hear, slow to speak, slow to wrath; for the wrath of man does not produce the righteousness of God." ~ James 1:19-20

"Be diligent to present yourself approved to God, a worker who does not need to be ashamed, rightly dividing the word of truth." ~ II Timothy 2:15

"And a servant of the Lord must not quarrel but be gentle to all, able to teach, patient, in humility correcting those who are in opposition, if God perhaps will grant them repentance, so that they may know the truth, and that they may come to their senses and escape the snare of the devil, having been taken captive by him to do his will." ~ II Timothy 2:24-26

"Let nothing be done through selfish ambition or conceit, but in lowliness of mind let each esteem others better than himself. Let each of you look not only for his own interests, but also for the interests of others." ~ Philippians 2:3-4

"As you therefore have received Christ Jesus the Lord, so walk in Him, rooted and built up in Him and established in the faith, as you have been taught, abounding in it with thanksgiving." ~ Colossians 2:6

CHAPTER 7

Boy Meets Girl

*B*oy meets girl, girl meets boy, and voila! There is a connection. And oftentimes a relationship! Your eyes meet, and you are drawn to each other like a magnet. There is chemistry. The heart strings are in motion. In fact, you can hear the music playing. You can't resist the impulse to make a connection.

Attractions and feelings are normal. They come and they go. How many have had relationships start with an attraction? Did you think he was the one? How many of those relationships were successful? I batted 0!

I still remember the way I felt when I met my first boyfriend. I did get sweaty palms and palpitations of the heart. It was exciting. But if I'm motivated by the flesh, I'm not letting the Spirit control my feelings. It's like jumping on a runaway train. Sure, those initial feelings took my breath away, but where did they lead me? Down a path of despair. I was involved in several train wrecks.

I wish I'd known the warning signs to look for. If I'd had a better grip on how the flesh worked, I'd have been more equipped to do the right thing. Sadly, we weren't taught how this process works. We weren't raised with a good understanding of what happens during puberty and beyond. We weren't warned of the incredible danger lurking in the distance. That's why a book like this is so important. It gives you spiritual insight. It gives you Biblical tools that can change the outcome of your relationships! It really can!!

Look to be Holy Spirit driven, as you seek to interpret things from a Biblical perspective. The lights are on and you are home. Don't let an individual into your personal space without God's stamp of approval on the relationship.

That's why you must be careful when experiencing heart flutters that tend to take wings. You don't want the relationship to take flight until you have a handle on your emotions. You can't be overcome by the euphoric feelings that can transcend common sense and intelligence. Don't let your feelings get the better of you. Be very prayerful about your next move. Seek Godly wisdom and counsel. Don't step into a friendship until you see true Godly evidence that Christ really does matter to Him. Ask the Holy Spirit to enlighten you!

Distractions, Distractions

One of the greatest things to impede your spiritual growth is getting caught up in a relationship with someone who isn't making Christ the central focus of their life.

If the relationship takes your eyes off Jesus, that is a serious indicator that the flesh and enemy are at work. Have you put so much time and energy into establishing a relationship that God is no longer the priority? It doesn't take long for that to occur. This is an important point to remember: God doesn't want you establishing a relationship with an individual that interferes in your walk with Him.

He wants you with someone who will encourage you to be more like Him. Remember that we have an enemy who tries to deceive us. He will seek to lure you away and use some tempting bait to do it! Remember the fruit in the Garden of Eden? It was beautiful to behold. Satan can make the temptation look like a special delivery sent from God. Things aren't always clear. At times, things can be very hazy. It's like walking through a fog.

But Scripture is always our guiding light. Just like a lighthouse directs a boat into safe harbor, the Word of God does the same thing for us! When we evaluate the story of Adam and Eve, there are two very important points. First, God gave them a clear directive not to bite the fruit. Second, the enemy was right there, ready to challenge the authenticity of God's Word. The spiritual battle was heating up for the heart of man.

Eve should have recalled the command of the Lord. She should have been contemplating what God had told her to do. The two conflicting messages should have been a red flag. Why did she listen to the enemy's lies? We see it all the time, ladies. Temptation is knocking at the door, and we open it. And then we wonder why the path has become so twisted and confusing.

We are going to find ourselves falling into many a trap if we don't allow the Word of God to illuminate our path. It will empower us to do the right thing. Please be aware of temptation and worldly distractions. They are all around us.

Is there a minnow currently being dangled in front of you? Does it seem to be calling your name? Please don't take your eyes off Christ. He has a specific mission for you to fulfill. So many women have missed amazing spiritual opportunities because they allowed a person to interfere in their walk with the Lord.

I counseled a woman who had been dating an unbeliever for 10 years. Her walk with Jesus had been deeply hindered by his influence. She was finally going back to church and wanting to get involved in ministry. She signed up to learn more about the children's outreach. The morning she got up to go to the event, the boyfriend had made plans to do something special. He had never done anything like that before. I was hoping she'd choose God's will over the guy. But, that's not what happened. She cancelled what God was leading her to do and went out with the boyfriend.

She came in months later so discouraged and disgusted with herself. The cycle in their relationship hadn't changed. She still felt empty and alone. I saw how he manipulated her so she wouldn't break free. I saw how he wanted to keep her under his thumb. God was trying to show her that the grass really is greener on His side of the fence. But she decided to live in the weeds, instead of discovering the lush tropical garden that awaited her.

So, be prayerful when you connect and engage with others. Our hearts are meant to be in community. And fellowship is very important. But the enemy will toss prey our way. He will muddy up the waters to make it harder for you to navigate through.

If the guy is a distraction, tell him that you have hung up your rod and reel! The "No Fishing" sign is on the door. You are tired of reeling in fish that end up having to be thrown back into the lake. You are looking for that prize catch. That is God's perfect pick for you! And you trust that He has one, and it's not him!!

The Maze

Relationships are very tricky! They're like walking through a maze. As you enter, there are different passages, but which is the right one to take? Which one will lead you to a healthy Christ-centered relationship? As you make your way through, it seems like you're going around in circles. You feel trapped. You have found signposts, but they lead you in the wrong direction. There are detours and U-turns. You can't seem to find your way out. As you walk through the maze, the confusion causes you to become anxious and afraid.

Where is the exit sign? I want out!

Isn't that how some of you would describe past relationships? We've gone through the maze and it hasn't been fun. We've experienced so much sorrow. There are many who have suffered deep wounds to the heart. And for some, the hurt has almost been unbearable. As you make your way out of the winding labyrinth, you're breathing a sigh of relief. It's finally over, thank God! But the experience has left you emotionally and physically drained.

You have so many questions. You want to know what went wrong. Why is this relationship thing so hard to figure out? Haven't you felt like you were doing everything right, and it turned out all wrong? How do you avoid relationships that will end up making you feel broken and alone? I know you don't want to get into another relationship and travel down that road again.

Prayer: *Help me know when I'm entering another maze, Lord. Protect me from going through the wrong door. Please pave a clear path for my feet! I want to know which way to go! I want to follow You, Lord, without distraction!*

The Ice Cream Parlor

I had a very attractive woman share a testimony from one of my classes. She always spent time in the church's cafe after the Sunday worship service. Each time she was there, numerous men showed an interest in her, and she was confused by all the attention. How would she ever know which was the right one?

There were so many suitors to choose from! It was like being in an ice cream parlor. There were just too many flavors on display. She shared how, as she went through the Guard Your Heart class, her eyes were opened, and she saw the attractions for what they were—a serious distraction.

She realized that God wouldn't bring so many different temptations at so many different times and in so many different forms. She was so thankful that she understood the distractions weren't from Him.

"Let no one say when he is tempted, 'I am tempted by God', for God cannot be tempted by evil, nor does He Himself tempt anyone. But each one is tempted when he is drawn away by his own desires and enticed" (James 1:13-15).

She believed that if God had someone for her, He'd make it crystal clear! He'd bring things together in a divine way, so she'd know it was from Him. He wants to receive all the glory for the amazing ways He works in people's lives.

Infatuation With A Capital "I"

I've had so many women tell me about guys who obsessed over them. They were bombarded with text messages and voice mails. These are signs of behavioral patterns that can cause serious emotional dependency. We know who the guy's world revolves around, and it's not Jesus. Does the woman see his obsession as an infatuation?

Many of you know the drill. The guy wants to be with you every minute of the day. He is consumed with thoughts of you 24/7. He can't get you out of his head. He's pledged his undying love for you within the first week. He's moving so fast that it makes your head spin. He showers you with compliments, and some of you are drenched to the point where you need to dry out.

There are some men who have asked women how many children they wanted and if they were willing to relocate. They've talked about how they'd make the perfect wife. Some guys have said things that sounded like he'd already planned a future with them.

Why would someone be talking like that after only a month of dating? The guy is busy whispering sweet nothings in her ear. Sad to say, nothing is oftentimes what it turns out to be. It's heartbreaking to hear that, within a few short months, he's gone.

Haven't we gotten our hopes up over relationships like that, only to have them dashed? Be wary of a man who makes all kinds of promises before even getting to know you. Be wary of someone who's constantly pouring on words of flattery.

Hey, compliments are wonderful, and they make us feel great. I recently wore a cute dress and three people told me I looked adorable. One woman said the color was perfect for me. That made me smile. It's a blessing to hear kind words from someone.

And it's important for women to encourage each other. Because there can be jealousy and competition between females, it's good to lay the pettiness aside and be supportive. It goes a long way in lifting a person's spirits and breaking down divisions.

Self-control is one of the fruits of the Spirit. Can the person control their tongue? Do they think before they speak? When you consider those in your circle of influence, would you say they exhibit self-control? It is a noble character trait that should be on display when developing friendships.

When a guy constantly talks about a woman's body, that reveals serious lust issues. The Scriptures tell us to avoid conversations that are not wholesome and edifying. What compliments has he given to you in the past week? Is anything making you feel uncomfortable? What is the focus on: mind, body or spirit? It's not wrong to say nice things. It's not wrong to compliment your looks or the way you're dressed. In fact, I would hope he'd do that.

But there are some guys who go completely overboard. You want to pray for wisdom to discern when the person might be infatuated with you. When there seems to be an unhealthy focus on each other. When the conversations center around fleshly desires, and not spiritual disciplines.

"Do not let any unwholesome talk come out of your mouths, but only what is helpful for building others up according to their needs, that it may benefit those who listen" (Ephesians 4:29).

The Warning Signs

I know it feels good to hear all those nice words. And it's wonderful to get all that attention. I know how you wait for the text messages every day. You love to hear how beautiful and special you are to him. His voice makes you smile. I know it's hard to draw boundary lines when someone is making you feel so good. I've been there myself, so I understand. It's hard to walk away from that. But ladies, this is infatuation. You need to put on the brakes!! This kind of behavior causes an unhealthy reliance on each other. And here you go again.

The definition for infatuation is a foolish and all-absorbing passion for something. Here are some signs of infatuation. Haven't you seen this behavior before, ladies? Infatuation.....

- focuses on feelings, emotions and self.
- is obsessive and compulsive.
- starts fast and usually ends fast.
- doesn't see the flaws of another.
- lacks self-control.

Have you ever gone on a roller coaster ride with a guy who quickly made a commitment, and then it was over? They moved into your life, and then they were gone? Neither of you could see anything wrong in the relationship. And even when problems arose, they were excused away.

When we are infatuated, we can act very foolish. We don't think clearly because our emotions have jumped into the driver's seat and taken the wheel. Each move made is generally based on feelings. When we are infatuated, we can act like teenagers in love.

And most of those immature relationships don't survive. That's why we want someone who talks about making a commitment. Who won't bring up the "D" word! That "D" is for divorce. They believe that relationships are worth fighting for. They don't give up when things get rough. They know that relationships require much sacrifice. Now remember, when sin is involved, we don't keep hanging around. We need to make a dash for the door instead of trying to wait for the bad behavior to stop! God doesn't want you around people that influence you in a negative way.

Does the person know the meaning of agape love? Do they understand what unconditional love really looks like? This is a good conversation to have with someone you are considering a serious relationship with. Are you on the same page when considering the spiritual depth of your relationship or are you on different levels? As much as you try, it might not be possible to see eye-to-eye.

Be Passionate For Christ

And, if there is a sense of desperation for someone, that is a serious form of idolatry. That's when the connection with the guy is more important than your relationship with God. The definition for idolatry is an "excessive or blind adoration, devotion or reverence for something." How many of you have been obsessed over a guy?

The feelings for him are consuming you. You can't stop thinking about him. How many have thoughts about him every moment of the day? And, even in your dreams? You are the one he longs to please, and you want to make him happy. Everything is based on the health and welfare of your relationship.

Ladies, in our flesh, we have followed the path of least resistance. It's not easy to stave off the emotions that are percolating below the surface. You're not usually trying to figure out how to resist the temptation; you're often trying to find out when you'll see him again. Be careful not to get swept up into another relationship. Don't let your emotions cause you to make unwise decisions.

So, are your thoughts and feelings focused on the Savior? God wants us to have that kind of devotion for Him. He wants us to be obsessed with thoughts of pleasing Him throughout the day. It's spiritually healthy to have a passion and awestruck wonder for Jesus. He deserves to be at the center of your universe.

He wants to fill your days with good things. He wants you to experience grace, hope and peace in a real, tangible way. Again, worldly relationships are not sent from Him. They are major interferences to prevent you from experiencing the power of God in your life.

You don't want a guy to become an idol. You don't want to put the person on a pedestal. Don't let pleasing the person be your main priority. God wants us to avoid things that cause our hearts to drift away from Him.

Let Jesus Take The Wheel

Imagine being in a canoe with your new boyfriend. As you hop into the boat and watch him grab the oars, you find yourself taken by him. You had never noticed just how handsome he is. And strong! You feel awestruck! This must be love. You're not even sure where you're going. But it doesn't matter, because you feel safe and secure with him by your side.

You cast off and down the river you go. The sights are beautiful to behold. The final destination will take your breath away. He tells you how wonderful your life will be with him. You are on this journey and there is so much excitement. Each vantage point brings a new fascination for the two of you. And a new discovery about each other. Could this get any more exciting?

There is so much beauty surrounding you. And you are drinking it in together. You never want the adventure to end. You feel like two lovebirds. Then, the current begins to change, moving the boat in another direction. What is happening? You wrestle with the oars, trying to fight the current. But it is too powerful and now the relationship has taken a different route. You feel helpless. Things seem to be out of control. You never imagined the journey would be so tumultuous.

At the end, the destination causes great grief and heartbreak. As you climb out of the boat and look around, he is gone. You can't believe it's over. The person ended up taking you down a path that led you far away from God. You had every intention on staying close to the Lord. You feel lost and alone. You are broken and confused. You are having to grapple with the reality that another relationship has failed. Your self-esteem has experienced another critical blow.

You have no choice but to begin again. How will you ever get back into another boat? Will there ever be another guy? How will you trust someone again? How will you ever recover from the rejection? You will. But first, you must learn to put your trust in Jesus, fully and completely. You must not let anyone steer you away from God.

When travelling down the river, weren't there red flags? Why didn't you say, "Stop here! I want to get out of this boat! I don't feel safe anymore!" But we ignored the warning signs that told us things weren't right. We avoided facing the truth.

We have experienced many broken relationships that have left us with more questions than answers. We have found ourselves bobbing in a sea of confusion. We are growing up in our understanding and knowledge of who God is. He wants us to learn and grow from our past experiences. The Scriptures say that He will take our pain and work it together for good. We can be confident of the promises He has given to us in His Word.

We can be assured that trusting in Him will lead us to a better destination. The Holy Spirit can fill your heart with comfort and peace, enabling you to overcome the loneliness and disappointment. Don't let the focus be on another relationship. Don't seek another relationship to fill the void that the last guy left behind. In the past, we tried to fill the holes in our hearts by starting a new romance. And where did it get us? It only left us feeling more broken. It only caused us to experience more feelings of insecurity.

And remember, a person can't fill the holes that will make you whole. Only Jesus knows where those broken places are. A new relationship will only create a deeper crevice. Allow God to fill those empty spaces with His Love.

Let Jesus be in control. Let Him be the Lord of your life. Let Him start to mend the cuts to your heart. Allow Him to pour on the salve that will bring healing to your soul. Allow the Holy Spirit to restore your wounded heart. Believe that He will give you a new identity! Think of Jesus. Isn't He wonderful? Just imagine how God wants to shape you to become more like Him. As you embrace your new identity in Christ, He will shine through you in ways you never dreamed possible.

Allow Him to show you the direction He wants you to go. Be excited about the adventure He's taking you on. Be encouraged that He knows what you've gone through and wants to rescue you! He is with you! He is beside you! He loves you! Don't let a smooth talker come along offering you a ride in his boat. Be careful! If Jesus isn't the navigator of your vessel, you will find yourself in very stormy and treacherous waters. And you can end up getting shipwrecked! I hope you've hung up your oars, at least for now.

"Little children, keep yourselves from idols" (I John 5:21).

Don't Trust Your Feelings

Rule #1: You can't trust your feelings. That's a rule you must always apply when evaluating relationships. I have such strong feelings for this person. I just want to be with him. It feels so right! Why would you say no to that? I mean, it's the way you feel. Don't allow your feelings to rule your life. Don't let your heart be led astray by passion and evil desire. That is the flesh wanting its way.

Watch out, ladies! You can act on your feelings and end up doing things you regret. Remember the river boat ride. The boundary lines can get fuzzy when you are overcome with emotion. You can do things that you never believed you would, could or should have done.

You have experienced much agony by opening the wrong door. There have been too many trails of tears that have been left behind. Keep your eyes on the prize! Jesus began and finished the race we are in. He is now seated at the right hand of God, the Father. So, make becoming a runner for the Savior your passion. Seek to make living for Christ the focus of your life.

> *"Therefore, since we are surrounded by such a great cloud of witnesses, let us throw off everything that hinders and the sin that so easily entangles. And let us run with perseverance the race marked out for us. Looking to Jesus, the author and finisher of our faith; who for the joy that was set before Him endured the cross, despising shame and is set down at the right hand of the throne of God"* (Hebrews 12:1-2).

Instead of being infatuated with a guy, be impassioned for the Savior. And remember the definition for infatuation: it is an all-absorbing passion.

I'd recommend running for the hills when you start seeing that kind of behavior. I've already lent out my Reeboks. Would you like to borrow my Nikes?

This doesn't mean that you won't have feelings and emotions for the person you are interested in. And it doesn't mean it's wrong to have them. But we still have our flesh to contend with, no matter how spiritually mature we are. We are human, and this can be a serious struggle. So, are the feelings you're experiencing under control? Is God being glorified in this area of your life? Are you praying for God to help you be controlled by the Holy Spirit?

"For you were bought at a price; therefore, glorify God in your body and in your spirit, which are God's" (I Corinthians 6:20).

What About Kissing?

Ladies, this is a very touchy topic, if you know what I mean. I teach classes on developing healthy, Christ-centered relationships to middle and high-schoolers. In one of the classes, I had an 8th grader ask a question about kissing. He said there was no place in the Bible that said kissing was a no-no!! Where is this boy headed? Sadly, this will create a very destructive pattern if his feelings aren't brought under control. The desires of the flesh start way too young.

So, what does the Word of God say? Is it silent? There is a passage of Scripture that helps shed light on this subject. The apostle Paul encourages the believer to *"put to death passion and evil desire"* (Colossians 3:5-6). We are wired for relationships. But, because of the fall, our passions are no longer for the things of God but for the things of the flesh. That's why we must be hyper-attentive to the thoughts and feelings swirling in our hearts and heads.

Because physical intimacy usually begins with kissing, why would I encourage a behavior that could lead individuals to sin? When there is an attraction for someone, the feelings can increase rather quickly. It's easy to say it's just a kiss. It's easy to say that there is nothing else to it. But a kiss often leads to other things. And many times, there isn't even a serious relationship established. We don't want to run headfirst into a situation without prayerfully considering the potential risks by moving forward.

When passion builds, it can lead a person to sin in thought, word and deed. There can be a burning inside. But look at it this way. That burning can turn into a very negative and harmful experience. The Scriptures warn us of what can happen when lust takes hold of a soul!

We are called to be holy as Christ is holy. The apostle Paul tells us to resist those desires that will bring shame, pain, and regret. We must combat those carnal feelings that consume the heart. He tells us to fight against those emotions that are going to produce immoral and unseemly behavior.

How many times did it seem innocent, but you regretted not putting up a wall of protection? It happened to me. Did it happen to you? If you want to live a righteous lifestyle, you can't let the flesh win!

Hopefully, you will have the spiritual strength to extinguish the fire before it rages out of control. Hopefully, you won't let the enemy tell you that it's not a big deal. Because it is! Are your passions and desires focused on surrendering to the Savior or are they moving you in a sinful direction?

"But among you there must not be even a hint of sexual immorality, or of any kind of impurity, or of greed, because these are improper for God's holy people" (Ephesians 5:3).

A Man Of God

The struggle with lust works both ways. But, because men are visual, they struggle more in this area. I do want to give the guys a break here! There are many men who aren't going to lead you on. They don't want to move too fast. They are fervently praying for God's sovereign leading in their relationships. There are men who are led by the Holy Spirit and not the flesh. They are looking to establish a pure friendship.

They are living a life of obedience to the Lord. They have a passion for God and His Word. His heart's desire is to experience God's best. He cares more about God's Word than anything else.

There are many people who think they are living for God, but they aren't doing it very well. The enemy has deceived them into believing they are close to the Lord. Is the person talking about wanting a deeper, more intimate relationship with Jesus? Is that their true desire?

They are out there, ladies. It's true. I married one of them. And I know many women who've married wonderful, godly men. Don't believe the lie that there aren't any decent guys left out there. Be encouraged. God is faithful! If He wants you married, it will happen. If He has someone for you, He will bring that person to you. You don't have to go searching for him. How successful has your search committee been so far? If your time is spent doing that, you won't be able to achieve all the great things He is going to do through you.

Question: Is serving and living for Jesus your heart's desire?

A Wise Move

A GYH attendee told me about a business luncheon she had with a prospective client. They weren't halfway through the meal, when he told her that they were meant for each other. He was already talking about marriage. He was gushing with emotion as he shared all the things he loved about her. He was pouring it on—thick! He was wearing the infatuation on his sleeve.

She was taken aback. She couldn't believe all the things he was saying to her. "You don't even know me," she quipped. He was surprised by her reaction. He apologized and said he was just smitten by her personality. That wasn't the only thing he was smitten with!

She wasn't comfortable doing business with him, and she kindly let him know it. That was a very wise move, and a good example of an act of discernment! She knew that there was too much of a focus on her. A business deal wasn't the only thing this guy was looking for. I was so proud of her for taking a stand and calling him out for his inappropriate comments.

There are some people who would have continued engaging with that individual. Since he's already so infatuated, where would it have gone from there? We should establish friendships based on mutual respect. You don't want someone pouring on the charm and leading you on. If you are feeling uncomfortable by someone's actions, it's alright to kindly let him know it. Each person has their own personal space. It's ok to draw those imaginary boundary lines so people know what you consider safe.

And don't feel guilty for telling someone no or that you can't see them anymore. It's important to do what you think is right, irrelevant of how it makes them feel. You can always be gracious and kind but confront those things you consider out-of-line.

There have been many women who have allowed people to stay in their lives and it's caused serious problems. There were many times you considered saying goodbye but didn't want to hurt their feelings. Feeling sorry for someone is not a good reason to remain connected to them. It's better to be honest and let them go. We can't develop friendships and stay in relationships that aren't following the blueprint of God's Word.

Not So Fast

We must be so careful in our friendships with the opposite sex. We must be mindful not to say and do things that tease and deceive. I've had women tell me things they've done to get a man's attention. They dressed in a provocative way that caught the guy's eye. They've said and done things that were very misleading.

There were times I flirted, wanting him to believe I was interested in a relationship. Some women have shared how they lied to a guy by giving them the wrong name and number. Sadly, some play with hearts like it's a game. It's wrong to string people along.

Ladies, can you relate to that? It was so foolish. I must confess that I made some very bad choices based on my flirtatious behavior. Where was that going to lead me? What would end up happening? I obviously wasn't thinking about doing relationships God's way. I was looking for attention, and sad to say, I found the wrong kind.

We don't want to manipulate people and situations with that kind of behavior. That is the flesh moving you in a very dangerous direction. If you want to establish a healthy friendship, don't do anything to lure him in! He is not a fish, and you are not bait! Relationships shouldn't be established by playing tempting and tantalizing games with each other.

We are praying for God to help us establish wholesome relationships that are focused on godly principles.

We want to treat each other like brothers and sisters in the Lord.

"Therefore, be imitators of God as dear children" (Ephesians 5:1).

Rule of thumb: Don't try to tempt the opposite sex to get his attention. Is that the only way he will notice you? PS: I wished I'd followed this rule in my younger years.

Two Hearts

I use two hearts to illustrate how we can get tripped up in relationships. The eyes connect and the two hearts meet. You're on guard because you don't want to get hurt again. The guy spends a lot of time talking to you. He starts calling you every day. He says and does all the right things. He is different from the rest. He's perfect for you! You are thankful to finally meet someone who can relate to you on so many different levels.

You slowly give him your heart. As time goes by, you begin to see changes in his behavior, and it isn't good. He's not calling you like he used to. He doesn't seem to care about your feelings. It's like he's putting your heart on a shelf. Then he comes back and acts like he cares, but then he withdraws again. It's as if he's playing with your heart, and it's beginning to ache. You don't understand what's happening. You feel so broken inside.

Then he returns, only to take your heart and throw it away. He doesn't want to see you anymore. You watch as it shatters into a million pieces. You look on as he walks away. He's gone. It's over! You bend down, and through the tears, slowly begin to pick up the pieces of your broken heart. I had several relationships where my heart was crushed. But I broke a few hearts myself. We all have caused heartache in past relationships. We've been very imperfect in the way we've treated each other.

Those relationships left us in a lot of pain. God heard my cry and healed my heart. He helped me learn to trust again. I have learned that my hope is in the Lord. That is the only thing we can have total confidence in. We must put whatever happened in the past behind us. It's time to move forward. Let your heart rejoice! He has redeemed us for His glory. There is nothing I've gone through that's been in vain! What an awesome God we serve!

> *"Bless the Lord, O my soul, and forget not all His benefits: who forgives all your iniquities, who heals all your diseases, Who redeems your life from destruction, who crowns you with loving-kindness and tender mercies, who satisfies your mouth with good things, so that your youth is renewed like the eagle's"* (Psalm 103:2-5).

Is He Really The One?

This is it! This is the one! Ah yes! How many times have you thought that? How many people have you believed were the one? Once, twice, maybe three times? I believed that most of the guys I dated were the one for me. How about that for a track record?

PS: I was wrong every time!

You can't assume that he is the one based on that thought. So, be wise. Be very cautious. It's like driving a car for the first time. You're not going to jump on the freeway when you've never been behind the wheel of a car. Why would you jump into some guy's car on the first or second date?

When *"This is it!"* pops into your head, remind yourself of how many times you've been wrong in the past. Consider how confident you were. You were convinced that this was your dream guy. Many women have gotten into a serious relationship because they believed a lie.

And just because a relationship started off on the wrong foot doesn't mean it's destined to fail. God can still work things out if the couple is determined to do things His way. But wouldn't you rather know that you had God's blessings going into the relationship?

Remember the old-fashioned days? When a guy would go to the father to ask for His daughter's hand in marriage? Well, consider that a requirement with the guy you are dating. He needs your Father's acceptance and approval. Because you believed that he was the one and you were mistaken, I pray you've relinquished this area of your heart over to the Lord's sovereign control.

Here are some questions to ponder: Maybe he isn't the one? Is this truly sent from God? Does he have an intimate relationship with the Savior? Do I see real spiritual fruit in his life?

Prayerfully consider these things at the very early stages of your friendship.

Ask the Holy Spirit to make very clear the problem areas that will cause serious complications to your life. It's wise to wait before you board another plane. He wants to protect you from adding more baggage to your already full cargo hold. In fact, there are many who need to take time to unpack some suitcases. This way your future relationships won't be as weighed down if you allow yourself to heal from past hurts.

And don't wait until the relationship is established before you realize that he's not fully committed to the Lord. And that he might not even be a true follower in Jesus Christ.

"But when He, the Spirit of truth comes, He will guide you into all the truth" (John 16:13). Meditate on these words. You can be certain that He will help you discern fact from fiction, what is real from what is fake, and His truth from the lies of the enemy.

Ask God to reveal the truth to you. Ladies, we've suffered so much pain because we took fleshly turns and ended up on "heartbreak row." We certainly don't want to go down that disastrous road again.

Don't Trust Every Spirit

"Don't believe every spirit, but test the spirits, whether they are of God" (I John 4:1). This is such an important Scripture to reflect on. You need to be very hesitant because not every person is sent from God. I have counseled many women who believed that God brought a relationship together, but it wasn't from Him.

He wouldn't lead you into a situation that was so spiritually unhealthy for you. You can't assume that God wanted you to develop a relationship with someone just because the timing seemed right. I met a guy, and I really believed he was the one. Because we had a connection, I thought it was meant to be. That was very faulty thinking.

I mean, it's not an accident or coincidence that I met this guy, right? I can't begin to tell you all the negative ramifications that occurred in my life because I did not test the spirits to make sure they were from God. I did not take this Scripture literally, and I needed to. The author of the book of James tells us that this spiritual principle must be applied when evaluating the people who come in and out of our lives.

We are instructed to not believe every spirit. Why? Because some come from God and some can be a temptation from the enemy. God's truth will lead men and women from a wayward lifestyle to one of righteousness. Those led by the Holy Spirit will reflect godly character. Those who belong to Jesus can testify that He is the Son of God and the Savior of the world. They know Christ in a personal way because His Spirit abides in them. They are led by His love.

This is the first place to start when testing a spirit to make sure it's from God. Does he believe that Jesus is the Son of God? Is the person a born-again believer in Jesus Christ? Is he confident that his salvation is in Christ alone? Does he believe in the Holy Trinity? And that the Holy Spirit dwells within a believer?

If you are praying for a spiritual leader, and he can't even answer yes to those questions, you cannot move forward in a relationship. I am sorry. In II Corinthians 6:14-18, the apostle Paul tells the believer not to bond with someone that does not have a personal relationship with Jesus Christ. This is not a request; it's a command from the Lord.

And in II Timothy 2:22, Paul instructs Timothy to "flee the evil desires of youth and pursue righteousness, faith, love and peace, along with those who call on the Lord out of a pure heart." That applies to us! We are called to be in pursuit of all that is holy and righteous. And we are to hang around those who are seeking after the Lord. Are you praying for relationships with individuals whose hearts have been smitten by the Savior?

Those who aren't living for God will defend the ways of this world. They will justify their sinful nature. They don't care what His Word says. They think that Christianity is a religion. They don't get that it's a relationship with Jesus. When you talk to them about being led by the Spirit, they are clueless and don't understand.

One guy I dated laughed at me when I talked to him about Jesus. That should have been an obvious indicator that there was a spiritual disconnect between us. But I still stayed in the relationship. We are told by the apostle Paul not to develop close friendships with these individuals.

How often did you stop to question whether a person was truly sent from God? Did you really pray for wisdom and discernment to know if he was a definite follower of Jesus Christ? Did you make sure that he truly believed that Jesus is the redeemer who offers salvation to all who trust in His name? I know. I didn't either.

> *"As obedient children, not conforming to the former lusts, as in your ignorance; but as He who called you is holy, you also be holy in all your conduct, because it is written, 'Be holy, for I am holy'"* (I Peter 1:14-16).

If the person is leading you astray in anyway, it's not from your Heavenly Father. The Holy Spirit is going to move you away from sin! He is going to make you more holy. Remember that! There are some who come "preaching and teaching" but their doctrines are not built on Jesus Christ.

There are some who even quote Scripture, but they aren't living a life of obedience to the cross. Actions speak louder than words. You don't want someone who's all talk; You want someone who walks the walk!

> *"Beware of false prophets who come to you in sheep's clothing, but inwardly they are ravenous wolves. You will know them by their fruits"* (Matthew 7:15).

Question: Can you see how you believed God's Hand was moving you in a certain direction, and it wasn't from Him? Can you see the enemy's lure? He is the father of lies.

Attractions Lead To Feelings And Feelings Lead To Actions

Attractions can lead to strong feelings and those feelings can lead to sinful actions, if not resisted. We know too well how this works. The glance that led to that first date. The connection that led to that romance. That's how many of our relationships began. I've already discussed how important it is to be "on guard" when you start feeling fascinated and captivated by someone.

Attractions aren't wrong. I mean, we are human. We all have them. We are talking about the physical contact that is moving you in an ungodly direction. You want someone who isn't pressuring you to move forward in this area. You want someone who exhibits restraint because of his relationship with the Lord.

There are Christian men who have told their girlfriends that it's abnormal to say no to a physical relationship. That it goes against our physiology. Well, you can say that if you are talking about relationships that aren't led and controlled by the Holy Spirit. Because we are children of God, we can overcome. We have been rewired. And because the Holy Spirit is in us, we can resist the evil influences that can cause severe havoc in our lives.

I think of how Potiphar's wife tried to seduce Joseph in Genesis 39. Don't you just love Joseph? He fought off her advances. He fled the scene. He proclaimed that he couldn't sin against God. His obedience to the Lord mattered more than gratifying the flesh. Don't you want someone who cares so much about Jesus that he acts honorably towards you?

We must seek to do our relationships God's way. We must focus on getting our fleshly feelings under control. They will steer you away from your godly potential if you aren't very careful.

Remember how you learned to do something by referring to an instruction manual? Well, God's Word works in the same way. You can't do life without His guidance. And that comes through experiencing more of Him through His Word. The Scriptures are not supposed to collect dust on a shelf. They're supposed to become an integral part of who you are and what you do.

I pray that you want to learn what God's Word says about how to resist temptation. I pray that you are meditating on Scriptures that relate to righteousness and holiness. I hope that His Words will bring a deep desire to break free of whatever sinful behaviors you are struggling with.

The battle begins in the mind. We must evaluate our thoughts throughout the day to insure they're lining up with the Word of God. We want to make sure the thoughts we are having don't cause us to sin against the Lord. If you have a lustful thought, rebuke it! You want to challenge those feelings that cause you to look at someone in an ungodly way. The enemy wants you obsessed with the flesh.

We must constantly remind ourselves that our bodies are temples of the Holy Spirit. We are brothers and sisters in Christ. Looking at each other in a sexual way is wrong. Remember, the clothes are to stay ON! If we allow that to happen, it will taint the way we see each other. We will become more focused on the physical qualities than the spiritual aspects of an individual. And the spiritual is what's most important.

Sure, lustful ideas will pop into your head. There'll be times when you'll wonder where those offensive thoughts came from. The enemy can and will do that to you. And you can have your own fleshly desires. If you allow those thoughts to take root, they will lead you to sin. If you ponder and play with those lustful ideas, you will do things that cause much regret.

That's a place He doesn't want you to go. Don't travel down that road again. Ladies, this isn't easy to do. That's why it's an intense struggle. But remember who your God is. He is strong! He is mighty! He is more powerful than the enemy! He is a warrior! He is Supreme! He is with you!!

"You have heard that it was said to those of old, 'You shall not commit adultery.' But I say to you that whoever looks at a woman to lust for her has already committed adultery with her in his heart" (Matthew 5:27).

Resist the Temptation

We must be careful when we start feeling close to someone. When fleshly emotions start to develop, God wants you to draw a serious boundary line. Fight the tidal wave of feelings that are drawing you into a physical relationship. You need to resist the strong urge to become intimate.

Remember how the apostle Paul instructs us to put to death passion and evil desire. That means saying no to what will prevent the Spirit from thriving in your life. The flesh doesn't like to be deprived of what it wants. It's hard to turn away from the longing to be loved. You will find yourself taunted by thoughts of him. Opposing those seemingly natural desires seems impossible to do. But that's how we've ended up getting so hurt in the past.

If you don't fight the temptation, those feelings will drag you back into another broken relationship. Remember the suffering you've already gone through. It's a good idea to ponder the brokenness you've experienced. It's not so you stay stuck in the past. Those thoughts should motivate you to stay on a godly path and follow Him, instead of the flesh. It will be a helpful reminder that stepping outside of God's plan will not prove fruitful in your life. Choosing righteousness will be the road you need to stay on.

The Holy Spirit will enable you to get control of this area of your life. He did it for me! And He will do it for you, too. The sooner you learn to say no to the flesh, the more you'll be able to see God's power working in your life.

No matter what stage of the relationship, you do not belong to each other. No matter how much time you've been together, or even if you're engaged, you don't have the freedom to get physical. It isn't until he slips the ring on your finger, and the two of you say I do!!

"Therefore, put to death your members which are on the earth: fornication, uncleanness, passion, evil desire, and covetousness, which is idolatry. Because of these things the wrath of God is coming upon the sons of disobedience, in which you yourselves once walked when you lived in them" (Colossians 3:5-7).

Ask the Holy Spirit to help you be Christ-minded. I encourage you to draw a boundary line in the sand to insure no one will cross it. No matter how much you desire a physical relationship, determine not to become one with a man who isn't your husband. If your feelings aren't moving you in a holy direction, then turn the other way. God's heart has been grieved by the way you have been taken advantage of in your life. He cares deeply about the pain you've gone through. He believes that you deserve so much better.

Do you believe that, too??

Niagara Falls

When you first start traveling down the Niagara River, it seems like there is no danger ahead. Along the way, there are signs telling people to turn back or they'll go over the falls. There are some who ignore the warning signs because it didn't look like anything negative would happen, and they've lost their lives.

I think of the falls when talking about the feelings that develop in the early stages of a romance. We must be so cautious. It can seem calm and serene the first few weeks you are floating along in your relationship. You are just holding hands and giving hugs. That seems innocent enough.

You had pledged to God that this time there would be no sex before marriage. You had promised God that you'd remain pure. You know how the desire begins to grow and the passion starts to build. Before you know it, you were overwhelmed by emotion and you fell into sin. And there you went, tumbling over the falls.

God doesn't want you in a boat with someone who is foolish and unable to heed the danger signs. You both need to have strong Biblical standards that protect you from getting too close to each other.

If you are in an ungodly relationship, you are floating down that river. God wants you to get out of the boat, before it's too late. You're not safe. His love is trying to spare you from experiencing more pain and heartache.

Some practical advice to follow: Stay in a public setting where other people are around. When you go out with someone, always make sure a friend knows where you are and who you are with. Never touch each other in an inappropriate way. There is to be no removal of the clothing. Always make sure that your conversations and behavior aren't leading you to a point of no return.

Bing, Bing, Bing!! That Is Your Warning Bell!

Can you hear the alarm? I've sounded it for thousands and thousands of people over the years that I've been a leader in ministry. I wish I could say that everyone heeded the warning to say no to temptation and were able to escape without injury. But there were people who didn't listen when the alarm bell went off.

I remember when I was little, and we used to have school fire drills. The alarm would sound, and the students would march out, single file, to a safe place. Well, the Word of God is our alarm system, and His Holy Spirit will alert us to trouble ahead.

God will move in some way that makes you aware that something isn't right. He will open a window or close a door. He will make a path of escape for you. He can keep you from falling. Don't think you can get into a vehicle without understanding who's behind the wheel. We must take responsibility for who we let into the driver's seat.

If you continue to advance and ignore the warning bell, you will suffer consequences. The car can speed out of control and result in a major crash and burn. The emotional, spiritual and physical results can be devastating. By God's grace, we can recover. But how many countless individuals would say, "If I had it to do over again...."

"No temptation has overtaken you except such is common to man; but God is faithful, who will not allow you to be tempted beyond what you are able, but with the temptation, will make the way of escape, that you may be able to bear it" (I Corinthians 10:13).

A Serious Red Flag

You'll know soon enough if this person struggles with lust and sexual desires that are out of control. He will eventually want more than just conversation and fellowship with you. There are some who won't waste any time making some fast moves. That is a red light! If he is moving this quickly with you, then you aren't the first one he's made sexual advances towards, and you won't be the last. So, tell him to move on down the pike!

A person who exhibits a lack of self-control is very selfish. They can have a wonderful personality, but they don't know what it means to truly love someone. Real love looks out for the best interest of the other person. They aren't going to put your life at risk, and they do everything they can to avoid causing you pain.

It isn't just the emotional heartache that can occur; it's the physical consequences we must be worried about. Pregnancy, sexually transmitted diseases, AIDS, sadness, guilt, shame, regret, depression, anger, and mistrust are just some of the consequences that can be inflicted if we don't abstain from our fleshly desires.

Look at that list of repercussions. How many have experienced some of the above? There are women reading this who are having to stop to catch their breath. You might still be experiencing the pain of regret. Maybe you are suffering with circumstances because of a choice you made. Maybe you are wondering when the pain will go away.

It's hard when you are having to live through the reverberations of a bad decision. It takes time to heal. But how long has it been? How much pain have you already gone through? I think it's time to let God revive your joy and heal your heartache!

I've talked about King David and his foolishness. He paid a huge price for his failings. He suffered great loss as a result. But when he repented, He rededicated His life to the Lord. He determined to live the rest of His days for God. He still had to live out some of those past sinful decisions. There was still pain and heartache that he had to walk through. God gave Him the grace and strength to do it. And, when David's life came to an end, the Lord was still His best friend.

A Priceless Gem

God wants you to look at sex as a priceless jewel that will be given to your husband on your wedding night. God wants you to preserve that part of the relationship for that special someone He has chosen for you in marriage. It is to be cherished, and it is considered holy. *"Marriage is honorable among all and the bed undefiled"* (Hebrews 13:4). Even though we might not have looked at the marriage bed as being sacred, it is!

He wants you to understand how a sexual relationship is a beautiful treasure. There are many things trying to destroy the marriage relationship. Don't let the enemy and the flesh have their way! If you've fallen, God will redeem your past. You can start over. You can begin again. You can set new boundary lines.

Maybe you've already fallen in this area. Maybe many times before. Maybe you feel like you don't deserve a man of honor. Well, let me shout this out to you. God thinks you do! God doesn't look at you as some kind of tainted vessel. He doesn't look at you like you are used property.

Your life is priceless to God. The sacrifice He made for you is real. His love for you runs deep and wide. In fact, His love is what placed Him on that cross. And we think we aren't valuable? In Him, we are. But what really matters is the heavenly cost that was paid for our eternal salvation. When we start dwelling on those truths, our minds and hearts will be renewed.

You don't have to stay in ungodly relationships. The next relationship can be one that reflects the holiness of God. You can be an example of how God can redeem the wrong choices that you've made.

And beware of those who pledge their undying love for you when there is no serious relationship. Love isn't based on a feeling; it's based on a commitment. That is real love. May the next person that claims his love for you be the one God has chosen to take your hand in marriage. That is my prayer for you.

A Living Sacrifice

We are going to be faced with major temptation in our lives. And sometimes it will be an all-consuming desire for someone or something. Our hearts will long for it. And we can find ourselves doing whatever it takes to satisfy those feelings.

When we face those struggles, God wants us to say no! This is what I call your "garden" experience. Remember when Jesus was in the Garden of Gethsemane? He was preparing to face the cross. As He prayed and sought strength from the Father, His sweat was mingled with droplets of blood. He was anguishing over what He was about to go through.

He is God, but He was still human. It wasn't going to be an easy journey. He asked for God's will to be done. His purpose was to die for you and me. That was His sacrifice for us. That is amazing love. He suffered a brutal death so we could have eternal life and be in close fellowship with Him. And just as Jesus had the strength to walk the road to Calvary, He will empower us to do what is acceptable in His sight. He will enable us to walk away from those things that aren't pleasing to Him.

Each time we say no to our sin nature, we are being a "living sacrifice" for Him. That's when we are saying no to behavior that is ungodly. At times, this will be very challenging and difficult to do. At points, it will be excruciatingly painful. It isn't called crucifying the flesh for nothing. We will have our share of garden experiences while on the earth. We will sweat, and the tears will fall. But our pain can't compare to the suffering He went through for us. No one understands what you've gone through better than He does.

As we say no to our fleshly desires, we will experience more intimacy with the Savior. Blessings will come as we learn to be obedient to His will. You're going to find that your no is the pathway to His Yes!

"For consider Him who endured such hostility from sinners against Himself, lest you become weary and discouraged in our souls. You have not yet resisted to bloodshed, striving against sin" (Hebrews 12:3-4).

"Beloved, I beg you as sojourners and pilgrims, abstain from the fleshly lust which war against your soul" (I Peter 2:11).

Flee Sexual Immorality

We are one with Christ! His Holy Spirit resides in us, and we are His temple! He has set us apart and consecrated us for His use. We are instruments that will be used in the Master's hand. You are not your own. You belong to God. He paid a huge ransom for you. God sacrificed His life to set you free so you could live a life of obedience to Him.

We are holy and righteous children of God. We need to value, above all else, our relationship with Him. When you asked Jesus into your heart, the two of you became one. The emphasis is on remembering your commitment to Christ. He is your husband. I encourage you to ask God to help you remain faithful to Him! Put your relationship with Him above everything else.

God wants us to run away from sexual temptation. He says to flee. We shouldn't try to linger or control the desires that are burning within us. If we play with fire, we will get burned. If we let our fleshly passions sweep us along, our hearts will be deeply wounded by the spiritual and emotional bond that occurs when the two become one. When we commit sexual immorality, we sin against our own body, declares the apostle Paul. I Corinthians 6:13-21 is a powerful section of Scripture that helps us understand the sacred and holy relationship we have with the Savior.

There is a deep emotional connection that occurs when a couple bonds on a sexual level. When that union is broken, there is a gaping hole left in the heart. I remember how broken I felt by those worldly relationships. It's a devastating process to work through. I've gone through this a few times and, at points, wondered if I'd ever recover, it was so painful. I praise Him for healing my heart. I am whole because of the awesome love my Savior has for me. And He has it for you, too! Thank God for His mercy and grace!

Meditate on the Scriptures below. Ask God to help you run from temptation! Tell Him you don't want to be in an ungodly relationship any longer. You want to be pure in mind, body and spirit! Continue asking Him for help in this area! It's a spiritual battle. Don't give up and don't give in. He can set you free. It is wonderful when you are no longer a slave to the things of the flesh. Being in Christ is liberating.

> *"Do you not know that your bodies are members of Christ? Shall I then take the members of Christ and make them members of a harlot? Certainly not! Or do you not know that he who is joined to a harlot is one body with her? For the two," He says, "shall become one flesh." But he who is joined to the Lord is one spirit with Him. Flee sexual immorality. Every sin that a man does is outside the body, but he who commits sexual immorality sins against his own body. Or do you not know that your body is the temple of the Holy Spirit who is in you, whom you have from God, and you are not your own? For you were bought at a price; therefore, glorify God in your body and in your spirit, which are God's"* (I Corinthians 6:15-20).

You Deserve Respect!

The sexual relationship establishes a bond that is like adhesive glue to the soul. The Lord never intended for us to go in and out of physical relationships. God wanted the consummation of a relationship to occur on the wedding night. *"For this reason, a man shall leave his father and mother and be joined to his wife, and the two shall become one flesh; so, they are no longer two, but one flesh. Therefore, what God has joined together let not man separate"* (Mark 10:7-9).

I remember seeing an illustration of two paper hearts that were glued together. Someone tried to separate them after they had dried. He couldn't do it without shredding the pages. When two people bond, it's as if their hearts are woven together. When the relationship ends, the fabric is torn, and the tears are like rips to the heart. God wants to protect us from this deep emotional heartache. I started over in this area, and you can too.

I had a Guard Your Heart attendee tell me about a wonderful guy she was dating. She came to the white-board and listed several spiritual things about him: he leads a Bible study, is in several ministries, he quotes Scripture, prays, and even witnesses. He sounds too good to be true.

He only had one character flaw. She listed it as item number 10. It was his desire for a sexual relationship. He seemed so right for her, but he wasn't—not with that kind of behavior. It was an eye-opening experience for her to see all the Scriptures on sexual immorality. She had been deceived into believing that the good outweighed the bad. She deserves someone that respects her.

And most of all, God wants her with someone that respects Him. He would want her to flee from a relationship like that! Remember, the will of God is your sanctification. If you are in a physical relationship, you are not being sanctified. You are not being made more holy. It doesn't matter how many great qualities the person has.

I have lent out my Reeboks and Nikes, but I can loan you my Adidas. I'm glad I used to have a closet full of running shoes. I'd invest in a pair or two, if I were you.

Look To Jesus

"You ran well. Who hindered you from obeying the truth?" (Galatians 5:7-8).

Has that happened to you? You were focused on God, and then you set your eyes on a guy, and your spiritual walk went downhill? The relationship got physical and now it's hard to break free. You are making excuses for the immoral behavior. You are trying to convince yourself that sex before marriage is ok. Could it really be wrong? Yes! God's Word says that it is.

God would never lead you into that kind of relationship. He would never want you to believe that a sexual relationship was acceptable to

Him. That goes against everything His Word says about purity (I Thess. 4:3-8). Because of our relationship with the Lord, we should have control over this area of our life. We should no longer be like those individuals who do not know God. They can't say no to their fleshly desires, because they don't have the Holy Spirit residing within them! But we do! And that makes all the difference.

A woman recently shared how she was with someone, and they were crossing physical boundary lines. She didn't want to leave him. Her attitude toward spiritual things began to change. She confessed that she had lost her godly focus.

Is your relationship moving in a physical direction? Is the guy tempting you to sin? Are you tempting the guy? Have sexual boundary lines been crossed? If the answer is yes to any of the above, God tells you to cast off the weights that are dragging you down. Don't allow yourself to be in bondage to sin any longer. We become slaves to the fleshly things that consume us. Remember, the enemy doesn't want us to experience freedom in Christ.

Question: Is there something that's weighing you down? Is it time to walk away? Is the burden becoming too much to bear?

We are to "lay aside every weight, and the sin that so easily ensnares us, and let us run with endurance the race that is set before us, looking unto Jesus, the author and finisher of our faith" (Hebrews 12:1–2).

"Do you not know that those who run in a race all run, but one receives the prize? Run in such a way that you may obtain it" (I Corinthians 9:24).

The Beautiful Butterfly

We have been influenced by family, friends, the media and the environment around us. We have certain belief systems that are etched in our brains. When we begin to meditate on His Word, we are being "transformed by the renewing of our mind." The Word will change our outlook on life. We begin to see things from a holy perspective. We won't look at ungodly things in the same way again.

For example, you might have thought living together was an acceptable practice, but now you know that God doesn't want you in that type of sinful relationship. You used to think it was alright to hang out in bars, but now you know that it's not setting a good example for others. You used to think that you could have a relationship with an unbeliever, but now you know that God would never want you in a relationship like that.

God is transforming your way of thinking. You are starting to have a zeal for righteousness. You don't want to bite the fruit. And it's because you love Him. You don't want to do things that will hurt your relationship with Him. You care about the oneness that you are experiencing, and you don't want anything to get in the way of that. You are being made new by the power of His Holy Spirit.

When you look at a caterpillar, you'd never believe that it would become a beautiful butterfly. So many of us look back and see what we once were, and we're amazed at the redemptive work He's done in our life. When butterflies come out of their cocoons, they can fly and reach the sky. And now we are like the butterfly, flittering around, reflecting His glory in what we do. It's a sight to see! We truly are new creations in Christ.

Question: What beauty is He creating out of your brokenness?

Our Great Protector

I know this is convicting for some of you. I understand because I've been where you are. I know how it feels. It's as if a veil has been lifted from your eyes and you're seeing how sinful your past choices are to God. It causes deep shame and regret. You feel embarrassed and humiliated. Your heart can ache as a result of your poor decisions. If you've accepted Christ, He loves you, and He is not condemning you. He doesn't want you continuing to focus on the past. He hasn't given up on you.

"There is therefore now no condemnation to those who are in Christ Jesus, who do not walk in the flesh, but according to the Spirit" (Romans 8:1).

He wants you to understand where you went wrong so that you can make it right. God brought people into my life to encourage me to seek repentance for my unconfessed sin. As I've drawn closer to Him, He's washed away all those painful memories from my past. I found that God really can restore the heart and heal the wounds.

It's impossible to go back in time. I know how many would like to, but that thinking is futile. God's Spirit will empower you to live for Him. The more you say no to the flesh, the more you will experience victory. And isn't that what you want? Don't you want to be free from the people, places and things that have kept you in bondage over the years?

You will see that the things you've done will, one day, be a faint memory that no longer has power over you. And you can tell people how He's delivered you from the pain and heartbreak in your life. He wants to redeem what you've gone through for His glory. That is my testimony, and I praise Him for it! Let it be yours, too!

> "If we say that we have no sin, we deceive ourselves, and the truth is not in us. If we confess our sins, He is faithful and just to forgive us our sins and to cleanse us from all unrighteousness" (I John 1:8–9).

You don't have to live with the shame of your past. You can experience acceptance because of His love for you. You can feel a sense of confidence and reassurance that He will redeem the pages of your life. A new chapter is being written in your book. How wonderful that it is being penned by your Savior.

Verses For Meditation

"For this is the will of God, your sanctification: that you should abstain from sexual immorality; that each of you should know how to possess his own vessel in sanctification and honor, not in passion of lust, like the Gentiles who do not know God; that no one should take advantage of and defraud his brother in this matter, because the Lord is the avenger of all such, as we also forewarned you and testified. For God did not call us to uncleanness, but in holiness. Therefore, he who rejects this does not reject man, but God, who has given us His Holy Spirit." ~ I Thessalonians 4:3-8

"For you were once darkness, but now you are the light (for the fruit of the Spirit is in all goodness, righteousness and truth), finding out what is acceptable to the Lord." ~ Ephesians 5:8–9

"The Lord knows those who are His," and *"Let everyone who names the name of Christ depart from iniquity."* ~ II Timothy 2:19

"For the grace of God that brings salvation has appeared to all men, teaching us that, denying ungodliness and worldly lusts, we should live soberly, righteously, and godly in the present age." ~ Titus 2:11–12

"Therefore, having these promises, beloved, let us cleanse ourselves from all filthiness of the flesh and spirit, perfecting holiness in the fear of God." ~ II Corinthians 7:1

CHAPTER 8
Freedom In Christ

We've all had things happen to us over the course of our lifetime that left deep wounds to the heart. We have experienced betrayal. We have felt neglected and abandoned. People have rejected us, and we've felt unwanted and unloved. We have been pushed to the side and walked over. We've been forgotten about.

I know that many of you have been through a wealth of traumatic experiences. It's been very hard to overcome. The heart is like a prison cell that is filled with unforgiveness. The walls are covered with anger, rage, sadness and despair. I understand. I've experienced all the above myself.

When I look around, I see so many unhappy faces. You can see the pain in their eyes. Life has taken its toll on them. In fact, some of you might feel that way right now. How many are still suffering with hurts from the past? How many are still trying to recover from a broken relationship? How many have lost their ability to smile?

There were times in my life when I'd muddle on, determined to persevere. I'd use the phrase "I'm pulling myself up by my bootstraps." Have you ever said that before? There are many who really do want to be all God intended for them to be. They don't want to be burdened with pain any longer. There are many who don't understand why they can't break free. Why won't the painful feelings go away?

The things that people have said and done have been like cuts to the heart. The negative things that have happened are like chains to the soul. As time goes by, the weights have gotten heavier and heavier.

God wants you to experience freedom from the burdens that have weighed you down. Let me share how God can enable you to walk in victory.

Waves Of Emotion

I want to share a little story with you. This isn't easy for me to talk about. I have no problem sharing this when I'm teaching or counseling, but in a book?!! As you can see, my pride can still rear its ugly head. My prayer is that someone will experience healing by what I'm sharing.

When we first got married, an avalanche of bitterness and anger was released in me and threatened to sweep us away. I was easily offended and had a very hard time letting go of hurts. I had been wounded from the past and hadn't fully healed. It was causing a very negative and emotionally charged attitude to surface.

So often I'd expect my husband to think and respond to a situation the way I would. I would want him to validate my feelings when I was hurt by someone. I'd want him to be understanding and sympathetic. He would tell me to forgive the person and move on. That was great advice, but not what I wanted to hear at the time. I wanted him to acknowledge my wounded heart by comforting and consoling me. Almost like a girlfriend would do. I wanted to talk about it...and talk about it. His personality is the opposite of mine. He does not think or feel the way I do. When he couldn't comprehend what I was trying to say, I'd lose it!

He thought I took things way too personally. He'd encourage me to not let the resentment take root! I needed to let things go, which I found impossible to do. When we had disagreements, I would withdraw and hold a grudge. I expected him to come back and acknowledge his lack of sensitivity towards me. I was so stubborn. He could not understand why I was having such a hard time. Why didn't he understand what I needed to hear? Why couldn't he say the things that would make me feel better?

So, the first year of our marriage was very trying for me, as I felt very frustrated and misunderstood. And that made me feel so broken inside.

And then I continued bringing up the offenses, determined to get him to see things my way. The thoughts continued playing in my mind, like a needle stuck on an old 45 record. Why couldn't I let the hurts go? Why was it so hard to forgive? I didn't have control of my emotions, they controlled me.

Our pastor set up a plan for us to meet once a month for a marital check-up. We were to discuss how things were going and get advice on ways to build a healthier marriage. I was thankful that we had set up the monthly appointments. I was so overwhelmed by what was going on that I couldn't wait for us to meet with him.

I was a little nervous when we got together, but I was sure the pastor would take my side. As I began to share, he quickly pointed out how unforgiving I was towards my husband. He said my heart was filled with unresolved hurts from the past. What!?? I practically fell out of my seat. It's not me, it's him!! The pastor continued with, "You have a very negative and judgmental attitude."

Why didn't he understand my feelings? He's a pastor and a counselor. Well, I assumed most men think alike. So, I felt that a female counselor would be better suited for me. He directed me to a woman he worked with. Boy, I was ready to talk with her.

Will She See Things My Way?

When we met, I was hopeful that we'd see eye-to-eye. You know, woman-to-woman. But she ended up repeating what the pastor said, practically word for word. I was floored. Not you too! I could not believe it. Did you talk to the pastor about me? She hadn't.

Why was it me? She helped me realize that my negative attitude and the inability to let go of offenses was a serious sign of unforgiveness. She helped me see that the more Christ's love dwells within a heart, the more mercy and grace will be shown to others. She helped me understand that drawing closer to God can enable a person to truly forgive. She helped me realize that when the Holy Spirit and the Word take hold of your heart, captives are set free! *"Therefore, be merciful, just as your father also is merciful"* (Luke 6:36).

I believed that I was a loving and gracious person. But the relationship with my husband revealed that I had a lot of bitterness and resentment stored up inside. Who knew?! I sure didn't.

The truth was, I hadn't forgiven those who'd hurt me. There were unresolved wounds that weren't healed. I could have worn a t-shirt that said, "Please be kind! I am super, super, sensitive." My heart was so tender that if anyone disappointed or disrespected me, I'd get angry and upset. There were times I'd lose control and find myself exhibiting some very ungodly behavior. What was happening to me?

The counselor said I was immature in my walk with the Lord and I needed some serious inner healing. How could that be? I thought she was wrong. I told her I'd forgiven everyone who had hurt me. I thought I had reconciled all the painful things from my past. I wasn't in denial—or was I?

I was so confused when I left her office. She encouraged me to pray about what I was going through. I wanted to know the origin of the unresolved sin in my heart. I needed to know why there was so much turmoil in my life. I was open to seeking God for an answer. I wanted the Holy Spirit to reveal truth to me. I began praying for God to show me why I was so easily offended.

Well, the next week someone said some harsh things to me, and I went home and cried like a baby. I found myself deeply wounded—almost to the point of depression. It was as if I had a button, and if someone pushed it, I'd experience all kinds of crushing emotions. I felt such a deep level of pain over things that shouldn't have caused so much hurt. And now, the struggle wasn't just with my husband, I was experiencing it with others.

Forgiveness Is The Key

Why did I take her words so personally? Why did they immobilize me? It was because I already had an emotional wound and the current insult had poured salt on it. It was triggering the unresolved feelings that were hidden deep within me.

Over the next several weeks, there were conflicts that left me broken. There were times I felt like I was drowning in a sea of despair. This overwhelming sense of rejection would sweep over me like a tidal wave. These were the same types of feelings I deeply struggled with as a young girl. How could I be feeling this same familiar pain? How could I be feeling this same sense of sadness? The desire to be loved and accepted was making itself known in a very vivid way! I would never have believed I was still that young girl that longed for validation.

I had tried to convince myself that I no longer lived for other people's approval. I thought I was done trying to meet other's expectations. I believed that I had broken free of the performance trap. I no longer lived to be a people pleaser. I thought that was all behind me. So, I didn't understand why I was so upset all the time, why I was so easily offended and why I had such a bruised ego. God knew, and in His faithfulness, He wasn't going to leave me with an unforgiving and prideful heart.

If I'd truly forgiven, then why was I still angry at that person? Why did I put up an emotional wall? Why couldn't I re-engage with them? Where was my unconditional love? Why didn't I show Christ-like behavior when I was insulted? Why did I justify and rationalize my bad behavior, thinking I had a right to be resentful?

I was learning that, because I was so easily offended, my heart still harbored the sin of unforgiveness. I began to understand that unresolved pain can be revealed by the way we respond to things. Whether it was a minor or major infraction, I found myself getting too emotional over it. I began to see how feelings can get buried for a long time and it isn't until a certain situation triggers those feelings, that we are even aware there is still an issue. Boy, those were light bulb moments for me. I tried to move beyond the past offenses, but they hadn't left me.

God was using our marriage to reveal my need to love and forgive those who had caused me pain. I wanted to finally be free of the unresolved hurts. I didn't want my behavior controlled by the things that had happened in the past.

The Power Of Prayer

The first step in the forgiveness process was to acknowledge the bitterness and resentment that still lingered in my heart. God tells us that we must forgive. If we choose to hold on to the offenses, we will pay a huge emotional and physical price. Letting the unforgiveness fester inside will only lead to more spiritual bondage. That's not what you want, is it? Don't you want to be free?

My counselor encouraged me to pray for those who had wounded me. I needed to ask God to give me a deep love and compassion for them. At first it was a challenge. There were some offenses that were very hard to release. I was so sad over some of the things that had been said and done to me. It brought back some very painful memories. I remembered the criticisms and condemnation like they happened yesterday. I felt a sense of brokenness that weighed heavy on me.

I was still angry at a few people who had caused deep pain in my life. I said that I'd forgiven them. But true forgiveness creates healing. And healing creates freedom. But I wasn't free. Even though it happened many years before, I was still weeping over it. I still felt the hurt. It was as if the pain had gripped me by the throat and wouldn't let go. I was choking. That's when I knew that the past still was affecting the present.

But then I began praying for them. I wanted to forgive and let go of the hurtful feelings. I wanted to feel love towards the individuals. I asked God to bless them. I earnestly prayed for their salvation. God began softening my heart and filling it with compassion. I found myself wanting what's best for them. I realized that if they had known better, they would have done the right thing. I understood that their past was broken, too. It was revealed in the way they treated others. God was teaching me mercy and unconditional love.

"Bless those who persecute you; bless and do not curse. . . . Repay no one evil for evil" (Romans 12:14,17).

This is what I had to do. And I am challenging you to do it too. Please go to God and ask Him to reveal the unresolved emotional wounds to your heart. Ask Him to give you the strength and courage to pray for those individuals. Ask God for compassion and love towards them. Pray for the gift of mercy. Ask God to help you let go of the pain from the past. Ask the Holy Spirit to heal your heart. Ask for God's grace to fill you up to overflowing so that it touches the lives of others. And enables you to see those people who hurt you through His eyes.

Tell him your true feelings. It's a sacrifice and can be very hard to do. Be honest about the struggle. I know it's tough. Cry it out! He sees! He cares! He knows! He understands! He's been rejected! He's experienced abandonment! He's gone through it! He was there when you experienced the pain. Just like God was with Jesus when He went to the cross. And, the Lord will bring glory out of your pain, just like He did with His Son. Nothing we go through is ever in vain when we are seeking to live for Him.

His limitless power can restore your aching heart. His boundless love can bring new life to the desert. So, earnestly pray for the desire to forgive. He will enable you to do this. Trust me, no trust Him on this. He'll never steer you wrong. His ways will always produce good things in your life.

There have been times that I've encouraged an individual to pray for someone that had caused them deep suffering. Some have broken down and realized they couldn't do it. They couldn't even consider letting the offender out of the emotional prison they had built for them. They had convinced themselves that the person had to apologize first. They believed the person needed to repent before reconciliation could occur. But, that's not what God's Word says. Forgiveness is not dependent on what the other person does. We are called to love unconditionally. And that means we must fully and totally forgive, whether they try to reconcile or not. The Holy Spirit can enable you to do it! He can remove the resentment and replace it with love.

> "Then Peter came to Him and said, 'Lord, how often shall my brother sin against me and I forgive him? Up to seven times?' Jesus said to him, 'I do not say to you, up to seven times, but up to seventy times seven'" (Matthew 18:21-22).

The Mercy Of God

Remember Jesus during His last hours on the cross. There were men beneath Him who were casting lots for His clothes. Here is the Son of God in agony. He had done no wrong! What was His response to their cruel behavior, *"Father, forgive them, for they know not what they do"* (Luke 23:34). Wow! He had gone through so much suffering and pain. And how did He respond? He showed compassion and forgiveness.

It's important to remember the forgiveness and mercy that He has shown to you. What if God held you responsible for all the ways you've sinned against Him? In Christ, we are totally exonerated. The slate has been wiped clean. That should bring great relief to our souls knowing that He no longer keeps a record of our wrongs. That is amazing grace. And that's what we must show to others.

> *"I, even I, am he who blots out your transgressions, for my own sake, and remembers your sins no more"* (Isaiah 43:25).

> *"For he has rescued us from the dominion of darkness and brought us into the kingdom of the Son he loves, in whom we have redemption, the forgiveness of sins"* (Colossians 1:13-14).

The Mighty Word Of God

When I was in counseling, she encouraged me to meditate on the Scriptures that dealt with forgiveness. It's more than just reading a Bible verse. It's taking the Words to heart and applying it to your situation. It's praying that the Scriptures will come alive within you. It's feeding on the Scriptures until it turns your hate into love. It's meditating on His truths until His desires become yours. It's wanting His Words of compassion to flow through your veins. It's wanting to show the same kindness that Christ exhibited to others.

I began asking the Holy Spirit to do a major healing in my heart. I was praying that the Word of God would cleanse my soul. I wanted to be empowered by His truth, so that I could do what He asks of me—and that was to love unconditionally.

There are people in our lives that we can't avoid. Our friends, family and co-workers, are just a few who might cross our path each day. God has a purpose for them being in our life. There will be frequent tests in the area of forgiveness. When you see the person again, are there still feelings of anger? Do you keep rehearsing what happened from the past?

Jesus says to bless those who persecute us. We are called to be peace-makers. The Lord wants us to exhibit care and concern when interacting with individuals. And, when we offer love instead of hate, the Holy Spirit can work to repair the broken relationship. You never know what will happen when you take that first step towards reconciliation. We mustn't let the enemy convince us that things will never get better.

Many relationships have experienced healing. How many more re-lationships could have been restored if we'd done things God's way? The Holy Spirit is mighty and is the one who transforms hearts and lives! We can't do this in our own power or else we will fail. We must pray for the Holy Spirit to wash the stains away and fill us with God's love.

How can you bless a person that has offended you? When the person crosses your path again, will you be gracious and kind? Who do you need to pray for today? How will the Holy Spirit work in your life as you submit to His will in this area?

Healing Is Possible!

I began to do the spiritual work needed to forgive, and God began cleansing my soul. I had to become very proactive in my desire to love and forgive. It was not automatic, and it surely wasn't easy. But I did begin to see a dramatic difference. I began to understand how the Holy Spirit works when we surrender to His will. He freed me from the pain of past hurts. I was so deeply wounded, and the Lord restored and renewed my heart. I am in awe of Him.

I knew true healing had occurred when I wasn't so easily offended. The insults no longer carried the same amount of emotional weight. My feelings were no longer controlled by the actions of others. I learned not to own an offense. I didn't want to receive the negativity and let it immobilize me, like it did in years past. I'd pray and reflect on it to see if I was wrong. If I was unkind, I needed to apologize and ask forgiveness. If I'd been hurtful, I needed to swallow my pride and seek reconciliation.

If I wasn't the one who caused the hurt, I wouldn't allow their bad day, or whatever they were going through, to weigh me down. I didn't want their actions to ruin my day. I wasn't going to let what they said make me feel unworthy or inadequate. I experienced a lot of criticism in my young life, and I took much of it to heart. It left me feeling very alone and rejected. I did not want to allow others to have that same kind of power over me any longer. What can I do? What can I say? Be kind. Be courteous. Be loving. Pray for them. Do not return evil for evil. Be a blessing instead!

"Do not repay evil with evil or insult with insult. On the contrary, repay evil with blessing, because to this you were called so that you may inherit a blessing" (I Peter 3:9).

I was growing in my spiritual walk. I was learning that He loves me unconditionally. I always have His love. And He always has my hand. And I can do the hard things He asks of me, because He wants me to be free. He alone gets the praise for giving me the victory.

We are human and our feelings will get hurt. We still must work through an offense. It can still sting. It can still burn. It can still knock us off our feet and take our breath away. We can't control what others do, but we can control our response. And that is the key.

In years past, I didn't know how to process the pain in a spiritual way and allow the Holy Spirit to help me forgive. I believed that all I needed to do was say that I forgave someone, and that was the end of the story. It was over. But it's not that easy, is it? It requires time and effort, as you seek God to help you be at peace with someone. We must always remember that the Holy Spirit will enable us to be obedient to the Word of God. The Holy Spirit has the power to renew and restore our shattered life.

When the hurt cuts deep, there might be more spiritual effort required to forgive. This isn't something that occurs overnight. The road to healing is a journey. As you pray and seek His Word, God will strengthen your heart. It's wise to seek godly counsel for Biblical advice when things are hard to work through. I've had people who directed me to His Word, and it changed my life. I pray you'll seek God and do whatever is necessary to find the spiritual and emotional healing you need to be whole. He will open doors for you. I can vouch for His amazing timing in my life.

But make sure that the people you go to for support and counsel are individuals who are mature in God's Word and believe in the power of the Holy Spirit. They need to be able to direct you to the spiritual work needed to move through the pain.

Unconditional Love

How was I not so tender to the touch? How did I learn to forgive those people that bruised my heart? I couldn't require a person to treat me a certain way. I expected too much from them. Why did I put demands on individuals? I believed that if I was respectful, they should be respectful too. If I had been kind, then they should be kind to me. I constantly focused on how others should treat me, instead of what God's Word said about how I should treat others.

When those we deeply care about have failed to return that love, we can't hold them accountable. We must accept people the way they are, without expecting change. That is how we love people unconditionally. In I Corinthians 13:4-8, the apostle Paul tells us that real love endures all things. Wow!! Is that even possible?

We don't have the ability to let hurts and offenses go in our flesh. We can't forgive on our own. We aren't going to love those who've hurt us. The enemy will keep bringing back the offenses. The memories can linger for a long time...sometimes a lifetime. But He can enable you to forgive! He can do it, if you'll let Him.

He will enable you to see them as imperfect people who need a perfect Savior. God doesn't want us spending time judging others for the things they've done wrong. He has forgiven us, so we must forgive them. If you think that your sinful behavior isn't a big deal, all you need to do is remember the cross. Christ died for you. His forgiveness for you never ends. His love is all consuming. I am sorry, but He wants us to love others like that, too. We've got work to do, don't we?

The Perfect Dad

When people bruise us, if we don't forgive them, a root of bitterness will take hold and disfigure our soul. It's like a weed that chokes the joy and peace out of our hearts. Those weeds can suffocate us to the point that we aren't able to fulfill our God-given purpose. The enemy is always trying to use the antics of others to cripple us.

I've counseled women who still have unresolved issues with their parents over things that happened many years ago. They share the heartache as if it occurred yesterday. The unforgiveness gnaws at their soul. It eats away at their heart and has spread like a deadly disease. You can hear it in all they say. Haven't you felt that way?

A woman shared how her father always expected perfection. She was constantly being corrected and reprimanded for what he considered unacceptable behavior. And he was tough! His criticism and hateful comments left her feeling angry and bitter. Now she believes that God expects perfection and nothing less. She is constantly worried that she needs to do everything right. She has fallen into the performance trap. Do you see how her dad's influence has caused her to live in fear that she will fail? She doesn't understand the meaning of the word grace because she didn't grow up receiving much of it.

Her father treated her the way he was treated. He exhibited the same sinful behavior that he experienced while growing up. We can't turn back the hands of time. The severely fragmented relationship with her father has caused her to doubt and question God's love. She needs to put her complete trust in the Lord. He will prove Himself faithful to her.

God isn't like her father. He isn't going to withhold His love from her. He doesn't expect perfection. That's the reason Jesus had to come. He is the perfect One! He is much more kind and caring than her father ever could be. He is the perfect daddy. God wants her to know just how loving a Father He is. He wants to show her the acceptance that she didn't receive from her earthly dad. She can be confident of God's unconditional love for her. He longs to bless and do good things in her life.

She needs to forgive her dad for the many ways he failed. She shouldn't allow the unresolved hurts to continue to ferment inside. She has carried the resentment around way too long. The many years of hostility have erected a huge emotional wall of anger and bitterness between them. And it has caused a ripple effect in her relationships with others.

When I sat down with her, she was not ready to extend an olive branch. She blamed the father for her many failed relationships. Because of the perfectionism, she had imposed unrealistic expectations on those around her. She had become just like her dad! She saw his abrasive attitude coming out in her and it was driving her nuts.

It's time to allow the Potter to reshape her heart. I began to share Scriptures on the love of God. I encouraged her to meditate on the truths of His grace. She needs to embrace His unfailing love. She needs to let the Living Water cleanse the deep wounds. She needs to accept the fact that she isn't perfect. It's impossible to do everything just right. You can do the best you can, but you must forgive yourself when things go wrong. And learn from them.

It took time, but she began to seek God for help to overcome the destructive behavioral patterns. She began to allow the Scriptures to be planted in her heart. She became more merciful and gracious. It was evident that the Holy Spirit was creating a new identity in Christ. It was awesome to see how she went from someone who was so stringent to one who was much more accepting of herself and others.

Only God can enable her to tear down the wall of separation. Restoration can't occur if she's not willing to pray for God to give her the grace to forgive. God can fill her heart with love.

"If it is possible, as far as it depends on you, live at peace with everyone" (Romans 12:18).

She was praying fervently for the ability to reconcile with her father. She began to focus on releasing the hurts and replacing them with words of healing. Her self-talk became much more Christ-centered. She was using God's Word to combat the constant onslaught of negative thoughts brought on by the enemy. She decided to no longer throw the past up in his face. She believed that love was the standard required to engage.

She was able to forgive her dad and move forward. It required a lot of humbling on her part. This was not an easy road for her. Even though their relationship is far from perfect, the bond is growing between them. She is taking baby steps. She has grown to understand his personality. She doesn't expect him to be different. When negative comments come, she responds with a soft word. But her change of heart has caused a softening on his part. The Holy Spirit is creating change. God is restoring their relationship. And the legacy left behind will be one of redemption.

We need to pray for an unconditional love that models the Savior. Ask God for the outpouring of His Holy Spirit. And for our words to be anointed by the One who can change even the hardest heart. May our kindness be a soothing balm that ministers to people's souls. Don't require change to occur in someone else. Be the catalyst that causes change. Jesus says you'll know a Christian by their love.

What would the people around you say about your attitude and behavior?

Prayer: *Lord, help us to believe in this amazing love that you have for us. And that you are restoring and renewing our hearts, as we cling to you through the healing process.*

"When my mother and my father forsake me, then the Lord *will take care of me"* (Psalm 27:10).

A Relationship Restored

I had a woman share an amazing praise report with me. She was frustrated with the relationship she had with her dad. He often said things that deeply wounded her. She never felt loved by him. It was sad to hear the hurt she had been through. She had lived a life of rejection.

I told her to start exhibiting unconditional love towards him. When he says the wrong thing, I encouraged her to respond in love. Do not argue with him or challenge the things he says. It takes two to tango, and that also applies to fighting. II Timothy 2:23-26 instructs the believer not to quarrel with others. We are to be kind and gentle.

Don't try to prove a point to win an argument. Don't get the nickname, "The Comeback Kid," because of all the clever and witty things you say in retaliation to someone's negative comments. That's pride! And we must swallow it. Pray for God to give you wisdom to respond in the right way. Instead of responding in kind, seek to de-escalate the argument.

"A soft answer turns away wrath: but grievous words stir up anger" (Proverbs 15:1).

When he hurts her feelings, she is to pray for ways to bless him. She agreed with the counsel but didn't think things would ever get better. She began treating her dad with love, care and respect. She'd ask for his opinion. She'd listen attentively, even when they disagreed. When things got heated, she'd tell him it was time to go. She'd end with an I love you, even when he didn't say it back. She was pouring on the love. And it felt good to her. She started seeing a huge difference in his attitude. She called it a miracle.

As the months went by, she witnessed an incredible change of heart. He wasn't the same person. He was so kind and gentle to her. She was in awe of what God was doing in their relationship. He was repairing and healing so many hurts. Their love began to blossom. Their relationship was being renewed. What a testimony of how God can work when we do things His way. She was overwhelmed by God's goodness and love. And she gave Him all the glory for repairing their broken relationship.

The Empty Well

We can't forget about mom, can we? Mother-daughter relationships are very complicated, aren't they? I have talked to so many women about the deep struggles they've experienced with their mothers. One woman told me she was angry at her mother and was finally going to set her straight. She had always longed for her mom's acceptance. She was tired of the criticisms and the way her mom made her feel stupid. I asked what she thought would be accomplished by confronting her. She wanted her mom to understand how she felt. She wanted to hear words of kindness come out of her mouth, for once.

I asked if she had ever told her mom about the way she felt? They had argued over it countless times in the past. I told her that it was unwise to confront her, but she was determined to do it. If you want to resolve conflicts by doing things your way, then it's not going to work out. God's Word gives guidance on how to be a peacemaker. When you follow in His footsteps, the chances are much better that things can be restored.

Take a look at the Scripture below:

> "And the Lord's servant must not be quarrelsome but must be kind to everyone, able to teach, not resentful. Opponents must be gently instructed, in the hope that God will grant them repentance leading them to a knowledge of the truth, and that they will come to their senses and escape from the trap of the devil, who has taken them captive to do his will" (II Timothy 2:24-26 NIV).

Consider this analogy: You can't draw water from a well that is empty. You can't pull water out of a well that has run dry. That's what we do when we try to make someone give us what we need. We hope that the demands will cause them to say what we long to hear, that we are loved and accepted. But they weren't told, so they don't know how to tell us. It doesn't mean that it can't happen. But don't go into the relationship expecting or demanding change.

You need to drop your expectations and raise your tolerance level. Pray through the process, while being loving and kind. If transformation happens, you will rejoice. If it doesn't occur on your timetable, then keep spreading the love. Keep seeking peace as you walk through the process. And always remember, God blesses those who are merciful and gracious.

And there is always hope for change (Romans 5:5). There are people who truly do change their ways. I am one of them! Are you? There are some that don't believe people can change! That's another lie from the enemy to keep you discouraged. God has created new identities in us, and He will create it in others.

All of us have been deeply wounded by individuals who said they loved us. Or they may never have uttered those words that you longed to hear. And those feelings of rejection have stuck like glue. It's time to forgive them for their lack of care and concern—for the pain and hurt they have caused in your life. Don't stay bound up by the failures of others. If God is with you, His love can fill you with compassion for them.

Your heart can be deeply grieved by the fact that they weren't told they were loved. You need to be sensitive to the pain they've been through. Pray for a heart of softness and tenderness. If we put ourselves in their shoes, you know, if we walk a mile in their moccasins, God can give us the ability to be empathetic toward them. We need to show goodness and grace. Allow the lord to help you give that love away freely, without conditions.

We can't require things from others. We can't expect them to do what we want. We must love them, just as Christ loves us. He has forgiven us for all our transgressions. When you realize just how much you've done to offend Him and how much He's forgiven you, then you'll understand why you must offer forgiveness to those who've caused you pain. And then you will understand why that is the same kind of love that He wants to exhibit through you. Isn't that incredible?

Forgive Men Their Trespasses

If it is possible, we must be at peace with everyone. We want to share the love that has been given to us, with no strings attached.

> *"Let all bitterness, wrath, anger, clamor, and evil speaking be put away from you, with all malice. And be kind to one another, tenderhearted, forgiving one another, even as God in Christ forgave you"* (Ephesians 4:31–32).

Dr. James Dobson shared a story on his radio program about a woman who was deeply offended by someone she loved. He encouraged her to bake brownies for the person. Who needs to receive some brownies from you today?

Are you still wounded over a past relationship? God wants you to forgive that individual. We need to take responsibility for our share of the sinful behavior in past relationships. Many women spend too much time blaming the guy for all that went wrong. That reveals some serious unforgiveness.

I can't blame another person for the decisions I have made. Why did I stay with someone that wounded me? Why did I allow such ungodly behavior in my life? It was because I lacked the spiritual strength and wisdom to leave.

I have had women complain about someone they dated for years. How could you have stayed with them for years? You must forgive them for the ways they mistreated you. But you must forgive yourself for allowing the abuse and sinful behavior to continue in your life.

I am sorry for the things I said and did in my past relationships. I, too, wasn't a good example for them. I should have drawn more boundary lines. I should have proclaimed my faith and stood my ground for righteousness sake. I didn't and for that, I'm sorry. But that is behind me. I have chosen to live a life for the King.

He has forgiven me, and I can move forward. I have repented of my past sinful disobedience. I pray that you choose to forgive those who have hurt you so you can experience true healing. There is freedom and liberation when a person chooses to forgive.

"Forgiveness is unlocking the door to set someone free and realizing that you were the prisoner." –Max Lucado

"For if you forgive men their trespasses, your heavenly Father will also forgive you. But if you do not forgive men their trespasses, neither will your Father forgive your trespasses" (Matthew 6:14–15).

The Apple Of His Eye

When I think of the word father, I think of a protector. A good father watches out for his children. God is the very best dad! He is the perfect Father. Don't believe that God is oblivious to the things you have gone through. Don't think that He is in a rocking chair passing the time away. He is on the throne and He sees and knows everything.

"For He who touches you touches the apple of His eye" (Zechariah 2:8).

The apple or pupil is the central part of the eye. Just like the pupil is deeply connected to the eye, we are interwoven with the Savior. Whoever touches you is messing with Him. You are valuable to God. Everything that has hurt you did not go unnoticed. He was there and He cares. Look at the Scriptures below. He is the judge. There is a day of reckoning. And it is coming!

> "God is just: He will pay back trouble to those who trouble you and give relief to you who are troubled, and to us as well. This will happen when the Lord Jesus is revealed from heaven in blazing fire with His powerful angels" (II Thessalonians 1:6-7 NIV).

We are not to play judge. One day each person will be held accountable for his/her deeds. Those who have not received Christ and repented of their sins will face the ultimate punishment, separation from Jesus for all eternity. But we pray for God to exhibit mercy on those individuals. God has shown great mercy towards us. We pray that they will receive Christ as their Savior before time runs out. It's not too late. Are they still breathing? Pray for their salvation.

To think that there is a place called hell and people will go there. That is a hard thing to comprehend. The thought grieves my heart. I pray it burdens yours too. Pray for a desire to share the Gospel with those you love. And, that the Holy Spirit will give you the boldness to do it.

What Are Your Blind Spots?

All of us have a sinful nature. We need to be made aware of the wrongful attitudes that still exist in our personalities. Ask God to show you behavioral patterns that need to be eradicated from your life. Are there things you say and do that are unkind? Do you respond in a harsh tone? Are you critical and negative? Can you be verbally abusive? How are your communication skills?

There are behaviors we have learned while growing up. It's as if we were programmed to respond a certain way. So, what does your wiring reveal about you? Are there ungodly attitudes that need some work on the Potter's wheel? You might not even be aware that the behavior is unsightly and unbecoming, but it is. You might not even know what they are, but they exist.

We all have blind spots. A local pastor told about a survey that his staff took to evaluate their perception of him. He was surprised when he got back their responses. He really didn't understand some of the low marks he'd received. How is that possible? He thought he was a terrific communicator. It didn't make sense to him. He decided to take a poll around the office. He wanted to know what people thought about his communication style, and the employees just smiled. Wow! So many people couldn't be wrong.

How many would even allow an evaluation like that to be done? It's humbling, isn't it? So where are your blind spots? What does God want to reveal to you today? What is it that needs to change? You can't compare yourself to someone else. God is speaking to you.

Make this your prayer to the Lord: "Show me, convict me, change me." This is a bold prayer, and one that reveals a heart that is open and receptive to the Master's transforming touch. Ask God to show you the sin in your life. Ask Him to reveal that to you. You want there to be conviction that produces godly results. You want there to be true repentance of the heart. Ask for a desire to turn away from behavior that does not reflect Christ. It's not the kind of conviction that produces pain and heartache that lingers on. It's the kind of repentance that produces a passion for the things of God. That's when you know there's been a true, Christ-like transformation.

> "Even if I caused you sorrow by my letter, I do not regret it. Though I did regret it—I see that my letter hurt you, but only for a little while—yet now I am happy, not because you were made sorry, but because your sorrow led you to repentance. For you became sorrowful as God intended and so were not harmed in any way by us. Godly sorrow brings repentance that leads to salvation and leaves no regret, but worldly sorrow brings death. See what this godly sorrow has produced in you: what earnestness, what eagerness to clear yourselves, what indignation, what alarm, what longing, what concern, what readiness to see justice done. At every point you have proved yourselves to be innocent in this matter" (I Corinthians 7:8-11).

And below is a section of Scripture you can pray over. What areas still need work? Let Him search your heart. Let Him reveal truth in the inmost places. Ask God to probe the depths of your psyche to reveal the deep wounds that are hidden away. He will get to those recesses and crevices that you can't see. Your prayer is, "Lord, please reveal these hurts to me so I can be free."

"Search me, O God, and know my heart; try me, and know my anxieties; and see if there is any wicked way in me, and lead me in the way ever-lasting" (Psalm 139:23–24).

I've Got Pride!

I was in a Beth Moore Bible study which asked questions on the issue of pride. I really didn't think that I was a proud person. I wasn't materialistic and never focused on wealth, so I didn't think there were any prideful ways about me. I asked God to reveal any haughty or arrogant ways that might still be a part of my heart.

Well, God took me on a road of discovery. It was an excruciatingly painful journey. The lessons that immediately came as a result of that prayer were painful and quite humbling. The first revelation was just how much pride there was.

I mentioned earlier that I'm a huge yard sale fan! I just love finding good deals. Early in our marriage, God provided through many a classified ad. I am a traditional kind of girl. You can't find a lot of Bassett and Ethan Allen furniture where we live. But God was blessing us with the things I love.

One evening, I saw this advertisement in the classifieds with lots of cool items for sale. We woke up early to head over to the home. It was a mansion with fancy cars parked in the driveway. I couldn't wait to get inside.

As we started touring the place, I struck up a conversation with the owner and asked what he did for a living. He said that he was an attorney who did things under the table. Why would he tell us that? I was surprised and began trying to find out just what kind of work he did. I pried a little too much. You'd have thought I was an undercover reporter. He thought I asked too many questions.

As he got defensive, I did too. Our voices began to rise and then he said, "The lack of respect you are showing reveals that you had a difficult relationship with your dad. And it's evident by your pride."

What! You could see my face turning red. And it wasn't from blush. My husband grabbed my arm and ushered me out of there. We jumped into the car and I broke down. I wept and wept. My hubby was dumb-founded. "What just happened back there?" he asked. I didn't have an answer. I was clueless on why I lost my temper so quickly.

God was using what happened to reveal my prideful attitude. It was an enlightening experience. I learned that pride is revealed when a person tries to justify, defend and rationalize their behavior. See, I thought I had every right to argue with this guy. I wasn't going to let him raise his voice at me. He wasn't going to disrespect me. I had to stand up for myself. Where did that thinking come from? It surely is not Biblical. His words triggered a lot of anger within me, and my Christ-like attitude flew out the window.

Would Jesus respond in anger? Would he defend Himself? He would rather I walk away before getting upset. He would want me to apologize for losing my temper. He wouldn't want me to quarrel with anyone. The Scriptures tell me that I must have a peaceful attitude toward others. I surely wasn't trying to live at peace with this guy.

And I learned a huge lesson. I didn't know there was pride, until I asked the Lord to reveal it. And now I understood how many people walk around totally unaware of their sinful behavior. There are countless individuals deceived into believing there's nothing wrong with them. Oftentimes they think the other person is to blame, and it's not them who needs to change. But they might very well be the one who needs the open-heart surgery. We must be willing to take an honest look inside to see if there is any element of pride.

"Humble yourself in the sight of the Lord, and He will lift you up" (James 4:10).

The Woman Who Washed His Feet

There was one woman who knew just how broken and depraved she was. In Luke 7:36-50, we find a harlot with a tawdry reputation. She was known around town for her promiscuous relationships. Her life was in shambles. She was a shattered woman. A woman in need of a new identity.

She had heard about a man named Jesus who is able to forgive sin and heal the brokenhearted. She had heard He has the power to set people free. Oh, how she wanted freedom from her captivity. In her desperation, she had to see him. She finally felt like there was hope.

She ventured out to find Jesus eating at the house of a Pharisee. In those days, men and women ate in separate locations. It wasn't acceptable for her to mingle with the men, but she didn't care what others thought. She had to get to Him.

It is said that the eyes are like mirrors to the soul, and hers reflected a wealth of pain and regret. She felt so unworthy and unloved. She had lived a life that had caused so much pain. Her heart was desperate for pure love and forgiveness.

She had heard that this was the man who was able to heal. She made her way to Jesus and stood at his feet, hot tears streaming down her face. Here, in front of her, was the Son of God. It must have taken her breath away to be in the presence of the Lord. She knelt, washing His feet with her tears, and wiping them off with her hair. She was bowing down before the only One able to cleanse her from all unrighteousness. He was her only hope of salvation. I can see the love in His eyes as He reached out to her and said the words that she longed to hear, *"Your sins are forgiven.... Your faith has saved you; go in peace"* (Luke 7:48, 50).

She found Jesus that day. The woman who was considered unclean and had been branded with a scarlet letter, was now washed clean by the Hand of the sinless One. She was ready for freedom, and on that day, He gave it to her. He forgave her sins. In that moment, in the twinkling of an eye, she was told to go in peace! Only God!

What a wonderful proclamation she received. I'm sure the townspeople were muttering their criticisms. And you could hear the pharisee pronouncing judgment, *"If this man were a prophet, he would know who is touching him and what kind of woman she is—that she is a sinner."* So many assumed that Jesus should keep His distance from her. That she should be shunned and treated as an outcast.

But we are all sinners, and God wasn't looking at where she had come from; He was focused on where she was going. What a wonderful feeling she must have had as she left. I can picture the change in her countenance. She had spent so much of her life trying to find someone to love and accept her, and now she had finally found the One!

Broken Over Sin

When I started going back to church, I read Scriptures that convicted me of so many things I'd done wrong in my past. As I did this, I experienced such a deep sense of sorrow and regret. I felt so ashamed. I felt like the woman who washed the feet of Jesus.

I knew the Scriptures said that I was forgiven, but I was having a hard time believing it. The enemy pounded me with thoughts from the past. The images played in my mind like they were on the big screen.

I was feeling guilty for having those past ungodly relationships. I felt awful about the lifestyle I had lived and the awful choices I had made. I was overwhelmed with grief. Has that ever happened to you? I was begging Him to wash the memories away. I no longer wanted to be plagued by the shame and guilt from the past.

He was the one who brought me to that place of repentance. I needed to be broken over the worldly, sinful behavior that had caused me to drift from Him. It was time to get right with the Lord. It was time to return to my father, just like the prodigal son did in Luke 15. The Holy Spirit was revealing the sin in my heart that needed to be acknowledged. I needed to see the sin for what it was, but more importantly, the sacrifice He made to enable me to be free from the bondage so I could live for Him.

He wasn't beating me up over the head or trying to destroy me. It wasn't His voice bringing up my past failures. God wouldn't belittle me and make me feel worthless. That's not from Him. That's not His style. His method is love. His ways of drawing us back will create a passion to live for Him. The repentance doesn't bring destruction, it brings deliverance!

"Or do you despise the riches of His goodness, forbearance, and longsuffering, not knowing that the goodness of God leads you to repentance?" (Romans 2:4)

"For as high as the heavens are above the earth, so great is His lovingkindness toward those who fear him. As far as the east is from the west so far has He removed our transgressions from us. Just as a father has compassion on his children, so the Lord *has compassion on those who fear Him"* (Psalm 103:10- 13).

Blessed Assurance

I finally understood that He had forgiven me. It just took me a long time to forgive myself. But through His Word I've learned how precious I am to Him. I am loved. He took all my sin on Himself. That is agape love.

He offers that grace to you through His Son Jesus Christ. He died for you. I've shared my past with you only to show how God has redeemed my life. I am praising Him for how He has guided me through everything. God wants to restore you. He knows that you've been deeply hurt. He knows everything about you. He has not given up on you. He can heal your broken life.

He is the great "I Am!" He doesn't desert and abandon His children. I'm proof of that! His promises endure forever. Thank God for His redeeming power or we'd be so lost. He tells us that we can be assured of who we are in Christ! What blessed assurance that is!

"And we know that all things work together for good to those who love God, to those who are the called according to His purpose. For whom He foreknew, He also predestined to be conformed to the image of His Son" (Romans 8:28–29).

Let's Make Up

I recently had a discussion with someone and we both said hurtful things to each other. We both apologized and asked forgiveness for our negative attitudes. I was feeling bad about the things that were said. I knew Christ didn't hold it against me. But I still felt awful about what had happened. Someone sent me a text that same morning with the song, "What can wash away my sin; nothing but the blood of Jesus." The sender didn't give their name.

But I knew it was a special delivery sent from the Holy Spirit. It's what I needed to hear to remind myself that He's washed the sin away. I played that song over and over again. And it gave me such peace. It wasn't long before I was smiling again. Thank you, Jesus, for your love.

But we must be very careful. Wrong actions and attitudes can leave an ugly stain and bad feelings can linger. Words can be like daggers to the heart. Insults can slash the soul. Let's take, for example, a tube of toothpaste. When you squeeze the tube, you can't return what has come out. So, be careful of what comes out of your mouth. May our tongues bring words that are like a soothing oil to the heart—words that are seasoned with salt.

"Let your conversation be always full of grace, seasoned with salt, so that you may know how to answer everyone" (Colossians 4:6).

Thank God we were both spiritually mature enough to talk things out and forgive each other. Reconciliation is something we must always seek after in our relationships.

"Now all these things are from God, who reconciled us to Himself through Christ and gave us the ministry of reconciliation, namely, that God was in Christ reconciling the world to Himself, not counting their trespasses against them, and He has committed to us the word of reconciliation. Therefore, we are ambassadors for Christ, as though God were making an appeal through us; we beg you on behalf of Christ, be reconciled to God. He made Him who knew no sin to be sin on our behalf, so that we might become the righteousness of God in Him" (II Corinthians 5:18-21).

She Touched Him

Do you ever feel worn down by all the things that are going on around you? We've all had to struggle through difficulties and challenges in our lives. Here's a story in Scripture that should give us great hope!

In Luke 8:43-48, we find a woman who had a flow of blood for 12 years. She'd spent all her money on countless physicians, but no one was able to help her. There seemed to be no cure for her ailment. What made matters worse was that her condition labeled her as an outcast in society. I am sure that despair filled her heart. There must have been seasons when she wondered, how much longer? We've all been in those seasons, haven't we?

She heard that Jesus was coming to town. She had heard that He could perform miracles. He had caused the lame to walk and the blind to see. She must have been so excited to think that He might be able to help her. Maybe He can heal her. That must have lifted her spirits. She ran out and made her way down the street. As the multitudes pressed into Jesus from every side, the woman was intent and determined to reach Him.

She moved through the crowd and was finally able to touch the hem of His garment. Then, at that moment, the bleeding stopped, and she was miraculously healed. Jesus knew that power had gone out from him. He looked around and said, "Who touched me?"

There was no doubt that He knew who did it. He just wanted her to acknowledge the miracle that had just occurred in her life. As everyone looked around, she came out, trembling with fear. She fell at his feet, and feebly responded, it was me. I did it. *Then she declared to Him in the presence of all the people the reason she had touched him and how she was healed immediately"* (Luke 8:47).

She met the Savior that day and life would never be the same. She had experienced the amazing power of Christ: the power to heal, the power to save and the power that sets the captives free!

Be Of Good Cheer

What an amazing illustration for us! No one had the answer for this woman. No matter how many doctors she went to and no matter how much money she spent, she had come up empty. He is our great deliverer. He reached out to her and said, *"Daughter, be of good cheer! Your faith has saved you, go in peace"* (Luke 7:50).

When He told her to be of good cheer, those weren't just empty words. He had done something no one else could do. He wanted her to finally be able to laugh again. Imagine how her heart felt. It must have been fluttering like a butterfly. I would have been dancing and singing in the streets. I can't even imagine the overwhelming sense of joy that must have consumed her!

My prayer is that you will find that He is the answer. We are all like the woman who touched the hem of His garment. We all need Him to heal our wounded hearts. We need the touch of His mighty hand in our lives on a continual basis. Help us, Lord Jesus!

Because we live in a fallen world, things won't be perfect until we get to our heavenly home. We will struggle with our fleshly desires, and we will battle the thoughts the enemy puts into our heads. There will be trials and tribulations. We will have difficulties with co-workers, friends and family. We will face obstacles. There will be times when life will be overwhelming. We will make unwise choices. We will suffer traumas. Just as the disciples experienced their share of challenges and heartache, we will too. But we don't have to fear, because God is with us.

"These things I have spoken to you, that in Me you may have peace. In the world you will have tribulation, but be of good cheer, I have overcome the world" (John 16:33).

How can you be of good cheer? By being confident that He will work through the situation. He's going to reveal His glory in and through your life. My prayer is for Him to *"Please, show me Your glory"* (Exodus 33:17).

We need to release our struggles into His loving hands! We need to study His Word and pray for help on how to trust Him in every situation. He is the Master Craftsman, and He has every single resource available at His disposal. He wants to work His heavenly power through your pain. He will show you what to do. He will help you.

The outcome will enable you to rejoice over how He has accomplished His purposes through your struggles. He will help you overcome! But it is all about resting in His care. He wants you to have confidence that He will move—in His time. Our prayer is to constantly focus on what His will is for our life.

"Therefore, do not cast away your confidence, which has great reward. For you have need of endurance, so that after you have done the will of God, you may receive the promise" (Hebrews 10:35-36).

You Have So Much To Rejoice About!

As we work through our trials and tribulations, let us give Him the praise and honor that He deserves. He is so worthy.

"Yet I will rejoice in the LORD, I will joy in the God of my salvation. The LORD God is my strength; He will make my feet like deer's feet, and He will make me walk on my high hills!" (Habakkuk 3:18-19).

Ladies, I'm changing the last words to read "high heels." He's talking to you. Those sacrifices of praise can break through the darkness. When we are in a sad and sorrowful state, it is hard to praise God. It is difficult to thank Him for what we're going through. But Scripture says that He inhabits our praises.

When we are sad and discouraged, we often find ourselves doing the exact opposite. God says that He will bless us as we lift up our praise offerings to Him. When you do that, you are trusting Him through the pain. You are learning to be thankful that He is with you and He promises to carry you through.

The enemy works during those times of despair, so you feel hopeless and helpless. He wants you to have a defeatist attitude. He wants you to give up and throw in the towel. Does your God really care? Is He even there? Does He even hear you? He makes us doubt who God is. He makes us question God's faithfulness to His children.

But He is faithful. He is good. And the Bible is filled with story after story of His unconditional love. And look around. There are countless testimonies of God working miracle's in people's lives. We must never give up! We must press on! Our God is a mighty God. We can be confident that He has a plan for our lives. Let Him reveal it to you.

"Greater is He that is in you than he who is in the world" (I John 4:4 NASB).

You Are Forgiven

You've been forgiven!! Go in peace! Rejoice that you have been chosen by the God of the Universe! He is your Knight in shining armor! He rides in on his white horse to rescue you. You have a valiant suitor that no one can hold a candle to!

Take His hand and let Him lead you to the wedding feast. You are His bride, and He loves you. Grasp how beautiful you are in His eyes! We have been transformed. No more shame, ladies! We are shining like the sun! He has delivered us and set us free!

The Angel of the Lord is encamped around us. We don't have to hide our faces anymore. We can look to the One who is able to keep us from falling, to the One who loves us more than life itself. His love surrounds you and will carry you through. You and the Savior are one! Rejoice, my sister! Sing praises of thankfulness to your King!

Verses For Meditation

"And whenever you stand praying, if you have anything against anyone, forgive him, that your Father in heaven may also forgive you your trespasses." ~ Mark 11:25

"If your enemy is hungry, feed him; if he is thirsty, give him a drink; for in so doing you will heap coals of fire on his head. Do not be overcome by evil but overcome evil with good." ~ Romans 12:20, 21

"You have heard it said, 'You shall love your neighbor and hate your enemy.' But I say to you, love your enemies, bless those who curse you, do good to those who hate you, and pray for those who spitefully use you and persecute you, that you may be sons of your Father in heaven." ~ Matthew 6:43-45

"Then Jesus said, "Father, forgive them, for they do not know what they do." ~ Luke 23:34

"Finally, all of you be of one mind, having compassion for one another; love as brothers, be tenderhearted, be courteous; not returning evil for evil or reviling for reviling, but on the contrary blessing, knowing that you were called to this, that you may inherit a blessing." ~ I Peter 3:8

CHAPTER 9

Encouragement For The Journey

*D*id you know that you have a calling? That's right! You have gifts and talents that God has blessed you with. You might not be aware of what they are, but you have them. God has programmed every one of us with a purpose. He has a great plan for your life. So often we wonder whether we can make a difference. Well, with the Lord's leading, you can do great things for the Kingdom of God.

> *"As each one has received a gift, minister it to one another, as good stewards of the manifold grace of God"* (I Peter 4:10).

It doesn't matter where you've come from or what's happened in your life. Every believer is important to the development of the body of Christ. Even the weakest link can be used for mighty purposes with God. He is in the business of working through our weaknesses.

> *"My grace is sufficient for you, for My strength is made perfect in weakness. Therefore, most gladly I will rather boast in my infirmities, that the power of Christ may rest upon me"* (II Corinthians 12:9).

Do you know what your spiritual gifts are? Have you prayed about what God is calling you to do? God wants to guide you to that place that is a perfect fit for you. He will prepare the way. He will reveal it to you as you seek to live for Him. It is an exciting journey that you are embarking on.

Pray for direction on which way to go. Ask Him to bring people into your life that will help lead you into the specific ministry He has chosen for you. He's called you. He has the key, and He will unlock the door. Trust in Him to fulfill His purposes in your life. Don't let the enemy tell you that God can't use you. Don't let Him feed you lies about the future.

An Answer To Prayer

I had been disconnected from the Lord for several years. When God began drawing me back, I started experiencing a stirring within my heart to serve Him. I was in my mid-20s when I recommitted my life to the Lord. I wanted to dive into ministry, but I had a dilemma. I had a part-time job that required me to work on Sundays. The extra money was helping pay off my credit-card debt. I didn't know if I should quit. I needed direction and divine intervention, so I prayed for God to show me what to do.

I am not kidding you. Within two weeks, the restaurant closed its doors. Wow! It was bought out by an Italian restaurant and was closing for 6 months. There was my answer. I was so excited to be able to attend church and get trained to be a Sunday school teacher. I wanted to work with children and teach them all about Jesus. God began giving me a passion for ministry. I needed clear direction, and He gave it to me. I had no doubt He had opened the door for me. When you want to live for Him, He will order your steps.

"The LORD directs the steps of the godly. He delights in every detail of their lives" (Psalm 37:23 NLT).

If you aren't attending a local church, pray for God to lead you to a Bible believing, Christ-centered fellowship where you can grow in your knowledge of Him. I have heard people say that they don't need to go to church. I wholeheartedly disagree! You don't have to go to church to be saved. It is by trusting in Christ alone that guarantees one's salvation and a relationship with God. But church attendance is an important element of your spiritual growth.

The pastor has much more Biblical knowledge than the average layperson. He is responsible for leading you to the Living Water, which is

Jesus Christ. You need to be sitting under a minister that teaches you how to study God's Word. Are you learning more about the Lord under his leadership? Are you growing in your spiritual walk?

Church is the place where we can experience rich fellowship with other believers. Spending time with our brothers and sisters in Christ helps us grow in the faith. We need to be with people who encourage us to be more like Jesus. It's a jungle out there. And that's no joke! The church should be a safe place to come and grow together.

"Not forsaking the assembling of ourselves together as the manner of some is; but exhorting one another: and so much the more, as ye see the day approaching" (Hebrews 10:25).

The church is God's house. Surely, we can worship Him wherever we are. We can talk to Him anytime, day or night. His phone never dies or has a busy signal. And that's a good thing. Pursue Him on every front. Seek Him in all your ways. Worship Him in His sanctuary! Praise Him in His house. *"Praise the LORD. Praise God in his sanctuary; praise Him in His mighty heavens"* (Psalm 150:1).

Small Groups

It's important that we fellowship with and get to know members of God's family. And that's where small groups come in. Our church has an abundance of small groups in all shapes and sizes. There are groups for married couples, singles, men and women. It's not hard to find a fellowship to join. Does your church have small groups?

I want to give you a few good reasons to get plugged into a small group. First, when you go through a traumatic experience, the people in your study will know about it. They will help you through the difficult time. They will pray for you and be a source of spiritual strength when you need it most.

Second, don't you want to develop godly friendships? Many individuals work in a secular environment. Many of their children attend public schools. Many are involved in extra-curricular activities with people who aren't Christians. We are called to love everyone. But you have a better chance of meeting godly friends by being connected to the body of Christ.

And what about small groups with men? If you've been hurt in past relationships, it's wise to be in a small group with women. If you are still longing for a relationship, fellowshipping with the opposite sex might not be a good idea right now. You need to make sure that's not the main reason for joining a group. There have been ladies who have done that and gotten very hurt.

They expected a Christian's behavior to be different from that of the world. They didn't think the relationship would end up leaving them drowning and gasping for air. People are still human. Sin is still a part of our nature. There are so many who haven't made peace with the brokenness inside. And because of that pain, their relationships reflect their unresolved issues.

Small groups will allow you to engage, no pun intended, with other believers. Make sure those around you are learning and growing in their walk with the Lord. And, that you are growing closer to Him through your time with them. Pray that God will use you as a stepping-stone in someone's life that enables them to experience more of Christ.

Rise Above

I know that some of you feel insecure about being in small groups. I used to feel the same way. You are self-conscious about sharing your thoughts with others. You worry about saying and doing the wrong thing. You don't want to be laughed at or made fun of. You worry about being judged. You feel very vulnerable. You don't feel safe. Yes, many have been deeply hurt by someone and it's hard to trust again. We've all gone through it.

When in the group, just listen to what others have to say. No one has all the answers. Even though some think they do. We are all growing in our knowledge of Him and His Word. If someone says something that offends you, pray for them. Ask God to bless them. Don't stop going to an activity or event because someone hurt your feelings. So many people do that, and it's sad.

God's Word tells you to go and make peace with that person. He wants you to reconcile. That is a major priority in God's Book. Don't let others control where you go or what you do, unless sin is involved. As you make the sacrifices and work through your struggles, you will find God enabling you to forgive and let go of the hurt.

"The discretion of a man makes him slow to anger, and his glory is to overlook a transgression" (Proverbs 19:11).

Ministry Matters

You will find rich fulfillment and meaning as you begin to fill your life up with Christ-centered activities. Are you involved in a ministry? Are you working with the teens? How about the women's ministry? One of the ways that we experience joy and contentment is by showing the love of Christ to those around us. Jesus didn't come to be served, but to serve. His desire is for us to use our God-given gifts and talents for His glory.

I had only been attending church for a few months, when I signed up for the nursing home ministry. On Sunday afternoons, I'd go with a group of people that reached out to the lonely and destitute. There'd be a message from God's Word, and then we'd lead them in song! What a joy it was to see them singing along and raising their hands.

After the service, we'd stroll the corridors and engage with the residents. It was heartbreaking to see so many alone, with no one to visit them. Even though we only went once a week, it really did bless their hearts. We spent a lot of time sharing the Gospel with these precious individuals. And many prayed to receive Christ as their Savior. Is there anything more special than that?

It doesn't have to be a convalescent home. It can be an outreach ministry at your church. Where is the need in your fellowship? Please find out. Offer your assistance. Be available to volunteer in some capacity. Start small, but at least get started!

Many women share that they have a hard time being content in their singleness. When I was going through that single stage, it wasn't easy. I spent many a night crying, with my head buried in a pillow. But I prayed for God to open ministry doors and He did. I found Him filling my time up with Godly service. And it was so enriching for me. I experienced great delight by being in service to our King. And I still do!

I don't know what I'd have done with too much idle time on my hands. I was used to being in relationships. If you have too much free time, please be careful. The enemy can use that to your disadvantage. God will give your heart a sense of peace and satisfaction as you stay busy for Him.

God will lead you. Pray for His divine guidance. Ask Him where you belong? What can you do to bring honor and glory to His name? How can you make a positive difference in someone's life? With the Holy Spirit, you are able.

"Commit your way to the Lord, trust also in Him, and He shall bring it to pass" (Psalm 37:5). Decide to step out in faith. Commit everything that you do to His sovereign leading. *"Lord, lift the light of your countenance upon us"* (Psalm 4:6).

Prayer: *We want Your face to shine on us, Lord. Let us feel the warmth of your embrace. May we sense Your presence. Be gracious towards us, Lord. As you shine Your light on us, we will radiate the hope that is within us! May You bring a soothing calmness to our heart. May you bless us and protect us. May your grace abound toward us, Lord. May your favor rest on our lives.*

"The Lord bless you and keep you; the Lord make His face shine upon you, and be gracious unto you; The Lord lift up His countenance upon you, and give you peace" (Numbers 6:24-26).

Personal Bible Study

A ministry leader shared something that helped me understand why it takes some individuals a long time to be transformed into the image of Christ. She talked of the different things people do to experience spiritual edification. They read devotional books. They listen to podcasts and radio programs. They watch Christian television. There is praise music to sing and dance to. These are all good and important things that will help in a person's spiritual growth.

She added that many people spend hours on the above, but they never really delve into the Scriptures. Are you meditating and planting the

Word of God in your heart? Please make sure that you are feeding on His truths! Don't let those other forms of ministry replace studying the Word. The Bible is our spiritual food and what is required for nourishment. It has power. It causes transformation on a radical level. The apostle Paul tells us that it is the only effective weapon to combat the enemy. It's great to fill your heart with those other things. I encourage you to do that. But make the Bible your go-to for spiritual guidance and edification.

I don't like to embarrass people or put them on the spot. But how will I know if a woman is studying His Word unless I ask a few questions. In class, I will ask the ladies to share their five favorite Scripture verses and tell why they are important to them. What are yours? Why are they your favorites?

Let's say you've been a Christian for five years, so, do you know five verses? That means you've memorized at least one verse a year. Now, you should be able to memorize much more than that over the course of a year, right? As the Word seeps into our souls, it enables us to stand and boldly proclaim His salvation to a lost and dying world.

"Study to shew thyself approved unto God, a workman that needeth not to be ashamed, rightly dividing the word of truth" (2 Timothy 2:15).

I am not trying to make anyone feel guilty. A counselor gave me the same quiz years ago, and I failed. But it really did spur me on to start meditating on His Word. And the more I learned, the closer I got to him. The more I prayed for the Holy Spirit to embolden me, the more I saw supernatural things happening in my life.

Some women tell me that the Bible isn't easy to understand. There are others who say it's too confusing and they don't know where to begin. While others claim that they've read it. If that's true, then we should see a dramatic difference in their lives. One that reveals they've truly had a divine encounter with the Savior.

I found that carving out personal time with Jesus every day really did cause a powerful change of heart. Why not consider doing your own personal Bible study? Here are some great authors: Kay Arthur, Kelly Minter, Lysa Terkeurst and Beth Moore, are just a few. These ladies have gone through much in their lives. They know a lot more about the Bible than we do. Their studies will help you dig deeper into His Word, as they break down the Scriptures. It will ask personal questions about your walk with the Lord. It will help you apply the spiritual truths you are learning to your daily life.

I remember the study, *No Other Gods*, by Kelly Minter. Wow! It spoke to me on so many levels. It was just what a needed at that time in my life. I learned so much from her. I am currently doing Susie Larson's, *Fully Alive*. I can't tell you the revelations that have occurred through my study time. Her Spirit-filled words have touched areas of my heart that I didn't even know still needed healing. Because it ministered to me so deeply, I am on my second round.

Which Bible study could you benefit from? Which one is God leading you to do? Bible studies are helpful tools that speak into our hearts in so many ways. Everyone is at a different season of life. Pray for the Holy Spirit to lead you to that message your heart needs to hear, in a life-changing way.

Can He Really Bring You A Godly Man?

If you spend a lot of time thinking about your single status, you will be miserable. Be thankful that you have this time to get closer to Jesus. Ask Him to help you be grateful for this quality time. Let it be about you and Him. Consider it a blessing.

Please realize that you have a companion, and He is with you every step of the way. You are never alone. Ask God to reveal Himself in personal, intimate ways. He is your husband. Let Him be the One who makes you happy. Let Him be the One that is your source of strength. Let Him be the One that provides for all of your needs. Pray about including Him in all your conversations. Make Him the One you long to serve.

"I have set the LORD continually before me; Because He is at my right hand, I will not be shaken" (Psalm 16:8).

And again, I want to be sensitive to the pain that some of my single sisters have and are going through. I know women that have never gotten married. It still doesn't mean it won't happen. You just can't predict what God will do. He can be full of surprises.

I have a good friend who got married a few years ago. She is in her 60s. She had struggled with being single for a long time. She was finally satisfied in her relationship with God. She didn't think she'd ever get married again. She was having fun living for Jesus. Little did she know, God had another plan. I love how she met her husband, and they now serve in ministry together.

"I know how to be abased, and I know how to abound. Everywhere and in all things, I have learned to be full and to be hungry, both to abound and to suffer need. I can do all things through Christ who strengthens me" (Philippians 4:12–13).

So, whether single or married, He can give you peace. We don't know what He has in store for the future. We must make living for Him our supreme purpose on earth. I encourage you to lay your dream of marriage down on the altar. It is a sacrifice to do this. I know how hard it will be for some of you. You are releasing your desires into His hands. If it is His will for you, He will bring it to pass. You don't want to be consumed with the dream. You want to be obsessed with the Savior.

Without Distraction

If you are consumed with the desire for a mate, you might compromise your beliefs because of your wants! You will settle for things because it is too hard to be alone. I've had so many women share heartbreaking stories because they got tired of waiting. And they regret the relationship they wandered into.

I had a woman who was celibate until she was 33. When she came for counseling, she was devastated. She had met this guy at church, and they hit it off. She thought he was "the one." But, after four months, he broke up with her. She had finally given into a sexual relationship because she was tired of waiting. I can't tell you the buckets of tears she shed. And the emptiness that she felt. She deeply regretted that relationship, and it took her a long time to get over. It wasn't worth the pain.

And for those who have already been in a physical relationship, God has cleansed you from all unrighteousness. You aren't a marked woman. You aren't labeled because of your past. That is behind you. Remember that you are one with the Holy Spirit. First and foremost, you are committed to Him. I'd encourage you not to give that part of your heart away until your wedding day. It is possible. I know. I did it!!

Ask God to satisfy the deep longings of your heart. I know the thoughts you have. I had them too. When I dwelt on what I didn't have, I only got depressed. I know that seeking and serving Him brings great joy. So, battle those negative thoughts that keep creeping into your head.

Thoughts like, "Why aren't I married? I want children. Are there any spiritual guys left out there? How long will this process take, anyway? My biological clock is still ticking." Again, praise Him for this time! He ordained it! He is sovereign over your life. You're only going to get more frustrated if you don't let it go and focus on Him. Pray through the tears. Ask Him for the strength you need to navigate through this season of your life. Make being obedient to Him your heartfelt desire.

When a couple ties the knot, the focus shifts to taking care of the husband and family. Marriage is a very good thing. But when you are single, you can totally devote yourself to Christ, without distraction.

> *"But I want you to be without care. He who is unmarried cares for the things of the Lord—how he may please the Lord. But he who is married cares about the things of the world—how he may please his wife"* (I Corinthians 7:32-33).

Marriage Causes Change

And if you are to be married, the person should help you grow closer to God. You'll see how the Lord will use that person to reveal behavioral patterns that need to be changed, for the glory of God. That is what happened in my life. I wasn't even aware of the unforgiveness, selfishness and pride that was buried below the surface. In fact, I didn't think I had a problem. I was much more spiritually immature than my husband, and I didn't even know it. But God did.

The marriage relationship caused a lot of unresolved, sinful issues to erupt. It wasn't easy, to say the least. In fact, it was downright painful to work through. But, without the friction, I wouldn't have realized just how selfish I was, and how much I needed to change. As I began seeking His Word, I was learning how to be more Christ-centered and selfless.

Don't be surprised when difficulties and challenges arise in your married life. God is showing you things that need to be transformed. Seek to be obedient to His Word. Make sure that your behavior is lining up with the Scriptures.

Are you honoring your marriage vows? Are you keeping the promises you made to God? Christ loves us unconditionally, and we must seek to love others in the same way.

After you get married, you can't turn around the next month and say it was a mistake. Sadly, too many people do that. It's important to understand the vows you are taking before the "I do." You aren't just promising to love your husband for better or worse, you are also making that promise to God. The Lord takes those vows you will make (made) very seriously.

If there is a struggle in your marriage, please seek godly counsel from a church that stands on the truths of His Word for guidance and direction in your situation. Make sure that you have a pastor who clearly shows you, from the Scriptures, what God says about your dilemma. And then follow what the Bible is telling you to do. God will bless you for submitting to His will.

I recommend reading *Marriage, Divorce and Remarriage* by Jay Adams. I have read several of his books. He does a tremendous job of breaking down the scriptures so we can understand them from a layman's perspective. He has helped me grow in my understanding of God's Word.

The Waiting Process

As painful as the waiting process is, it's more heartbreaking to be with someone who isn't good for you. God can give you discernment. I struggled for several years because I wasn't married. After I broke up with my ex-boyfriend, seven years passed before I met my husband. I had been with a guy ever since I was a young teenager. I was used to having someone around. I had to learn to depend on Jesus. We do long for companionship. But if it's not happening, we shouldn't try to force the issue. It's gotten us into so much trouble in the past. Keep your eyes focused on Christ. Stay busy doing the work of the Lord.

"Therefore, my beloved brethren, be steadfast, immovable, always abounding in the work of the Lord, knowing that your labor is not in vain in the Lord" (I Corinthians 15:58).

One of the things that helped during my singleness was remembering the brokenness that I had experienced in past relationships, and I surely didn't want to go through that again. I wasn't going to jump into another relationship. I didn't want to develop a friendship with the opposite sex if it wasn't a Christ-centered relationship. I also decided not to have sex until I got married.

The milk was no longer available without the full and complete purchase of the cow. I was going to have to draw some serious boundary lines. I was tired of guys coming into my life that were controlled by their flesh. I didn't want any more broken promises. I didn't want to be an idol in anyone's life, ever again.

The Dating Game

So many women ask me what I think about dating. I just don't trust the dating game. And it is not in the Bible. It is a 21st century worldly practice that places the responsibility of finding a mate into the hands of an individual. What generally happens is you spend time with someone to see if there is a connection. How many have gone in and out of relationships and it all started with a first date? Is that what God wanted you to do? Was that His plan? Did He really want you in those relationships that caused so much brokenness?

When you go on a date, you always want to make a good first impression. And that's OK. You put on your best dress and he looks dapper in his new duds. It looks like the two of you belong on the cover of a dating magazine.

You are both on your best behavior. You are very careful not to say or do anything to turn the guy off. And vice versa. One thing I want to stress is, BE YOURSELF! Don't pretend to be someone that you're not. You need to allow your true personality to shine through. That's being honest with yourself and with him.

It's sad how quickly couples have become exclusive. It seemed so right. The two of you were so happy. You both had so much in common. You laughed at each other's jokes. He likes to go kayaking and so do you. You like to read, and he does too.

There seemed to be such a deep connection, and sometimes on every level. Because things moved too rapidly, you really didn't have enough time to get to know the person. Now you are in a serious relationship.

It can be weeks or even months later, and then everything changes. If there are sinful behavioral patterns in either one of you, they're not usually going to present themselves on the first or second date. As time goes by, the couple settles into the relationship and their sinful struggles begin to surface. So many women, including myself, desperately clung to relationships that were unhealthy. We must not allow ourselves to enter a relationship without a Christ-centered focus.

If you go out with him and he ends up not calling you back or you don't hit it off, don't sweat it! If things don't work out, let it go. The wiring was off and that's ok. Don't let your fear of being alone, cause you to hang onto relationships that aren't healthy. The evaluation process must be made by seeking the Holy Spirit's direction and guidance.

God, My Provider!

After I broke up with the last boyfriend, I decided that I wasn't going to date. I wanted to get to know someone through ministry. Now, you don't have to be in the same ministry together, but he needs to be serving the Lord in some capacity. I'd recommend not getting serious with someone who doesn't think that being in ministry is a priority in their relationship with the Lord.

I wanted someone who had a heart of service for the King. I wanted him to come alongside and encourage me in this race to the finish line. I wanted a spiritual man and godly leader.

"Now the overseer is to be above reproach, faithful to his wife, temperate, self-controlled, respectable, hospitable, able to teach, not given to drunkenness, not violent but gentle, not quarrelsome, not a lover of money. He must

manage his own family well and see that his children obey him, and he must do so in a manner worthy of full respect" (I Timothy 3:2-4).

When I was single, there were numerous guys that asked me out, but I wouldn't go. There were a few that said God told them to approach me. My response was, "He didn't give me the same message." They were wrong. They didn't become my husband.

I wasn't going to be pressured, pushed or prodded. No! Not anymore! I determined that the next relationship wasn't going to look like the ones I'd had in the past. I wanted to know that it was from God, and that He was bringing the two of us together. I really wanted God to write our love story. I wanted to see His divine Hand in it. I wanted to be able to tell people that it was from Him, because He does the impossible. And His timing is perfect.

I knew that God had provided my ministry, my job, godly friends, and direction in my life. I trusted Him to bring me my husband. And if it wasn't going to be clear, I wasn't going to move forward. If He wanted me married, He'd have to show me the way. He'd have to put him smack dab in front of me. I just didn't trust myself or my feelings. And I'd been deceived by the enemy too many times before. He is faithful. Until then, my goal was to live a life that pleased my Savior. I wasn't going to be led down another rabbit trail.

The Perfect Match

I was told by the pastor that God would bring me a godly man, and He did just that. If I had it to do over again, I'd rather wait my whole life for God to bring me that special someone than go through the pain and heartache I experienced because of trying to do relationships my way. I was used. I was abused. I was deeply wounded. And I caused deep pain to others. I sought people to fill my desire to be loved.

It never worked. It never did. I had drifted off course, but He brought me back into the race. He rescued me. My Savior loves me. I am His. He is my King. I praise Him for His mighty work in my life.

You don't have to be on the lookout for Mr. Right. That is a distraction. God wants "all eyes" on Him. When my husband came along, we were friends first. We were involved in the same ministry work, so we were able to get to know each other that way. We had a lot of common interests. We became friends.

He began to initiate spending time together outside of the ministry. He talked about wanting something more serious, but he didn't want to move too fast. We wanted to take it slow as we prayed and sought God about the relationship. We got godly counsel on how to move forward. The pastor encouraged us to start reading books and listening to audio tapes on marriage. We both agreed and spent a lot of time trying to learn as much as we could about how to treat each other in a marriage relationship. We got married approximately two years after we met.

If you start moving forward in a relationship, make sure that there is nothing in Scripture saying you can't proceed. Remember to make sure He is a true believer in Christ. Don't try to manipulate and control the way things happen. And don't let him control you.

Remember, he might not be the right one. So, don't move too fast. Make sure that you draw serious boundary lines. Don't let him lead you on and move you into a physical relationship. Be a woman of purity. God loves you. You are His princess. He wants you with someone who will love you unconditionally.

He has a glorious plan for your life. The Potter is creating a beautiful masterpiece. Surrender your rights! Submit to Him! Seek His face with a passion. Fill your heart with His truths. The piece of artwork that He is creating will have such an incredibly powerful story, that others will be drawn to you...and to the Savior. Isn't that incredible? I can't wait to see what it looks like. I can't wait to see what He will do! I can't wait to hear how God will rescue you!

Here is a list of reminders to ponder. Ask God to help you set these standards in your daily walk with Him.

Reminders:

- Test your thoughts to make sure that they are lining up with the Word of God.
- Make sure you're involved in a Biblically based, Christ-centered church.
- I encourage you to spend time with Jesus every day.
- Start memorizing and meditating on His Word.
- Make sure that your friendships develop with a focus on the Lord.
- Remember that God wouldn't move you into a relationship that takes your eyes off Him.
- Guard yourselves against spending too much time with someone in the friendship stage.
- In the early stages of a friendship, make sure you stay in groups.
- Don't trust your feelings.
- He must know for certain that Christ is His Savior.
- How long has he been walking with the Lord? How has God transformed his life?
- You want a Godly man and a spiritual leader.
- Does he go to church, read the Bible, pray and serve in ministry?
- You want a person who is living for Jesus because he loves the Lord, not because you told him to.
- Is he willing to get godly counsel?
- God wouldn't want you in a relationship with someone who causes you to sin.
- Is his desire to remain pure until marriage? Was that desire initiated by him?
- Does he have similar beliefs? Does he have a Christian values system and worldview?

And The King And His Bride Lived Happily Ever After!

They say that fairy tales don't come true. But Christ is my King. He rescued me and set me free! He redeemed my life for His glory. He has shown a love for me that makes me feel so special. I'm loved by my King. And He wants you to experience that love, too! Heaven is a place where there is no more sadness, pain or heartache. We will be with the King of kings, and we will live happily ever after. Dreams do come true!

CHAPTER 10
Salvation is the Key

*D*o you know for certain that if you died today, that you'd go to heaven? That is the most important question that you will ever be asked! Everything hinges on whether you know the answer to that question. What is your response?

I love to tell people about Jesus. There are many that I've talked to that believe they are good enough to get to heaven. But it's not by works that a person is saved! God offers us eternal life as a "free gift" (Romans 6:23). You don't have to work for something that is free, because we could work from now until eternity, and we still wouldn't be good enough.

How sad that people try to achieve salvation through their good deeds. *"But we are all like an unclean thing, and all our righteousness are like filthy rags"* (Isaiah 64:6) Love isn't based on performance. If that were the case, we'd never make it to heaven. His love is unconditional. It is by grace that we are saved! You couldn't do enough to earn or deserve eternal life (Ephesians 2:8-9).

And it is a pretty proud person that thinks they can stand before God and tell Him how great they are. There will come a day when people get to heaven and say, *"Lord, Lord, I did all these mighty acts in your name."* Jesus responds, *"Depart from me, I never knew you"* (Matthew 7:21-23 paraphrased). Many are deceived! What a sad day that will be! There are some who will get to the pearly gates and recite their list of good behaviors. It won't impress Him. He requires a humble, repentant heart.

We are separated from God because of sin! And that sin prevents us from having a relationship with the Lord. His amazing love caused Him to sacrifice His Only begotten Son on the cross for us. He watched, as His Son suffered a punishment that He did not deserve. Jesus went willingly. He lovingly laid down His life for the sheep. What a great Shepherd we have!

"Greater love has no one than this, than to lay down one's life for his friends" (John 15:13). The ultimate sacrifice! It was the only way for us to be one with Him!

Jesus Is The Key To Heaven

Jesus is the only way to heaven. It is faith in Christ that unlocks the door to eternal life. *"That if you confess with your mouth the Lord Jesus and believe in your heart that God has raised Him from the dead, you will be saved"* (Romans 10:9). When we accept Him as Savior, our names have been written in the Lamb's Book of Life. He doesn't erase it every time we sin, or that's all He'd be doing.

I am a child of God! A daughter of the King! I've been adopted into His royal family. He chose me from the foundation of the world. I am called to go into the world and represent the Savior. I am considered an Ambassador for Christ. There is no greater honor than for God to use His children to do great things for the Kingdom.

> *"Now then, we are ambassadors for Christ, as though God were pleading through us: we implore you on Christ's behalf, be reconciled to God. For He made Him who knew no sin to be sin for us, that we might become the righteousness of God in Him"* (II Corinthians 5:20–21).

There is no longer a wall separating us from God. The wall has been torn down, and we have free access to God, the Father. We no longer must wait to enter into the Holy of Holies, as the priests did in ancient Israel. We are now able to come to the Lord, just as we are. We have a direct connection to the Lord. He is always there for us.

"Therefore, brethren, since we have confidence to enter the holy place by the blood of Jesus, by a new and living way which He inaugurated for us through the veil, that is, His flesh, and since we have a great priest over the house of God, let us draw near with a sincere heart in full assurance of faith, having our hearts sprinkled clean from an evil conscience and our bodies washed with pure water" (Hebrews 10:19-22).

How awesome is that? You have been redeemed by the grace of God and the blood of the lamb. *"You have been sealed for the day of redemption"* (Ephesians 4:30). We are joint heirs with Christ. His Holy Spirit dwells within us. We are wired for greatness because of who He is and what He wants to do in and through us.

Give Him Your Whole Heart

Don't get me wrong! The Bible says that faith without works is dead. John 14:15 says that if you love Him, you will keep His commandments. If we have the Holy Spirit within, it should be reflected by a changed heart and life. One should be able to see a transformation of the soul. But that takes time. And we need grace. In our humanness, we can do some foolish, sinful things. But remember, God is the one who redeems and restores. And His promises of faithfulness are guaranteed for you. *"I will never leave you nor forsake you"* (Hebrews 13:5).

"My Father, who has given them to me, is greater than all; no one can snatch them out of my Father's hand. I and the Father are one" (John 10:29-30).

I love Him because He first loved me. I owe Him my life. What I do for Him is out of the gratitude and love I have for my Savior. He has been faithful and true. I'm so blessed to be in this relationship. I praise Him every day for choosing me. As I seek to live for Him, He gives me the desires of my heart.

I pray that you have received Christ as your Savior. If you haven't, this is an opportune moment to do that. If you don't, you won't be with Jesus when you die. Don't you want to go to heaven? Hell is a real place, and I don't want you to go there. Eternal life is free! All you need to do is acknowledge that you are a sinner in need of Jesus. He's the only way you can have a relationship with God. He is the answer.

The Sinner's Prayer

Just say: *Dear Lord, I'm sorry for the things that I've done wrong in my life. I know that God sent You, Jesus, to die for me. I am totally unworthy of Your mercy and grace. Thank You for sacrificing Your life for me. Jesus, I ask You to come into my heart and become Lord of my life. Please protect me from the evil one. Help me to live for You. Help me to apply the Biblical principles in this book to my life. I want to serve You. I've wasted too much time. Guide me in the direction that you want me to go. Help me to trust You, Lord.*

I'm so thankful that He's adopted me into His family. We are sisters if you have received Christ as your Savior. I hope you have done that, my friend. You won't ever regret it. In fact, it is the best thing you'll ever do in your life.

I pray that I've been an instrument that He has used to minister healing to your heart. I hope that the stories I've shared have brought strength, comfort and hope to you. I pray that my words have been Holy Spirit anointed and that they've helped transform your relationship with Christ. And that you truly believe that He has an amazing purpose and plan for your life.

He wants to experience an intimate relationship with you. I pray you understand that He is the only one able to satisfy the longings of your heart. Our Savior deeply loves you. He proved that on the cross. He laid it down so you could be lifted up to bring honor to His name—so you could do great things for the Kingdom of God.

Let His light shine through you. It will radiate that spiritual warmth that enables others to see that God is real, He does exist, and they too can experience a relationship with Him. You are a child of God! A daughter of the King! You are beautiful! You are amazing! Believe the truths of His Word and not what the enemy says! Rebuke his lies and receive His truths! I am praying for you. I am trusting that you will discover the path He has for you. And that your story will be one that brings Him great glory! Praise God, my sister.

The Light of the World

"You are the light of the world. A city that is set on a hill cannot be hidden. Nor do they light a lamp and put it under a basket, but on a lampstand, and it gives light to all who are in the house. Let your light so shine before men that they may see your good works and glorify your Father in heaven" (Matthew 5:14-16).

About the Author

Tewannah Aman has been executive director of Broward Right to Life for over 20 years. An active Bible teacher, she presents Guard Your Heart, abstinence and sanctity of life presentations throughout South Florida. She has reached thousands of individuals with biblically based, Christ-centered teachings. Her passion is to share God's truths with women and young people so they can embrace the life-changing, transformational message available through the Scriptures.

Having experienced so much insecurity and brokenness in her past, she understands what women go through and the struggles they face. She has helped many women, through counseling and mentoring, experience healing and restoration by developing a closer, more intimate relationship with Jesus Christ. As she puts it, "Without Him, there is no hope for healing. With Him, we can experience freedom from all the hurts and pains of our past."

She has been involved in the local prison ministry for many years and is pursuing a bachelor's degree in theology and biblical studies.

One of her happy places is the beach. She loves walking on the pier and hanging out by the seashore. Tewannah loves travelling with her hubby and discovering new changes of scenery. She is a workout instructor and loves to create dishes in the kitchen. She is married to John and they reside in sunny, South Florida.

Connect With Me

I want to spread the *Guard Your Heart* message to women and young ladies. I am available to speak at women's functions, Bible study groups, youth events and church congregations.

Please contact me to discuss the possibility of presenting the GYH series to your group or organization.

Find out about the latest GYH happenings at
www.guardyourheart.net

Check out my YouTube channel at Tewannah Aman

FB @ Tewannah Leticia Aman
Instagram @ Tewannah Aman

Please send your questions and comments to
tewannah@guardyourheart.net. I'd love to hear from you.

To purchase copies of *Guard Your Heart*, please send a check for $15.00 (S&H is included) to Tewannah Aman at

Tewannah Aman PO Box 24342
Fort Lauderdale, FL 33307

Made in the USA
Columbia, SC
04 June 2023

17338344R00148